Praise for *Communicating Globally*

"In the 21st century, the ability for ad agencies to provide worldwide, integrated marketing services for their clients will become essential. Only those marketers and agencies with the ability to brand products and services globally will thrive. *Communicating Globally* provides a roadmap on how to do it right."

O. Butch Drake, President-CEO
American Association of Advertising Agencies

"At last . . . a book that truly lives up to its claims of an integrated approach to marketing. It has no peer within marketing literature and its practitioners are similarly rare, despite many protestations to the contrary. Advertisers and agencies alike can only founder if they fail to eschew and heed its messages."

Juliet Williams, Director
Strategic Management Resources

"No one can provide a guaranteed formula for future success, but *Communicating Globally* comes awfully close. By combining an astute knowledge of the global marketplace, emerging trends and technologies, and good old common sense, Don Schultz and Philip Kitchen illuminate the path for successful brand building in the 21st century."

Ed Faruolo, Vice President
Corporate Marketing Communications
CIGNA Corporation

"Global corporations are no longer just in business—they are in the "relationship" business. As Schultz and Kitchen's pathbreaking book shows, customer acquisition, retention, and loyalty are now pivotal to 21st century global business strategy and brand building. Schultz and Kitchen comprehensively define the strategic and operational imperatives required to implement a global marketing communication plan. Their work is exceptionally well grounded theoretically as well as being useful practically."

Sylvia D. Meli, Group Planning Director
Grey Advertising Ltd.

"Don Schultz has done it again! His unique and highly readable approach is a must for companies looking to market globally in the new century. *Communicating Globally* offers an important road map through the maze of global marketing communications."

James R. Gregory, CEO
Corporate Branding, LLC

"This book is important because it brings the concept of integrated marketing communications (IMC) into full international focus for the first time. This focus is maintained throughout the whole structure and it makes the book a truly conceptual work. The case studies that illustrate the practical ramifications of international IMC yield significant general as well as specific lessons."

John Philip Jones, Professor
Syracuse University

"The 1990s introduced integrated marketing—understanding and communicating relevantly with customers by using information. *Communicating Globally* now takes the same principles and adapts them to today's dynamic global marketplace. Even better, it is written in a style that makes it easy for a non-marketer to fully understand the importance of managing a brand."

John R. Wallis, Vice President of Marketing
Hyatt International Corporation

"Just as IMC was a revolution in the '90s, *Communicating Globally* is the road map to becoming a successful company in the global marketplace of the new millennium. A must for doing business globally."

Miguel Rafael Mendoza, Director
Business Administration & Executive Development Program
University of Chile

"For more than a decade Don Schultz has been the prophet of integrated marketing communications, with many disciples around the world; I'm one of them here in Brazil. This new and outstanding text addresses the necessary evolution of marketing and communications and is a welcome addition to a world immersed in the irreversible globalization process."

Rafael Sampaio, Executive Vice President
Association of Brazilian Advertisers
Founder and Editor, About *Magazine*

COMMUNICATING GLOBALLY

AN INTEGRATED MARKETING APPROACH

Don E. Schultz

Philip J. Kitchen

NTC Business Books
NTC/Contemporary Publishing Group

Library of Congress Cataloging-in-Publication Data

Schultz, Don E.
    Communicating globally : an integrated marketing approach / Don E.
Schultz, Philip J. Kitchen.
        p.   cm.
    Includes bibliographical references and index.
    ISBN 0-8442-2522-3
    1. Export marketing.   2. Export marketing—Management.
3. Communication, International.   4. Export marketing Case studies.
I. Kitchen, Philip J.   II. Title.
HF1416.S35   2000
658.8'48—dc21   99-43187
                                                                                CIP

Interior design by Hespenheide Design

Published by NTC Business Books
A division of NTC/Contemporary Publishing Group, Inc.
4255 West Touhy Avenue, Lincolnwood (Chicago), Illinois 60712-1975 U.S.A.
Copyright © 2000 by NTC/Contemporary Publishing Group, Inc.
Printed in the United States of America
International Standard Book Number: 0-8442-2522-3

00 01 02 03 04 05 LB 18 17 16 15 14 13 12 11 10 9 8 7 6 5 4 3 2 1

With grateful thanks to our wives, Heidi and Diane, for helping us work through the concepts and ideas represented in this text.

We also acknowledge with gratitude the many individuals and companies who have assisted in any way in providing insights for this text and in allowing these to be cited.

Contents

Transitioning into the 21st-Century Marketplace

The challenge facing most marketing organizations as they enter the 21st century is how to transition from traditional functions and operations to the new world of the 21st century and the global marketplace. We argue that the best mechanism for making the adjustment to the new marketplace realities is integrated marketing communication. Therefore we start with the transitioning process. Exhibit 1.1 illustrates the challenge.

Most marketing and communication organizations know their current location; that is, they understand the marketplace they occupy, the prevailing competitive framework, the target markets they serve, and so forth. As a result, most firms and managers have fairly well-established patterns for communicating with customers and prospects and investing in processes and systems, and they have some idea of the return they can likely expect from those investments. Although they may not consider these conditions ideal, most managers clearly understand where their organization is in today's marketplace.

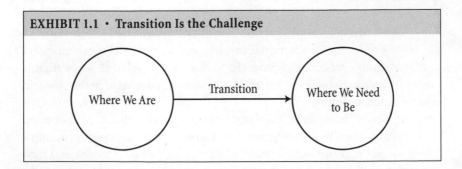

EXHIBIT 1.1 · Transition Is the Challenge

Where We Are → Transition → Where We Need to Be

By the same token, most organizations have some idea of where they need to be or where they would like to be in the future. While the view may be a bit fuzzy because of unknown market or technological changes, for the most part senior management knows where it is trying to drive its organization one, three, or five years out.

Marketers and marketing managers also have a fairly clear understanding of where their firms and brands are in the marketplace. For example, they have many guideposts marking present success such as market share, sales performance, profit and loss accounts, and the like. These tell them how they are doing. In addition, most marketing people have some vision of the future or where their marketplace is going and how they might fit.

Thus the challenge for both senior managers and marketing managers is not "Where are we today?" or "Where do we need to be in the future?" but "How do we get there?" That, in our experience, is the transition with which they are struggling. And that transition faces every senior management team and every marketing manager in every organization around the world.

The same transitional challenge confronts most marketing communication managers. They generally know what communication programs are in place now. They also know what seems to work and what doesn't, but often not why for either. Therefore most know what they can and can't do with communication to influence customers and prospects in today's marketplace. In addition, most communication managers can wax eloquent about what the marketplace of the future will or might be: electronic systems, interactive communication, information on demand, World Wide Web, and so on. But, like senior management and marketing managers, most have difficulty identifying how they might get to this new marketplace and what needs to be done to make the transition. There are so many variables. So much change. Such dynamic structures. The traditional "plan, develop, execute, and evaluate" model doesn't seem to work anymore. The old models are less and less relevant given the challenges of a global marketplace where border-crossing, new cultures, new languages, and new media abound. Yes, how and in what ways, or with what mechanisms, to make the transition to the new global marketplace is the question and the challenge.

That's what this book is about. How to get from here to there. How to get from a domestic or a national or even an international marketing and communication process and program to one that is global in scope, that is customer focused in orientation, and that takes full advantage of the new and emerging technologies.

This book, however, is not about technology. It is about how to develop and execute effective and efficient marketing communication programs. True, we will make use of the new technologies, but new media and new technology will not drive our focus. Instead the new media and the new technologies will be used to make the transition from where firms and brands are to where they need to be. Thus we will focus on controlled and controllable technology and how it can and will be used to create global communication systems and global marketing communication programs.

GLOBAL BUILDING BLOCKS

To illustrate the marketplace transition, we start with some basic tools of the new global marketplace. In our view four major interrelated elements or building blocks are driving changes in the marketplace and thus marketing and marketing communication: digitalization, information technology, intellectual property, and communication systems. All have contributed and will contribute to the development of the global marketplace and the global marketing communication programs that must be developed for organizations to succeed. These global building blocks form the backbone for the major communication renaissance that is affecting marketing communication everywhere. Each is discussed in some detail on the following pages. The impact of these building blocks on the development and implementation of marketing communication programs will become more apparent in later chapters.

Digitalization

There is little question that digital technology has had a sweeping impact. The ability to convert almost all types of knowledge, information, and materials into 1s and 0s and to manipulate those digits through computers and other electronic systems has literally changed the world. The computer, which was originally conceived as a sort of electronic abacus that could be used to simplify and take over mundane, repetitive tasks such as accounting, calculating, and record keeping, is now recognized as one of the most creative tools man has ever devised. However digitalization is used—whether to develop computer-assisted design and manufacturing systems, to store and manage huge sets of data, to analyze disease and uncover new treatments, to create new logistical and distribution systems, or to organize and manage satellites thousands of miles in space—our ability to convert almost everything man does into a digitized form has changed and challenged almost everything in society, even business and human relationships.

The impact of digitalization on businesses and their marketing and communication activities has been so immense that we seem scarcely to have scratched the surface of the changes it will create. Just look at the impact of digitalization on Eastman Kodak, the photography giant. Eastman Kodak, for all intents and purposes, invented, developed, and brought to market the entire field of consumer and pleasure photography. Using the basics of film, paper, and chemicals, Kodak built a global business in photography and, in spite of tough competition from Fuji and others, still controls more than half of the world's sales of film and developing. Today, however, the traditional film-, chemical-, and paper-based photography market is challenged by digital photography. Digital photography requires no film, no chemicals, and no paper, only electrons in the form of 1s and 0s. Think how radically digitalization has changed and will continue to change the traditional photography business. Think what type of impact the shift to digitalization will have on Eastman Kodak, its manufacturing facilities, and certainly its marketing communication activities. How successfully Eastman Kodak handles the transition will determine how successful it will be in the 21st-century global marketplace.

Information Technology

By *information technology* we mean all those devices, techniques, and capabilities that allow human knowledge, data, or experience to be transferred quickly and easily between organizations or individuals around the world. Information technology is comprised of new electronic forms of data storage, transmission, analysis, and distribution, ranging from mundane tools such as customer databases and the Internet to the most complex forms of mathematical analysis and calculation. The basis of information technology, however, is the formalization of methods of data transfer that allows knowledge to be distributed to all levels of interface. The growth of the World Wide Web is only the tip of the information technology iceberg. Today, for less than $1,000, a consumer can buy a computer with Internet access. Suddenly consumers can literally shop the world for products and services. They are not limited by space or time to fill their wants and needs. How dramatically is this changing the marketing arenas in which most organizations operate? Just look at what Amazon.com has done to the retail book business. It has literally made every book currently in print available to consumers. It has made logistics and information technology, not retail locations and store ambience, the keys to book-selling success. Indeed, upstart Amazon.com is forcing traditional book super-retailers such as Barnes & Noble and Borders Books & Music to match its systems and processes, not the other way around. And the same is true for the Charles Schwab brokerage house. In stock market transactions and brokerage, Schwab has rewritten the entire book on how this business operates. On-line trading is rapidly becoming commonplace. Such is the power of information technology now and into the future.

Intellectual Property

Historically, nations, business organizations, and individuals have been valued on the basis of their tangible assets—raw materials, land, factories and buildings, and even cash and precious metals. Today the new wealth is knowledge, experience, understanding, and capabilities. Yesterday countries that controlled raw materials or converted raw materials into finished products were wealthy. Today wealth is created by the human mind: books, music, art, movies, computer programs—all are the new corridors to wealth and power around the world. For example, the largest export of the United States is now entertainment in all its forms and formats, not traditional manufactured goods or even services, and that trend will likely continue in the future.

Communication Systems

While one might argue that communication systems are part of digitalization or information technology, we consider them separately because they are so critical to the future of marketing and marketing communication. Historically, communication systems have been linear, developed, organized, and delivered from a single source, whether that was a newspaper, a radio or television station, or a magazine, to masses of listeners or readers or viewers. There was a single originating source, in many cases controlled or at least regulated by various levels of government. Communication systems were designed to distribute identical content, that is, either entertainment or information, to large groups of people, commonly in single geographic areas. Thus we saw the development of the mass markets and mass audiences that many advertisers believe are desirable and still grapple for today.

Communication systems, however, have changed dramatically in the last few years. Primarily they have increased greatly in number. Increased competition has forced most of them to become more targeted and focused on specific groups of consumers or viewers or readers. In addition, many forms of media have become interactive; that is, audiences can be both receivers and senders of messages and information. There are fewer and fewer passive audiences of the past. These two changes have radically altered how people and organizations and even businesses communicate.

With this quick review of the four building blocks—or, better said, *driving forces*—that are behind the development of the global marketplace, we next look at the marketplace transitions that have already occurred. Then, in Chapter 2, we relate those to the new global marketplace we see developing.

MARKETPLACE, MARKETER, AND MARKETING COMMUNICATION TRANSITIONS

To explain and illustrate the various marketplace, marketing, and marketing communication transitions that have occurred or are in the process of occurring, we have identified four specific market structures: the manufacturer-driven marketplace, the distribution-driven marketplace, the interactive marketplace, and the global marketplace. In the following sections, we describe and discuss the first three. We hold the fourth marketplace, the one we call *global,* for Chapter 2 since that will form the crux of this book.

As will be noted in the following paragraphs, while we separate the four marketplaces for discussion, we do so only for the convenience of the reader. In many cases the organization finds itself in some type of blended or evolving marketplace. That simply means that while we define and describe the various marketplaces, there are generally shades and variations of several marketplaces in which individual organizations are operating. For example, there are major differences in marketplace structures in the United States, Japan, and Poland. Yet international organizations may market successfully in each. By the same token, organizations may be producing and marketing a wide range of products, some sold directly to end users and others using very complex and complicated distribution systems, with each individual market appearing to be successful in its present state. The same is true for communication systems. In the United States, for example, choices of media modes and manners for reaching customers and prospects are almost unlimited. In India, however, mass media are still emerging, and there is still much reliance on local forms of media such as outdoor, cinema, and even street demonstrations and sampling. Thus the structures we describe next are meant primarily as illustrations. They outline the basic marketplace structures and serve as departure points for explanation of the changes and dislocations global marketing and marketing communication managers will find themselves addressing as they make the transition from "where they are" to "where they need to be" in the 21st-century global marketplace.

To complicate the discussion further, many marketing and marketing communication managers will find their organizations operating in all of the marketplaces described here at the same point in time. That might include various product or service lines, or it might be on the basis of various countries and markets. Indeed the transition from one marketplace to another is not, in most cases, linear or even clearly defined. Even worse, there is no real end in sight. That is, in our view, no organization will "achieve globalization" in marketing and marketing communication and be done with it. Instead managers will face continuing change, continuing response to customer needs, continuing challenges from competitors and technology, and continuing change and evolution in relationships and ways of doing business.

The following marketplace descriptions will be useful as we define and illustrate how marketing and marketing communication must transition to the new global marketplace.

The Manufacturer-Driven Marketplace

Most marketing history and certainly most of today's marketing activities assume a marketplace in which the manufacturer or producer of products and services has most of the marketplace power. From the earliest forms of commerce, the manufacturer (or producer or grower or maker) took his or her wares to market. Buyers met sellers at the market or bazaar. From the ancient souks of the Middle East to the shopping malls of today, the marketplace has been driven by what producers have offered and what customers have been able to purchase. Buyers searched for what they needed. If those needs were not filled, they simply did without. Sellers, on the other hand, controlled the supply and thus the marketplace. We illustrate these traditional marketplaces in Exhibit 1.2.

   As shown in our illustration, sellers brought their goods and services to the marketplace, where buyers came in search of the things they needed. Pricing, distribution, and marketing communication occurred on the spot and instantaneously. Because the manufacturer or seller controlled the supply of

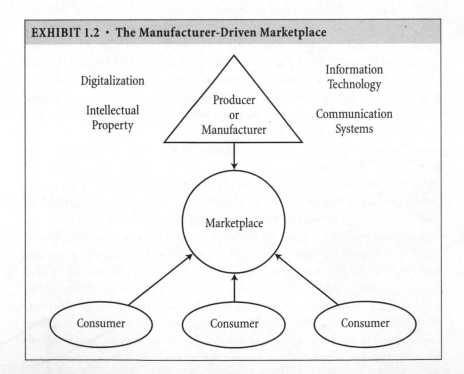

EXHIBIT 1.2 • The Manufacturer-Driven Marketplace

Digitalization

Intellectual Property

Producer or Manufacturer

Information Technology

Communication Systems

Marketplace

Consumer   Consumer   Consumer

products or services, it also exerted control over the marketplace. Indeed, in these simple buyer-seller relationships, sellers always control the four major power elements in the marketplace. They control facilities to produce, make, or assemble product or service offerings. (In our 21st-century global model that would be the digitalization and information technology building blocks.) In the past producers also controlled information technology, crude as it was, necessary to create a marketplace in which the products or services could be offered. (In our building block model, we call these *information technology* and *intellectual property*.) Producers also controlled the communication systems that existed in the marketplace simply as a way of advising or informing customers of the availability and location of products and services being offered. By controlling these four building blocks, sellers dominated channels and consumers or buyers. For example, even in ancient times, farmers owned the land and thus the production of food and clothing. With this control the farmer could decide when and where and what bazaar to visit, what products to offer at that time, at what price, and whom to tell about availability. Thus makers or manufacturers or growers or weavers controlled the marketplace.

Such markets still exist today, although we may have added extensive distribution systems involving intermediaries and facilitators. For example, pharmaceutical companies produce medicines presumably designed to heal the sick or cure various diseases at a profit. The pharmaceutical company decides which diseases to focus research on. It then decides what physicians it will tell about the developed drug and through which distributors (e.g., pharmacies or chemists) it will make the drug available. It develops the price for the drug and controls the amount it will supply in alignment with the government legislation of the day, of course. Patients who suffer from the disease must accept the form and manner in which the pharmaceutical company wishes to market its products. Thus we might say the pharmaceutical company is an excellent example of a manufacturing organization that controls the manufacturer-driven marketplace.

Today, in many situations, manufacturers of all types of products and services still dominate the marketplace. They decide how much they will make in their plants or what plants they will build to produce what goods or services. They then bring those products or services to market, deciding during the process how much they will make, how they will price it, how they will distribute it, whom they will tell about availability, and the like. Almost all of our present-day marketing and marketing communication systems have been developed to support this manufacturer- or producer-controlled model. The most common model is based on the famous 4Ps (extended to 6Ps by Philip Kotler) model of marketing: product, price, place (distribution), and promotion. It is a linear, single-focus model based on transactions and exchanges between sellers and buyers that is used, or at least adapted, by many types of organizations around the world.

In terms of our four building blocks of today's marketplace, the selling organization controls the development of digitalization, deciding where and when such technology should be applied in the development of the product or services. Information technology is also under the control of the seller, whether that technology is used to enhance the manufacturing of a product, the handling of data, or the billing of customers.

The same is true of intellectual property. The knowledge or wisdom or experience of the organization has much to do with its success in the marketplace. The ability to develop new products, to obtain patents, to develop unique manufacturing skills, and the like gives the marketer great power in the marketplace. In addition, the marketing organization certainly controls the communication systems. Almost all media are designed to cater to the needs and wishes of the marketing organization. That is, media gather audiences that they then either rent or sell to marketing organizations as vehicles and methods of promoting their products and services.

Since we are specifically concerned with marketing communication in this text, we have illustrated how communication occurs in the manufacturer-driven marketplace in Exhibit 1.3.

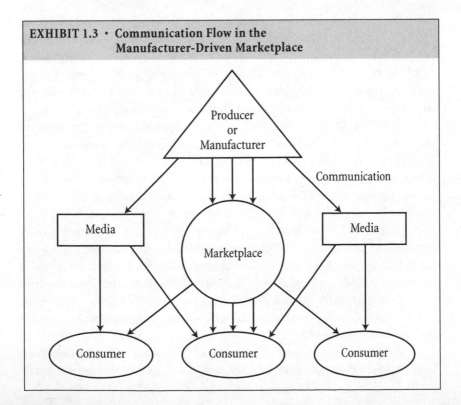

EXHIBIT 1.3 • Communication Flow in the Manufacturer-Driven Marketplace

As shown, in the manufacturer-driven marketplace, the seller or producer or marketer has almost total control over the communication systems. The buyer or consumer comes to the marketplace seeking goods, but the search is totally up to him or her. The marketer or seller controls that information as it sees fit. Thus almost all communication is outbound, and it is almost all linear in structure; that is, it flows out from seller to buyer with little or no return loop.

In this arena the producer is always looking for media systems that can be used to inform buyers. Producers continually seek media that are inexpensive and broad ranging since the seller generally never knows who potential buyers might be. This is how traditional forms of mass media developed, and it is still the basis for much traditional advertising and promotional activity throughout the world. It is designed for a seller trying to influence a buyer, the marketer convincing the customer of the value of the product or service. Thus the goal of the communication demands that the messages almost always be persuasive in nature. Most valuable to our analysis, this is the basic marketing model from which all organizations and all managers are or will be trying to make a transition.

The Distribution-Driven Marketplace

Over the last thirty or so years, the traditional manufacturer-driven marketplace has evolved into what we now call the *distribution-driven marketplace*. This has come primarily as the result of retailers, distributors, wholesalers, or other forms of channel organizations gaining control of the four marketplace building blocks. In most developed economies this type of marketplace is represented by the example in Exhibit 1.4.

As shown, the distribution-driven marketplace is now in the center of the system. From that central location, channels control marketplace power. That is, channels now dominate sellers *and* buyers. This control in the retail area is a result of huge investments in real estate and other place-based facilities along with major changes in various forms of technology. These retailers, whether they be physical or virtual, have made wide varieties of products and services available to buyers. In other words, retailers have created marketplaces for themselves, often becoming destinations in and of themselves for the actual end users. The Mall of America in Minneapolis is an excellent example of this development of retail. Today the Mall of America is the third most visited location for overseas visitors to the United States. Moreover, these large-scale, edge-of-town malls are becoming commonplace throughout the developed world.

As shown in the illustration, many distribution-based organizations have captured the traditional role of seller that originally was controlled by

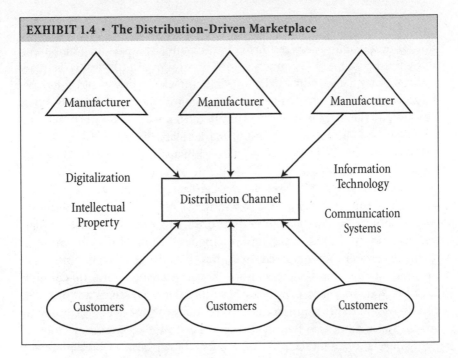

EXHIBIT 1.4 • The Distribution-Driven Marketplace

the manufacturer. They have thus captured the interface with the consumer or end user, allowing them to obtain large amounts of marketplace data and information. In addition, the commodification of products and services has enabled the distribution channel to take marketplace power from the manufacturer. This is increasingly true in many consumer product categories and increasingly in the business-to-business arena as well. Examples of these types of dominant retailing or distribution systems abound—Wal-Mart, Carrefour, Marks & Spencer, Tesco, IKEA, Toys Я Us, and so on.

While one might argue that retailers or forms of retailing have always existed and have always had marketplace power, it has been only within the last twenty or so years that they have begun to concentrate and consolidate into massive, logistically driven distribution systems that control dominant shares of many total retail markets. Much of this concentration and consolidation has come as a result of channel or distribution organizations mastering the four building blocks we have been discussing.

Beginning in the 1970s, the development of Universal Product Codes (UPCs), electronic point-of-sale (EPOS), scanners, and increased computer capability allowed retailers and distributors to capture, store, manage, and analyze massive amounts of market data at the retail and even at the individual market level. These data allowed retailers to track product movement, determine effective pricing margins, and know what customers bought and when they bought. They provided a much better understanding of the flow of products and services through the channel systems than had previously been possible. As channels gained control over close-in marketplace information (that is, individual market and often even household consumer level data and individual customer level data in the business-to-business market), marketplace power quickly shifted from manufacturers to retailers or channels. This massive amount of marketplace data generally came as a result of the rapidly developing digitalization and information technology. From this, channels have been able to create tremendous amounts of intellectual capital in terms of how the marketplace(s) works, what consumers respond to, what they are willing to pay, and so on. They have leveraged this information against manufacturers who often have only broad ideas of market demand, consumer needs, and pricing levels. In addition, because the channels have greatly improved the source, knowledge, and shopping convenience of consumers and end users, they have created powerful communication systems, many of which are simply the retail stores and facilities themselves. Thus distribution channels of today use not only the traditional media systems but also the retail facilities as forms of communication to bring buyers to the marketplace and to fulfill their needs. Consequently in market after market, channels or distribution systems have gained marketplace power and now in many instances can dictate the rules of transaction to product manufacturers.

In terms of marketing communication, the present-day marketplace is controlled by or at least greatly influenced by the retailers, channels, or distributors. That influence is shown in Exhibit 1.5.

Distribution is now in the center of the marketing communication system. Manufacturers or producers, while they still try to speak to or communicate with consumers and end users, generally through forms of mass media, increasingly have focused their communication efforts through their distribution channels. Thus they have become dependent on the channels to provide information about usage and purchases of their products or services by ultimate consumers or end users.

At the other end of the communication system, consumers or end users have come to rely on the channels or distribution systems to provide the products and services they want or need. Being in the middle of this communication exchange system, the retailer or distributor is now the dominant element in this distribution-driven marketplace. As illustrated in Exhibit 1.5, most marketing communication is controlled by the distribution system operator, who communicates upstream to the manufacturer or producer to obtain needed products. This is then matched against expected or anticipated demand downstream to consumers and end users to advise them of available products and services. Thus, while there is some interactive communi-

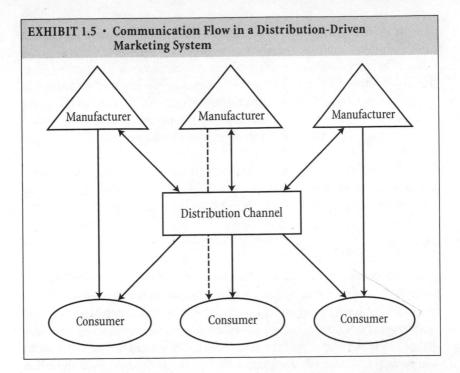

EXHIBIT 1.5 • **Communication Flow in a Distribution-Driven Marketing System**

cation, primarily between producers and distributors or channels, most of the communication is still outbound and one way, from the channel outbound to the consumer or end user.

The communication systems that have developed in this marketplace are also generally one way and outbound. For the most part these communication systems are still fairly traditional, relying on established media systems such as newspapers, radio, television, and magazines. Interestingly, however, the use of targeted communication from the channel to known customers is increasing, often to encourage continuity of purchase. This occurs as the distribution channel learns more about the end user through various forms of digitized data gathering. Retailers have made substantial investments in databases, data management, and targeted communication approaches such as direct mail and telemarketing as they attempt to leverage the marketplace knowledge they have accumulated over time to make their communication programs more relevant to consumers.

In an attempt to maintain some type of relationship with the consumer or end user, manufacturers or producers commonly supply retailers or channels with money and promotional materials in hopes of encouraging the retailers and distribution systems to favor or promote or display their products through their stores or channel systems. Indeed, in the United States and other advanced nations, many consumer-product manufacturers now invest

75 percent or more of their total promotional and communication dollars against the retail trade compared to only 25 percent against end users or consumers. In the business-to-business arena, manufacturers may invest all of their promotional efforts against the channel or distribution system in an attempt to gain its marketing support. Thus, in our view, much of today's commerce in the developed markets of the world operates in this distribution-driven marketplace. We believe this model will be the one that will continue into the immediate future.

There is, however, a new model emerging, which we define as the interactive marketplace. This marketplace is driven by the shift of control of the four building blocks. We discuss this rapidly emerging marketplace next.

The Interactive Marketplace

Although the interactive marketplace is still emerging, it is now possible to see how the system will likely develop. The basic structure of this marketplace began to develop in the early 1990s with the growth and expansion of various forms of electronic communication such as the Internet, the commercialization of the World Wide Web, and the development of E-commerce. As will be shown, this new marketplace will be radically different from those that have gone before. Most important, it will, for the first time, put marketplace power in the hands of consumers rather than with the traditional producers or channels. One need only compare Exhibit 1.6 with the illustrations of the manufacturer-driven and channel-driven marketplace examples shown earlier to see the dramatic differences.

The most obvious change, of course, is the manner in which consumers or end users can access information that enables them to acquire needed products or services. Rather than being at the mercy of the manufacturer or distributor, based on what is offered or available in geographic or time-constrained marketplaces, in the interactive marketplace the buyer or consumer actually initiates his or her own search for products and services. The consumer can even search *globally* for the availability of products and services from both the manufacturer and distribution channels. Indeed, in the interactive marketplace, the consumer or buyer controls the four marketplace building blocks.

Perhaps the most interesting change in the interactive marketplace is the revision of traditional linear marketing systems. Instead of flowing from producers to consumers, goods and services can flow through the interactive marketplace in or from any direction. Producers can contact buyers directly. Alternatively, buyers can contact manufacturers directly or through distribution channels or even through media systems. Of greatest importance, however, is the give-and-take nature of this new marketplace. It is

EXHIBIT 1.6 · The Interactive Marketplace

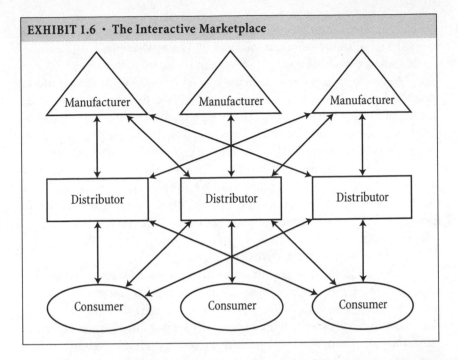

interactive: there is a flow of product and service knowledge up, down, and throughout the entire system, not just the outbound system we have observed in the manufacturer-driven or distribution-driven marketplaces of the past. There is really no beginning or end to this new system. It flows and it moves, consolidates and disaggregates, based on the needs of the various members.

The reason buyers have gained control of the interactive marketplace is the transition of the four marketplace building blocks. Digitalization and information technology today have been made available to consumers in the form of computers, electronic commerce, logistics and transportation, and electronic communication. These systems and approaches take many forms and are developing continually. From a marketing standpoint, however, the most important changes are that the marketplace has been expanded. No longer are consumers dependent on products or services that were presented to them in traditional marketplaces such as retail stores or shopping malls or sales force calls. Instead they have radically different alternatives that enable them to fill their wants and needs *at their convenience and under their own conditions.*

As a result of the shift of control of the four building blocks, manufacturers and retailers must become response driven, not product or service driven. The primary task of manufacturers and channels in the future will be to respond to the needs and wishes of consumers. Manufacturers and retailers must ultimately provide what the customer wishes or desires, not what the organization is able to make or produce or supply. This, in and of itself, creates a major change in the way the marketplace operates.

Again, this power shift is being driven by the four building blocks described earlier. In the new interactive marketplace, the consumer has access to the full range of the marketplace through the development of digitalization and information technology. These electronic systems, driven by computers and modems, enable the consumer to access marketplace information on demand. This change puts every supplier or seller in competition with all other sellers everywhere in the world for the purchases of the end user. Admittedly, this marketplace is not here *yet*. But it is on its way, dynamic, powerful, and irresistible. All technology associated with communication and media, whether for information or for entertainment, is rapidly being coalesced into new, more interactive hands.

Inherent in this power shift is the equalization of manufacturers and channels. Thus, rather than either one of these traditional market brokers having marketplace control, both are now and will be driven by the needs and requests of consumers and end users. This is not a marketplace in which senior management, marketing management, or even the communication manager has much experience. This may be the most difficult transition for managers and organizations, for they have no previous experience or history in operating in a marketplace in which the consumer or end user has control.

Marketing communication changes dramatically in the interactive marketplace as well. As shown in Exhibit 1.7, traditional flows of information through marketing communication now become two way rather than linear. That in itself is a major change for most marketing organizations.

As shown, the major change for the marketing organization is that it must develop skills in responding to marketing communication inquiries from customers and prospects, not just in developing messages and information that it wants to deliver or send out to the marketplace. In other words, the organization must be able to listen, not just talk. That is a major transition for most marketing organizations since they are accustomed to finding potential benefits for the product or service being offered and then developing forms and methods of sending messages about those benefits to prospective customers or users. In the traditional communication systems that were dominated by the manufacturer or producer or the channel or retailer, the marketing organization traditionally has had total control. It decided what products it wanted to offer, what means of communication it wanted to use, to what audiences its messages would be directed, with what volume, and at what noise level. All that control slips away when the orga-

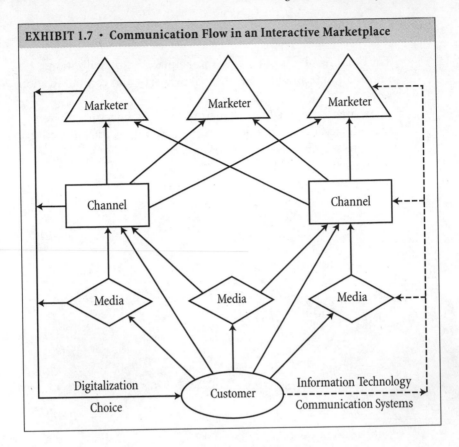

EXHIBIT 1.7 • Communication Flow in an Interactive Marketplace

nization becomes customer or prospect responsive. With the consumer in control of digitalization, information technology, intellectual property, and media systems, a totally new communication system must be developed. No longer will efficient delivery of messages or incentives be the driving force in marketing communication. Instead the challenge is how quickly and completely the organization can respond to consumer or customer requests or needs. No longer is the goal of communication to cut through the clutter of competing messages. Instead it becomes a question of how to involve the customer or prospect to obtain some sort of behavioral response that will lead to an action or affirmative response.

There is, of course, the fourth marketplace, which we have termed the *global marketplace.* This new marketplace that we see emerging is an amalgamation of the three marketplaces just described. Since that is the heart of this book and really defines the various transitions that all organizations must address, we discuss that new marketplace in detail in Chapter 2.

CONCLUSIONS

- The building blocks of the new marketplace are digitalization, information technology, intellectual property, and communication systems.
- There are four marketplace structures: the manufacturer-driven marketplace, the distribution-driven marketplace, the interactive marketplace, and the global marketplace.
- Get ready for change!

Understanding the Emerging Global Marketplace

Without a doubt the balance of power among the three current marketplaces—the manufacturer driven, the distribution driven, and the interactive—has shifted in recent years. But it is the emerging 21st-century global marketplace that bears deep investigation, because it will be the environment in which most businesses will be operating sooner than they think.

THE GLOBAL MARKETPLACE

Many organizations believe they already operate in the global marketplace. They may have created cross-border production, distribution, and marketing systems that they are currently using to serve some clients. In marketing communication, typically, they have centralized communication development with one headquarters group and pared the agency list to one or two global suppliers. Through those efforts they have created what they call "global advertising campaigns," generally based on some type of "one sight, one sound" marketing communication approach. They may have even appointed "global managers" to oversee the programs they have created. However, these approaches have not reached the level of global customer focus, integration of marketing and communication, and development of relationship approaches we believe will be necessary in the new global marketplace. In the true sense of global marketing communication, as we define it in this chapter, these companies have not yet moved into many of the realms of marketing and communication that we believe will be critical. Those include (1) using an outside-in approach, that is, identifying and valuing customers and prospects that the organization is able to serve; (2) allocating finite corporate resources against the most important customers and determining how much and where to invest those resources; (3) finding new ways to balance the improvement of shareholder returns with service to customers on an ongoing basis; (4) building ongoing relationships with current and prospective customers that provide benefits to both parties; and (5) totally integrating the marketing and marketing communication activities of the organization, both internally and externally, to create ongoing, useful, interactive communication systems that bring the organization and its customers closer together.

Many of the organizations that have claimed to be "global" have not reached full global capability, certainly not in marketing or marketing communication. Instead they have simply aggregated a number of national markets, coordinated them in some way, and offered the results to customers and prospects. The typical approach has been to aggregate the world into some number of convenient geographic groups—regions such as Europe, Africa, and the Middle East; the Americas; Asia-Pacific; and so on. The focus, of course, has been to consolidate the multidomestic operations of the organization to make them more efficient, at least from the company view. Commonly this type of "globalization" provides little or no value to the customer or prospect and often simply creates another layer of management for customers to deal with.

To succeed in the 21st century, global organizations must organize around customers and prospects and their operations and activities, not around geographies and certainly not around products and services. Simply consolidating activities generally does not provide the type of integration or coordination that will be needed to operate in the new global marketplace. The following example will illustrate the point. (Note: We have masked the names of the marketing organization and the channel customer. The situation is, however, real and will be recognizable to a large number of organizations that are presently in the throes of globalization.)

Whiz-Bang Stores and Marvel Products: A True Global Marketplace Story

The manufacturer of a wide variety of consumer products sold a substantial amount of its product lines to a very large retail organization that was expanding rapidly outside of its traditional domestic base. For convenience, let's call the manufacturer Marvel Products and the retailer Whiz-Bang Stores. Marvel Products was organized by product lines, manufacturing plants, and dedicated sales forces. It deployed its resources against Whiz-Bang Stores in the same way that it was structured and organized—by product line.

Marvel Products had a sales force representing the Sticky Product line, another representing the Grinder Product line, another representing Roller Stuff, and so on. Behind these sales forces were production and operations groups that manufactured the products, distributed them, billed and accounted for them, and handled other tasks. Each product line was operated as a separate profit center and was generally unrelated to the other groups in the Marvel Products organization.

The sales people for the Sticky Product line called on the buyers of this category of products at Whiz-Bang Stores. Back at the Sticky Product line plants and offices of Marvel Products, separate groups produced the Sticky Product line products, organized their shipment to the Whiz-Bang Stores, billed and invoiced for the products, resolved disputes, and so on. Each of the other divisions of Marvel Products operated in approximately the same way. Every product line for Marvel Products was separate, and Marvel management liked it that way. They believed it gave them better control over the operations and they could quickly identify which product line was doing well and which wasn't.

From the Whiz-Bang Stores view, the operations of Marvel Products were acceptable since they were organized by stores and geographies and product lines as well. Since Marvel Products and Whiz-Bang Stores operated in approximately the same geographic areas and with the same structures, the system seemed to work for both of them.

As Whiz-Bang Stores expanded its operations, it added products from the Grinder line, Roller Stuff, and so on. As had been the case with the original Sticky Product line, Marvel Products assigned a separate sales force to work with the managers at Whiz-Bang Stores. Since Marvel Products was organized by product lines, that meant additional salespeople calling on Whiz-Bang buyers even though Whiz-Bang buyers often purchased multiple lines of Marvel Products. It also meant additional invoicing, accounting, and billing systems and additional delivery systems and product management. Still, the systems worked since Whiz-Bang was not a large customer and was willing to adapt its operations to fit its suppliers.

Whiz-Bang Stores grew very rapidly. As they did, they started to restructure for global expansion. That meant consolidation of functions, more electronic and systematized logistical systems, increased emphasis on proper stocking for specific stores in specific geographies, and so on.

As Whiz-Bang started to expand into other countries, it naturally wanted to offer Marvel Products in those markets as well. Since Marvel Products was organized not only by product line but also by geography, as Whiz-Bang Stores opened stores in new countries, Marvel Products naturally assigned its local national sales force to call on the Whiz-Bang buyers in that area. It did the same for logistics, invoicing, shipping, and the like.

While this created some problems for Whiz-Bang Stores because it was centralizing and consolidating its operations, Whiz-Bang agreed to the Marvel Products system.

One day Whiz-Bang management realized that a considerable amount of time, effort, and energy was being spent contacting and being contacted by the various levels of supplier companies in all the different geographies. Therefore Whiz-Bang management reorganized its operation on a global basis. Using the four building blocks we described in Chapter 1—digitalization, information technology, intellectual property, and communication systems—Whiz-Bang Stores organized itself into a global structure. Its goal was to have one representative for each product line, rather than having a separate contact for each of the Marvel lines.

Thinking that it had solved its internal problem, Whiz-Bang Stores contacted the top management of Marvel Products to suggest that it could organize itself in the same way or at least in some way that would fit with the new structure of Whiz-Bang Stores. Couldn't Marvel Products have one contact person or a contact team that could represent all the Marvel Products to Whiz-Bang Stores around the world, that is, one person who could represent the Sticky Product line, the Grinder Product line, and the Roller Stuff line? Along with that, couldn't Marvel Products also have one sales force that represented all Marvel Products rather than an individual sales group for each product line? And, while they were at it, couldn't Marvel Products also provide one invoicing and billing system for all Marvel Products and also arrange to have all Marvel Products orders consolidated and shipped to all Whiz-Bang Stores in one delivery rather than multiple deliveries from Marvel's various plants and facilities?

Marvel Products had over the years become a very successful company. Its organizational structure, sales force allocation, and billing and distribution system had worked very well. Marvel liked the way it was organized and, to a certain extent, resented its customer, Whiz-Bang Stores, for suggesting that it change the way it did business just to suit Whiz-Bang. After all, Marvel had other customers, and none of them had raised any questions about the procedures Whiz-Bang Stores was challenging. So the senior managers of Marvel Products met with the senior managers of Whiz-Bang Stores. Their goal was to explain how Marvel Products operated, how successful it had been, why its structure worked for Marvel, and why it really couldn't comply with Whiz-Bang's requests.

Whiz-Bang managers listened to the presentation. They agreed with Marvel Products that its marketing program and systems worked for Marvel. The problem was, they didn't work for Whiz-Bang Stores. And, since Whiz-Bang was the customer, they thought Marvel Products should try to do something to help them grow and expand globally. They suggested that as partners such cooperation would work to the benefit of both parties. In other words, Whiz-Bang Store managers said: "You either find a way to work with us on a global basis—that is, all products, all stores, all geographies, all billing, and all delivery—or we will have to find another supplier. We don't believe your system or approach is good for our business, and we don't believe it will help us meet our goals and expectations. We understand why you are what you are. We respect that it works for you, but it doesn't work for us."

To say that the Marvel Products management was chagrined is a vast understatement. They had just wandered into the global marketplace. They were not prepared to meet the Whiz-Bang Stores request and, quite honestly, weren't at all sure they wanted to change their business to fit their customer's needs. When they got back to their home office, Marvel Products managers reevaluated their situation. Whiz-Bang Stores was a major, fast-growing, profitable customer, likely to become even more important in the future. But Marvel Products wasn't prepared to operate in the global marketplace. It was organized and prepared to market primarily in the manufacturer-driven marketplace in which its business had developed. It didn't like the change, but it recognized the transition it needed to make if it was to become a global marketer—that is, developing the ability to respond to customer needs.

The story does have a happy ending. Whiz-Bang Stores and Marvel Products were able to work together to resolve the problem. Each side was able to change and adjust its processes and systems so that they were responsive to mutual needs. They developed interlocking ordering, distribution, and billing systems that saved each group substantial amounts of money, time, and energy. Most of all, they both moved to a marketplace built on relationships, not transactions, which requires buyers and sellers to come together to provide mutual benefits.

GLOBAL MARKETPLACE DRIVERS

One of the best explanations of the developing global marketplace and the changes existing organizations need to make to operate in that venue has been provided by Professor Jagdish Sheth of Emory University. Sheth suggests that almost all organizations began initially as domestically oriented firms. As they grew, and as the markets for their goods and services expanded, organizations tended to evolve from their initial structures and operations on a replicative basis. That simply means that as organizations expanded beyond their initial geographic base, they replicated their domestic structure in other areas. They became *multidomestic organizations*, where managers simply transferred products, organizational structures, operating systems, and programs to other countries or geographies.

When these multidomestic organizations developed, senior management typically established the new company as a separate entity and operated it as a division or unit with its own management structure and profit goals. While sometimes this separation was required by the foreign government in which the unit was located, often it was done simply because it was what the management of the domestic organization knew best. Thus each country's company became a mirror image of the home company or as close as possible to that model, recognizing, of course, that some modifications based on government policies, cultures, languages, and the like were necessary. Exhibit 2.1 illustrates the global evolution model.

As shown, the x-axis is time and the y-axis is global evolution. Based on the model, once the organization grows from the domestic base to a multidomestic organization operating in multiple geographies, the next step is for the organization to become a global company. The problem is, of course, that global companies are radically different from the domestic or multidomestic organizations that call themselves international organizations. Sheth argues that organizations that operate internationally or multidomestically are driven by a number of "contextual determinants." These are factors that drive how organizations operate outside their domestic marketplace. Some of those determinants are illustrated in Exhibit 2.2.

At the center of the model are the "Determinants of Internal Marketing," factors that drive how the organization markets to its own employees, suppliers, distributors, and others. Those determinants are generally based

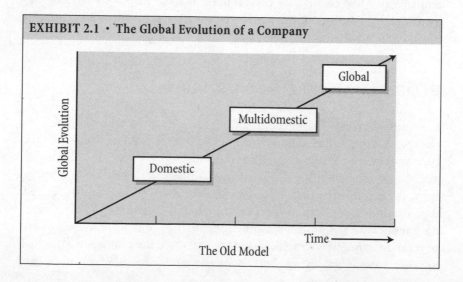

EXHIBIT 2.1 · The Global Evolution of a Company

Global Evolution

Global

Multidomestic

Domestic

Time →

The Old Model

EXHIBIT 2.2 · The Contextual Determinants of International Marketing

on the type of product or service offered, the manufacturing or production facilities, employment practices, management style, and similar factors.

There are three general external determinants:

1. The Cultural Context: This context includes such factors as cross-cultural differences between the organization and the market in which it is operating, the level of market development, and the political stability of the region.

2. The Entry Context: This is how the organization has entered or has been allowed to enter the new market. For example, government policy has much to do with how the organization can be structured and how it might operate in the new market. Another important consideration is the ideology that drives the economy. That ideology can be political, religious, or perhaps simply a unique way in which the country or geography operates and the beliefs held by the population. Fear of imperialism often drives countries or economies to set up specific laws and regulations that restrict the ability of the organization to grow, develop, and derive profits.

3. The Operational Context: This context includes items such as infrastructure adjustments that might be necessary for the organization to apply its operating systems or hiring practices in the new country. It might also include functional adjustments—circumstances that cause the organization to rethink or reorganize the functional structures it uses both internally and

externally. Product life cycle management also has a great impact on how the organization will operate in the new economy. These contextual forces have a great deal to do with how an organization operates as it moves from a multi-domestic to a global approach.

The major change for an organization as it moves from a multi-domestic approach to a global system is how it views the creation of value. Sheth uses the measure that he calls "shareholder value" to determine the success of the organization. Exhibit 2.3 illustrates the necessary transition from past to future success.

As shown, past success in delivering shareholder value for multi-domestic organizations involved some type of domestic portfolio management: organizations created shareholder value in domestic markets by managing a variety of brands or products or services successfully. Often there were economies of scale in such an approach, and success came from dominating a domestic category such as detergents or dental care or ready-to-eat cereals. Examples in the United States might include Procter & Gamble, Colgate Palmolive, and Kellogg.

In the near future, global success will be driven more by a focus on the core business or core capability of the organization and its ability to drive that success in other markets around the world. In other words, the firm must become "world class" in its area and be able to deliver that capability globally. Examples of this type of global organization might include Ericsson in telephony, Philips in electronics, and Nestlé in foods, all of whom have devel-

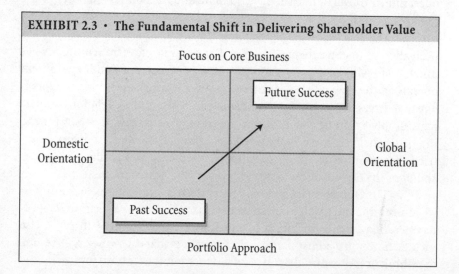

EXHIBIT 2.3 · The Fundamental Shift in Delivering Shareholder Value

Focus on Core Business

Future Success

Domestic Orientation

Global Orientation

Past Success

Portfolio Approach

oped recognized worldwide expertise in their specific areas. The creation of shareholder value in the global marketplace will be dramatically different from that in the domestic or international marketplace.

Finally, the global marketer must develop integrated systems and processes that can be applied around the world. That concept is illustrated in Exhibit 2.4.

Inherent in a globally successful marketing approach will be the ability of the organization to develop and provide seamless, transparent products and services to customers and prospects around the globe. That will require an integrated approach that, as shown, will start with an understanding of global commerce. (Recall our example of Marvel Products and Whiz-Bang Stores earlier in this chapter.) This effort will require global products that are adaptable for use in multiple markets around the world. Those products and services will need to be backed by globally recognizable brands using some type of global account management system that will be run by global managers. The global managers will require global production, operations, and logistical processes and global systems. And, to succeed, these global systems will require global sourcing of ingredients, raw materials, or skilled employees along with the development of global logistical systems.

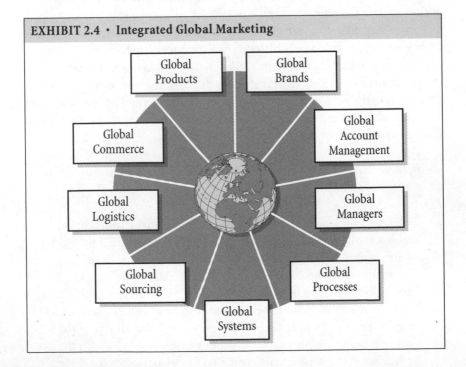

EXHIBIT 2.4 • Integrated Global Marketing

REQUIREMENTS OF A GLOBAL MARKETING ORGANIZATION

In 1988 Christopher Bartlett and Sumantra Ghoshal published the first edition of their text, *Managing Across Borders*, the landmark book on the structure and management of what they called the new "transnational organization." Bartlett and Ghoshal identify three major forces that they suggest drive the strategy of organizations competing across borders, boundaries, and cultures:

1. Global Integration: "The past decade or so has been an era in which global political boundaries were re-forming. Regional blocs were emerging, technological advances were changing, the economic structure that underlay industries and competitive dynamics were reformulating the rules of the game in industry after industry. All these forces for 'global integration' required companies to be more integrated and coordinated across national boundaries."

2. Responsiveness to National Environments: "As any international company well understands, there are other forces that require sensitivity and responsiveness to national environments. Most obviously, consumers differ country by country; national infrastructures differ; competitors vary market by market; and host-country governments require companies to accommodate the interests of each particular nation-state."

3. Administrative Heritage: "The many aspects of a company's past— its home-country culture, its history, the influence of specific individuals— collectively constitute a company's 'administrative heritage.' It is vital that a company understand its administrative heritage for two reasons: a company's strengths lie deeply embedded in this heritage, and a company must recognize those strengths to protect them. But, at the same time, administrative heritage can be the biggest barrier to change."

Using these three forces, Bartlett and Ghoshal describe what they define as a transnational company:

This trend (companies must become more globally competitive, and, at the same time, more sensitive and responsive to national differences) has given rise to what we call transnational industries and transnational companies. What is different about a transnational company? This type of company expands the dominant strategic asset created through its particular administrative heritage into multiple sources of competitive advantage, layered one on top of the other. Leading multinational companies have started to match the efficiency of global companies, while leading global companies have begun to match the local responsiveness of multinational companies. And as these companies match each other in efficiency and responsiveness, they have begun to build a third source of competitive advantage—the ability to learn and innovate on a worldwide scale. This requires them to view the world not only as a collection of marketplaces but also as an enormous source of information and expertise. These companies are able to sense technologies and consumer trends that emerge anywhere in the world; to tap into local resources, capabilities and entrepreneurships; and to leverage the resulting innovations throughout their organizations. So, transnational companies compete on the basis of global efficiency and national responsiveness and the ability to develop innovation on a worldwide basis.

Using these "three forces," Bartlett and Ghoshal develop a strategic format that helps managers identify the basic competitive framework, illustrated in Exhibit 2.5, on which the organization can or should compete in the global marketplace.

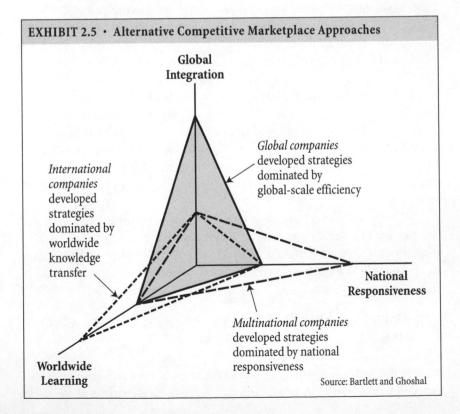

EXHIBIT 2.5 · Alternative Competitive Marketplace Approaches

Global Integration

Global companies developed strategies dominated by global-scale efficiency

International companies developed strategies dominated by worldwide knowledge transfer

National Responsiveness

Multinational companies developed strategies dominated by national responsiveness

Worldwide Learning

Source: Bartlett and Ghoshal

Bartlett and Ghoshal suggest that an organization must either focus on or dominate the marketplace in one of the three basic competitive advantages that organizations can develop—global integration, worldwide learning, or national responsiveness. Further, emphasis on one area necessarily reduces the requirements in the other two. As shown, for example, international companies tend to develop strategies dominated by worldwide knowledge transfer. In other words, the organization competes in how well it can transfer knowledge from one branch or country or region to another. Multinational companies become expert at responding to national needs and requirements. This is done by continuously monitoring countries and markets and developing strategies and approaches to provide the best possible solution in that market. Then, by making those solutions available to allied companies in other countries, these organizations succeed in becoming the global supplier with standardized and coordinated products and services around the globe. Global companies achieve global integration by developing strategies dominated by global-scale efficiency. In other words, they become the best in the world at what they do. (Compare this to Sheth's idea of "core capability" described in the preceding section.)

At this point the manager should take stock of the organization. Using Bartlett and Ghoshal's concepts of competitive advantage, managers should identify where and how the organization can compete in the new global marketplace. While few organizations are purely international, multinational, or global, this approach does provide a useful framework for thinking about where and how the organization is today and where it might need to be in the future. It is useful to think about the current status and what transition needs to occur in terms of both marketing and marketing communication for the company to truly succeed in the 21st-century global marketplace.

Likewise, Sheth's concept of creating shareholder value can be used to assist in determining the type of transition that needs to be made so that the organization can compete in the future. That naturally will lead to considerations such as the integrated global marketing structure presented earlier, in Exhibit 2.4.

As you read about how we see organizations developing marketing and marketing communication programs for the 21st-century global marketplace in the following section, refer to Case Study 3 at the back of the book as an example of a current successful global organization, Dow Chemical.

MARKETING AND MARKETING COMMUNICATION IN THE GLOBAL MARKETPLACE

As discussed in the beginning of this chapter, we see the 21st-century global marketplace as essentially one in which customers, consumers, and end users will dominate the system. As in our example of Marvel Products and Whiz-Bang Stores, the marketing organization will have to know and understand how the customer wants to be served, not just how the organization wants to operate. In other words, the marketing organization will play a different role in the global marketplace, that of supplier of identified customer and prospect needs, not producer of products and services, as illustrated in Exhibit 2.6.

In the 21st-century global marketplace, digitalization, information technology, intellectual property, and communication systems will shift to the control of the consumer in most marketing systems. This shift will put the customer at the center of the system. The consumer, not the seller, will control the marketing system. Further, customers will be able to access the marketplace through any of the three previous marketplace systems—the manufacturer driven, the distributor driven, or the interactive—depending on their orientation and needs. This will put tremendous pressure on traditional marketing organizations, for it means they will have to maintain all three systems to serve the entire market. Few organizations will be able to cope with this marketplace complexity.

EXHIBIT 2.6 · The Global Marketplace

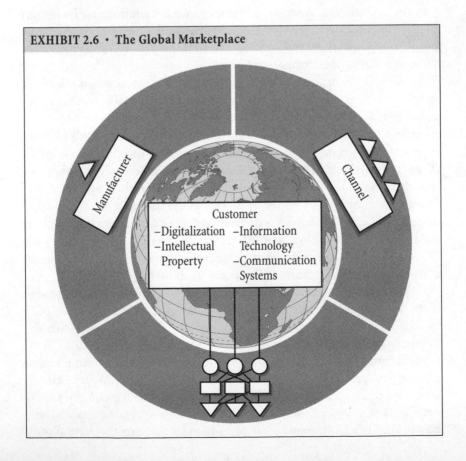

Some consumers may prefer the traditional approach—a manufacturer-driven marketplace in which the consumer is a passive recipient of the marketing efforts of the seller. This is more likely to be the case in less-developed countries where channel systems are still somewhat underdeveloped. Alternatively, some consumers may well choose to obtain products and services through the distribution-driven system. That is, they still prefer the personal shopping experience where they can examine and evaluate products and services. In some cases, particularly in the service arena, the distribution-driven system will likely continue. It is difficult to imagine how dental services or emergency room hospital services could be delivered anywhere other than at some place-based location.

Of course, some consumers will want to use the rapidly developing interactive systems that are becoming available through the Internet. While this area will continue to grow quite rapidly, logistical and payment method problems remain to be solved. Pictures and words displayed via the Internet will not always provide sufficient information for consumers to make decisions about the products or services offered there. For example, consumers will usually require the experience of smelling perfumes and colognes before they make a purchase. Also, some customers are not comfortable giving out their credit card numbers over the Internet. We do, however, expect large numbers of consumers and end users to shift their purchasing patterns to these new forms of electronic commerce.

As might be expected, customer control of the marketplace will create major transition problems for many marketing organizations. Those that currently market through the manufacturer-driven system will have to decide whether to migrate initially to the distributor-driven system with a planned expansion to the interactive marketplace later on, or to attempt to leapfrog directly to the interactive marketplace. Whichever decision it makes, the marketing organization will face substantial transitional challenges. Likewise, those organizations that currently market in the distribution-driven marketplace will find the transition much easier to the interactive marketplace. Indeed, we already see much of this transition in retail organizations such as Land's End, L. L. Bean, Sharper Image, and others that have added interactive capabilities to their traditional catalog and retail operations.

For those organizations such as Amazon.com, Charles Schwab, CDNow, and Cygus Technology, which have chosen to enter the interactive marketplace by selling primarily through electronic forms of marketing, the question will be whether or not they need to go back upstream and develop systems in the manufacturer-driven or distribution-driven marketplaces that would allow them to serve customers who prefer those forms of commerce. We have already seen this occur in traditional direct sellers such as Eddie Bauer, Talbot's, and Pottery Barn, which, although they started business as catalog retailers, have now opened substantial numbers of place-based retail stores that have allowed them to service customer groups who prefer to shop in a "touch and feel" store. Again, much of the marketing organization's decision will rest with *how* the customer wants to do business. If the marketer is unable to provide the desired system, the organization may not be able to compete in that marketplace. Thus the major transition for most organizations will be to understand the various customer groups they wish to serve and then be able to deliver the type of marketing system those customers prefer.

Inherent in the new global marketplace will be the growth in importance of various forms of marketing communication. As we outlined earlier, the consumer will have control of the four building blocks of the marketplace. Digitalization has already shifted into the hands of the consumer through the multitude of products driven or managed by computers or other digital systems. Information technology in the form of computers, modems, the Internet and intranets, global telephony, satellites, and the like all provide the consumer with very sophisticated levels of information technology. The availability of these information and communication systems presage a marketplace in which consumers will quickly start to develop their own forms of intellectual property; that is, they will develop systems and approaches to the marketplace that will allow them to maximize the return on the various marketplace investments, whether that be time, money, value, or something else. In the global marketplace, it will be the consumer who drives the marketer, not the other way around.

In all three marketplaces, marketing communication will become the key element that allows the customer and the marketer to come together. Marketing communcation will be the glue that holds buyers and sellers together over time. It will be the basis for the relationship market in which the buyer and seller agree to exchange information for the benefit of both parties. Unlike the traditional manufacturer-driven and distributor-driven marketplaces, where buyers and sellers were often at odds, or at least cast in competitive positions where one side won at the expense of the other, the global marketplace will be one of relationships and continuous give-and-take among all parties. It will be a marketplace of shared values.

This change in importance of marketing communication will be a major transition for many organizations. Historically, marketing communication has been used to support various types of business activities, not to lead the marketing effort. Thus most marketing communication managers have been either staff positions or under the direction of marketing or product managers. As consumers become more important and more emphasis is placed on understanding customers and prospects, and as more focus is directed toward building long-term customer relationships, marketing communication will become one of the most important areas of the entire organization. Indeed, how to develop and manage marketing communication will become one of the basic strategic decisions that senior management will have to make.

CONCLUSIONS

- You may think your company is global but it's probably multinational or even multidomestic.
- Don't make the mistake of operating in other cultures with a domestic strategy.
- Customers now have the power of choice, making marketers take notice.

How Marketing Communication Works

Marketing communication theory was originally based on the functional specialty areas of advertising, sales promotion, public relations, and direct marketing. Each of these areas evolved into a major but separate industry, and only in the last decade have they started to amalgamate to reflect the need for integrated approaches. Although marketing communication is the major element of communication expenditure, a corporate communication industry has also evolved from early roots in public relations to serve consumer interest in what companies are and do, rather than just the brands they market. The late 20th century has seen the marketing communication industry mature at the same time as media and markets have fragmented.

From a global perspective the marketing strategies and tactics deployed by corporations have undergone radical and consistent change. Mass markets have shrunk and fragmented, and one-to-one marketing is now possible. In fact technological developments have underpinned movement to new forms of one-to-one communication. The Internet is about individuals—with unique and diverse hopes, needs, desires, and cultural backgrounds—more so than it is about mass marketing or markets. The Internet is not one big market of 100 million people—it's 100 million markets, each made up of one individual.

Over the last two years international and national economic fluctuations have shown the extent to which markets are interrelated. But the major development has been the emergence of global markets on a previously unimaginable scale. The phenomenon of globalization, and how corporations respond to this, is crucial to our argument.

THE CHANGING ROLE OF COMMUNICATION

Within an increasingly crowded global market focused on organizational restructuring, return to core competencies, and competitive jockeying and turbulence, marketing communication is still charged with responsibility to move products and services *forward*. Integrated approaches to this goal are undeniably important, but it's also critical to understand how changes have taken place in terms of both communication and communication technologies. This is conceptualized in Exhibit 3.1.

Consumers throughout the developed world have grown up surrounded by, but not necessarily inured to, mass media systems. National television channels, radio stations, magazines, newspapers, mass retail distribution systems, point-of-sale displays, and billboards are all part of many cultural backgrounds. These systems tied countries together and helped underpin the mass marketing systems on which so much of modern marketing is based. Just about everyone in many advanced nations heard or saw the same messages repeated through mass communication systems.

From around the mid-1980s, emerging evidence indicated that consumers were no longer passive recipients of marketing messages. Indeed consumers were becoming savvy, streetwise, and sophisticated. Suddenly, specialized products were desirable, delivered via nonconventional distrib-

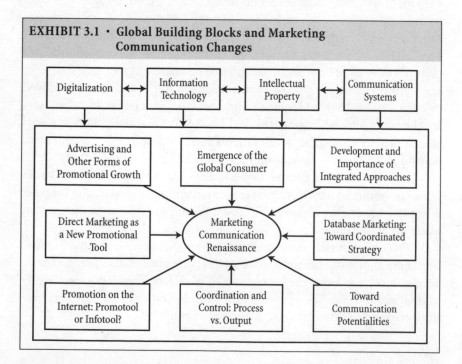

EXHIBIT 3.1 · Global Building Blocks and Marketing Communication Changes

ution channels, while communication altered to meet the needs not of the mass but of targeted segments, niches, and micromarkets. The mass had irrevocably evolved to the micro; market segmentation and target marketing became the order of the day. While the causes of this splintering process are relatively easy to discern on a national basis, they are more problematic when viewed from an international or global perspective. Factors that have impacted marketing communication from that wider perspective can be divided into the following seven categories.

Global Growth in Advertising and Promotion

Advertising and other forms of marketing communication activity have become powerful and pervasive forces around the world. Advertising, sales promotion, marketing public relations, sponsorship, Internet communication, and forms of corporate communication activity form a significant and recognizable cultural ambience in every country. By 1993 worldwide expenditure on advertising had risen to $218 billion versus $276 billion on all forms of below-the-line promotion. Meanwhile, the only country to have resisted the trend to below-the-line promotion was Japan. Even here, by 1995, advertising spending had risen to ¥3,503 billion versus ¥1,907 billion on sales promotion. It can be argued that following the Asian economic meltdown that there will be further development in below-the-line promotion.

A number of coalescing forces have underpinned growth in these areas: increasing costs of advertising (leading to increased below-the-line activities); saturated mature national markets (the only way to grow sales is to take sales away from the competition); burgeoning price competition and price comparability in many markets (more emphasis on trade and consumer promotions); and balance-of-power shifts toward retailers who are buttressed favorably by the rise in scanner technology and consumer databases (providing more leverage for manufacturer-supported sales promotion). The same retailers have in many countries moved toward private label and, in some cases, generic product lines, thereby producing three-tiered pricing structures. Further developments include the growth of database marketing (supportive of the entire promotional activity, including direct marketing) and changes in the media buying system that have significantly affected the fossilized commission-based reward system.

These changes are all driven by supply-side considerations, or market dynamics. From a demand-side perspective, consumers are exercising increased powers of choice and discernment, underpinned by access to suitable alternatives. While there seems little doubt that advertising, sponsorship, and marketing public relations do underpin and support nonrational brand loyalties, it is the totality of brand *and* corporate messages through a bewildering multiplicity of contacts that affect communication effectiveness. Thus changes in advertising and promotional activities of all forms *and* in consumer behavior have led to the birth and rapid growth of integrated approaches.

Emergence of the Global Consumer

In a milestone *Harvard Business Review* article, Theodore Levitt trumpeted that "the world is being driven towards a single converging commonality . . . the emergence of global markets for globally standardized products." He sought to differentiate between old-style multinationals versus new-style global firms that saw the world as one market to be reached with a distinct marketing mix. But the "world" in 1983 was really the areas identified as "the triad" by Kenichi Ohmae—North America, the European Community, and nations spearheaded by Japan in Asia. The other constituted nations of the world were grouped under COMECON and the then underdeveloped or Third World nations. As we move into the 21st century, the triad still forms a powerful trading bloc that dominates world trade. Inside the triad, presumably global corporations operate with resolute constancy, as if the world were one market. However, Warren Keegan and Mark Green (1999) also noted that these firms "standardize where possible, but adapt where necessary." Many firms now exemplify the global approach—McDonald's, Levi Strauss, IBM, Caterpillar, Komatsu. But in 1983 Levitt was roundly criticized by Phil Kotler for "setting the marketing clock back" to a setting associated with production and sales orientations. For Kotler and many others, the marketing clock has moved inexorably forward from mass to niche marketing, underpinned by the principles of market segmentation and target marketing, leading to a greater focus on product differentiation as a means to create and sustain successful exchange.

There is strong evidence that homogeneous segments of demand exist within heterogeneous global markets, especially for items such as jeans, burgers, cameras, cars, sunglasses, and many other product categories. Product categories and brands can be standardized, but that does not necessarily mean that global demand can be created by global (universal) appeals. Many global marketing texts indicate that global firms take advantage of global opportunities when available, reap the advantages of learning and experience curve effects where possible, but also *adapt* when and where necessary. This is especially important in the cultural domain where perception of the same advertisement or other promotional activity may be radically different. Moreover, the "world" envisaged by Levitt has been joined by China (1.2 billion consumers), Eastern Europe (300 million consumers), India (600 million consumers), and newly industrializing countries such as

Indonesia, Thailand, Singapore, and countries in South America such as Chile, Argentina, and Brazil.

Development and Importance of Integrated Approaches

One way of considering marketing communication is as a group of disparate functional activities. The problem is, unless these activities are orchestrated carefully, consumers may see one brand but hear a number of discordant messages. Integrated approaches presuppose strategic marketing communication planning, based on a sound understanding of the dynamics of behavioral segments, with a clear set of procedural methods for analyzing effectiveness, and preferably underpinned by an organizational design not driven purely by functional specialization. However, the drive for integrated approaches is underpinned by changes in communication generally. Marketing communication success depends on building and sustaining brand loyalties—in other words blending marketing communication tools and activities to meet consumer needs, wants, and desires. From our perspective, brand management (i.e., brands and managerial processes), interaction between corporate communication and marketing communication, and realignment of media services (structures, offerings, and compensation) will have to be adjusted if corporations wish to achieve the benefits of integrated approaches to markets and publics.

Direct Marketing as a New Promotional Tool

Direct marketing, for so long regarded as an adjunct of advertising and the unloved stepchild of marketing communication, has enjoyed significant growth in the 1980s and 1990s. In the European Community, expenditures for 1997 were 32b ECU, an increase of 10% from 1996. Monitored spending exceeded ECU 1 billion in six markets, with Germany being the largest followed by France. In the United States, direct marketing expenditures rose from $28.5 billion in 1985 to $135 billion by 1999. Part of this growth has derived from packaged goods manufacturers such as Heinz and Procter & Gamble integrating direct marketing alongside marketing activities. Direct marketing as a marketing communication function is difficult to identify since no current definition is accepted universally. All agree, however, that it is concerned with activities that yield a direct, measurable response. Direct marketing agencies have multiplied throughout the developed world, and in many cases advertising agencies have acquired or developed direct marketing services in response to client demand for integrated marketing communication approaches. Direct marketing has progressed through at least three stages: sales orientation, image building, and, the current stage, direct marketing as part of an integrated marketing communication system. At this stage direct marketing is underpinned directly, as are all other marketing communication elements, by database marketing.

Database Marketing: Toward a Coordinated Strategy

Database marketing accesses and uses the power and reduced cost of computer technology to use customer data in new ways. Database marketing, however, is much wider in scope than direct marketing since it uses technology to drive consumer-oriented programs in personalized, cost-effective ways. It does this by analyzing consumer characteristics and purchasing behavior, allowing development of personalized attitudinal and behavioral databases, which can be reformatted to help drive integrated marketing communication approaches. Database marketing allows global firms to underpin promotional programs with informational resources. Database marketing has the potential to change the basis of competition, strengthen relationships with customers, overcome supply-side problems, support barriers to entry, or generate new product ideas. Database marketing is crucial to developing integrated approaches to marketing communication, but not just as a vanguard for expansionist direct marketing. Instead it underpins the entire range of marketing communication activities, as we will discuss in Chapters 8 and 9.

The Internet: Promotional Tool or Informational Tool?

By mid-1998 it was estimated that more than 100 million people worldwide were using the Internet. Marketing is about to transition into "webonomics," "the study of production, distribution and consumption of goods, services and ideas over the World Wide Web," according to Evan Schwartz, author of *Webonomics*. Notably, this definition excludes marketing communication. There is a debate as to whether multinational firms view the Web as a promotional tool or an informational resource. The problem really concerns the nature of Web users—they are mainly male (65 to 80 percent), eighteen to thirty-five years of age, college educated, earning higher than average incomes, and white collar—in other words, typical Web users are *entirely unrepresentative of most known markets*.

However, most corporations are moving toward a realistic assessment of Internet potentialities, which really means marketing in a *consumer-controlled* electronic environment. Thus marketing on the Internet is distinct from advertising and direct marketing in the sense that it speaks to a consumer as advertising does, records a response as direct marketing does, and also *responds* in real time. It is, however, only at the behest of users that websites are accessed. Thus it is an integrated mechanism driven by receivers, not senders.

What seems evident is that the Internet as used by clients and agencies is just beginning to be understood. The Internet is an informational or directive medium; it is not yet a promotional medium, though we suspect that once the computer, television, and telephone are technologically unified in the near future, the diffusion rate among users will accelerate exponentially. And despite the fact that current users do not fit into any known market, an entire generation of teenagers in the developed world is growing up with top-of-mind awareness and usage of this new medium.

Coordination and Control: Process Versus Output

Given the previous points, many firms need to reconsider the ways in which marketing communication approaches are developed in the age of globalization. The debate concerning standardization of adaptation of marketing communication is long standing. However, our recommendation is that any firm planning marketing communication needs to take into consideration potential adaptation so as to gain the benefits of standardization while paying attention to local differences. Most marketing communication agency personnel around the world do perceive adaptation of campaigns as vital to retain effectiveness. However, the driver for adaptation is not based purely on consumer criteria but also on legal, political, infrastructural, and service provisions. The second factor of coordination and control relates to new media development, particularly the World Wide Web, where many corporations offer virtual meeting places, among them Levi Strauss, American Express, Coca-Cola, and Pepsi-Cola. Examples gained from leading firms lead us to surmise that communication, particularly advertising, is both integrated *and* standardized but is also *adapted* where needed based on company and environmental criteria. Thus we argue that the *process* of communication is the same worldwide but the *output*—messages, media, and measurement—will likely vary in accordance with internal company criteria and external environmental considerations.

THE CHANGING ROLE OF CONSUMERS

We will look at two aspects of marketing communication. The first is the extent to which marketing communication is integrated and the underlying rationale for that. The second is the extent to which marketing communication is standardized (global) or adapted (domestic).

The extent to which communication is integrated or unintegrated, domestic or global in scope depends on several underlying factors. Our view is that these factors will include at least the need to think globally, manufacture regionally, and be perceived (by consumers) as acting locally; to take advantage of regionalized or globalized marketing communication agency capabilities; to consider the move from marketplace to marketspace; and to be cognizant of consumer sophistication in developed economies. Thus the extent to which globalized or integrated marketing communication approaches can be deployed depends not on corporate edict but on perceived marketspace realities, the stage of life cycle or brand development a product may be in, and corporate philosophy. Of these, one major marketspace reality is consumer needs, wants, and desires.

In *Integrated Marketing Communications* by Don E. Schultz, Stanley I. Tannenbaum, and Robert F. Lauterborn, the authors referred to four major changes impacting consumers that have spelled change for marketing communication, shown in Exhibit 3.2.

The four changes shown in Exhibit 3.2 did not occur just in the United States, the focus of Schultz et al., but are reflective of major and far-reaching aspects of the global marketing scenario. Many major corporations focus on visualization in terms not of what products do but of what they mean. Words and symbols represent meaning, and meaning is, of course, the essence of marketing. IBM, Coca-Cola, American Express, Virgin, Intel, Microsoft, Nike, and Reebok are represented not only in verbal form but also in terms of vision

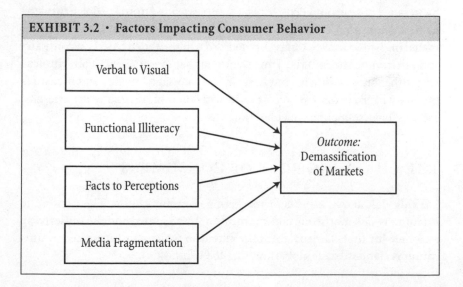

EXHIBIT 3.2 • Factors Impacting Consumer Behavior

Verbal to Visual

Functional Illiteracy

Facts to Perceptions

Media Fragmentation

Outcome: Demassification of Markets

and sound. As stated earlier, a whole generation of teenagers in the triad are growing up with icons, signs, signals, and symbols top-of-mind. Even those trained in an age before computerization and digitalization are moving through a world of representational images each and every time a computer is turned on. What is being communicated is an image, representational but also powerful and meaningful. The move from words to images is on a continual, accelerating curve.

Functional illiteracy is growing in all societies, but the real point is that icons, graphics, pictures, and sounds are mechanisms that communicate to not just the illiterate but to all consumers. Consider, for example, what consumers are exposed to at an average shopping mall, at a sales presentation, during a business lunch, in a radio advertisement, in a direct mail piece crammed into the average mailbox, or on the train or subway. Signs replacing words to communicate meaning is not a possible future development. It has already happened.

Media fragmentation continues to accelerate. Recent decades in all developed and less-developed economies have witnessed the steady and continuous infiltration and multiplied diffusion of broadcast, cable, and satellite television channels; video recorders; computer systems; radio stations; billboards; point-of-sale promotions; and integrated telephone systems. These, coupled with the proliferation of brands, brand extensions, and attempts at global brand franchising, have created a world awash with symbol, color, and sound.

Yet the very proliferation and fragmentation of media goes hand in hand with the splintering of markets into smaller and smaller units; hence the earlier reference to one-to-one marketing. Thus, while audiences become harder and harder to reach and evaluate with broadcast and mass media, the need for integration of all communication messages becomes more and more paramount. Consumers tend to lump all messages via every medium into public relations or advertising, and every message, planned or unplanned, positive or negative, stands for the brand, the company, or the marketing organization. This ties into the idea that perception, not facts, drives so much of consumer thinking and behavior.

Think of the many companies, brands, ideas, and individuals that have achieved marketing success. Most decisions to buy or not buy, support or not support are *not* based on a carefully systematized process. Despite the popularity of cognitive processing and the intuitive appeal of elaboration likelihood models, most consumers base decisions on perceptions, not facts. Put simply, for all consumers there is too little time and too little interest, and there are too many competing messages for any of them to have any communication impact. Instead, what consumers receive are small pieces of information that add to or subtract from memory organization concepts.

What this means from a global context relies on an understanding of how communication works.

How Communication Works

A simplified model of how communication works was put forward by Harold D. Laswell in 1948 and then extended and amplified by Wilbur Schramm in 1971, as illustrated in Exhibit 3.3.

Since these two models were presented, we have become aware that both senders and receivers encode and decode thoughts, or something one party wishes to communicate to another party. Also, it is now clear that the receiver can transpose position and become the sender, transmitting information back to the original sender (now the receiver).

Market research and marketing information systems serve as mechanisms enabling senders to develop and transmit decodable messages more accurately. In the absence of extrasensory perception, exact transmission of thought is impossible. The best result that a sender can hope for is that some elements of the sender's thoughts are retained in the consumer's long-term memory, where they can be tapped during purchase decisions. Thus, if there is a key to communication from a consumer perspective, it lies in the domain of memory and the way in which messages are decoded and meaning is allocated to appropriate stimuli by consumers. Remember, the average con-

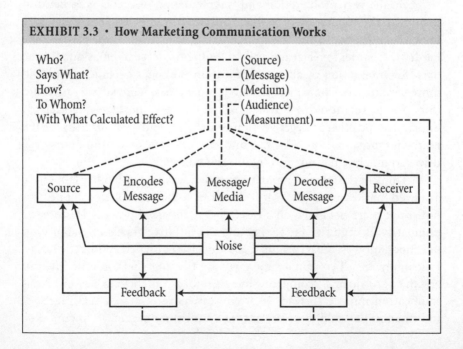

EXHIBIT 3.3 · How Marketing Communication Works

Who? ---- (Source)
Says What? ---- (Message)
How? ---- (Medium)
To Whom? --- (Audience)
With What Calculated Effect? (Measurement) ------------

sumer is exposed to about 2,500 commercial messages a day, most of which are automatically screened out as irrelevant. From all available messages, consumers select those they wish to pay attention to. A very basic model for the way consumers process messages is shown in Exhibit 3.4.

All marketing communication can be measured against this model. First, marketing communication can have no effect unless it reaches the sense organs of those who are to be influenced. However, exposure alone is insufficient to ensure communication has taken place. Consumers must allocate processing capacity to the incoming message or stimulus. Here the memory determines what is relevant or irrelevant. For attention to be allocated, the message must be relevant, meaningful, and preferably creative, because the more times the same message is transmitted through the same media the less communication effectiveness it has. At this stage the memory is operating in short-term mode, and the problem here is that the short-term memory (STM) has very limited processing capacity. Any message that is not paid attention to will be lost within thirty seconds.

Assuming the message is attended to, it must be comprehensible; that is, it must correspond or fit what the receiver already knows or has stored away in long-term memory (LTM). Let's suppose the message is unusual. Say a particular brand fails to live up to expectations, or price rises markedly, or the company is enjoying negative publicity. Each of these circumstances may create a new node or belief in LTM, which may act in helping consumers behave differently, say, to purchase a new brand. This is another reason for integrated approaches to marketing communication.

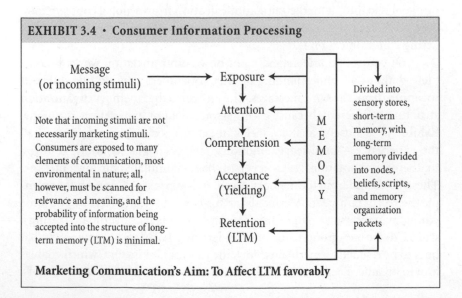

EXHIBIT 3.4 • **Consumer Information Processing**

Message (or incoming stimuli) → Exposure → Attention → Comprehension → Acceptance (Yielding) → Retention (LTM)

MEMORY

Divided into sensory stores, short-term memory, with long-term memory divided into nodes, beliefs, scripts, and memory organization packets

Note that incoming stimuli are not necessarily marketing stimuli. Consumers are exposed to many elements of communication, most environmental in nature; all, however, must be scanned for relevance and meaning, and the probability of information being accepted into the structure of long-term memory (LTM) is minimal.

Marketing Communication's Aim: To Affect LTM favorably

Let's assume that the message is understandable and meaningful (it fits in). It must then either be accepted as part of a person's cognitive structure, rejected, or yielded to. Yielding is recognizably a function of persuasion, and persuasion is the essence of marketing communication. The majority of consumers do not want to be *told*. Marketing communication is never about creating the loudest marketing voice; rather it is about meaning. Meaning is not in messages, nor is it in media vehicles. Instead, consumers allocate meaning to messages. Senders transmit intended meaning; receivers decode received meaning. When there is yielding or acceptance to a communicator's message (or positive meaning is received), the essence of the message must undergo something analogous to an unconscious filing system in the LTM.

The nodes, beliefs, schemas, scripts, and memory organization packets into which long-term memory is divided are simply ways of describing associated links or connections among knowledge structures, beliefs, and information. Each of these may be activated during information processing and either is screened out or accelerates or retards meaning allocation. Marketers attempt to provide information that will facilitate consumer learning either by strengthening linkages among memory concepts or developing entirely new linkages. One can see how important it is to develop messages that will deliver intended meaning, then review to see if such meanings have been decoded.

This cursory review has not done full justice to three other models—the cognitive processing model, the hedonic experiential model, and the elaboration likelihood model developed by Richard Petty and John Cacioppo. These models are also useful. They are not reviewed here because our goal is to look at marketing communication from a global context; however, all three are reviewed extensively and excellently in Terry Shimp's marketing communication text.

Of course, no understanding of how communciation works is complete without an understanding of why consumers may decode different meanings from the same messages. The answer is that memory organization structure is different, because each person's field of experiences is unique. Exhibit 3.5 is a useful analogy. Fields of experience are the sum total of all the experiences—knowledge, emotions, feelings, signs, symbols, gestures, mathematical notations, etc.—a person has accumulated during a lifetime. These fields underpin the memory organization packets. Consider for example the recent European "Mermaids" ad for Levi's 501 jeans. Here a handsome young man wearing a pair of Levi's preshrunk 501s falls overboard during a storm. To the background music of "Underwater Love" we become aware that he is to be rescued by mermaids. First, the mermaids kiss him, which enables him to breathe. Then their attention switches from the young man to his 501s,

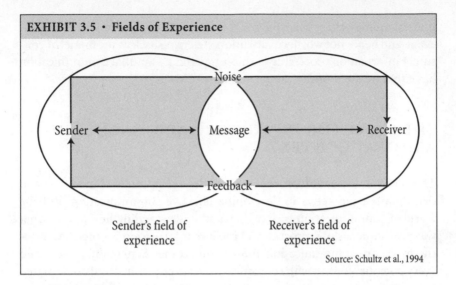

EXHIBIT 3.5 · Fields of Experience

Noise

Sender ←→ Message ←→ Receiver

Feedback

Sender's field of
experience

Receiver's field of
experience

Source: Schultz et al., 1994

which they try to remove. He escapes and swims to the surface, to the disappointment of the mermaids. Based on the fields of experience concept, what is going on here? Do the mermaids want the young man, his jeans, or what's inside the jeans? From a decoding perspective, we realize the young man is attractive because he's wearing the 501s. The young man is a means to an end. The mermaids want to be part of the Levi 501 generation. Further decoding reveals that in mythology, when mermaids love a human, they can leave the water and have their fins replaced by a beautiful pair of legs. Such legs need, of course, to be covered to get by in today's world. All these underlying associations support nodes and beliefs relating to Levi 501s as being a brand that is trendy, a bit daring, and attractive to the opposite sex.

But what if this message is presented to an audience with no background culture regarding mermaids or 501s? What if the message is presented to an audience with a rather puritan outlook? The sensual elements of the message would be have to replaced with something more conservative. Plainly, the extent to which communication is effective depends on the extent of overlap between fields of experience. Or, put in another way, effectively decoding messages is dependent on the receiver's fields of experience, which in turn may act as proxy for memory organization packets.

It is not enough simply to place a message within a field of experience. As we argued earlier, meaning is in the mind of the receiver. Hence, the greater the overlap between a sender's field of experience and the receiver's field of experience, the greater the probability that messages encoded by the sender will be decoded appropriately. Likewise, the smaller the overlap between the sender's and receiver's fields of experience (based on lack of understanding), the greater the probability of messages being seen as irrelevant, and hence not worthy of attention. Referring back to the model of consumer information processing (Exhibit 3.4), this means that communication has either misfired or not progressed into LTM.

THE DRIVE FOR INTEGRATED APPROACHES IN A GLOBAL CONTEXT

The field of information processing provides a rich source of modeling and data to assist marketers in developing effective communication. But the world of communication is changing, and understanding how and in what ways consumers store, process, and retrieve information is crucial to effective marketing communication. Information comes from many sources, and every potential contact with consumers needs to be planned and orchestrated to reinforce positive associations. There are at least four additional reasons why marketing communication should be integrated *and* standardized whenever and wherever possible.

First, control of information is passing from senders to receivers of messages. The old idea of consumers mesmerized by a flickering cathode ray tube and consuming soap operas, sitcoms, and advertisements has already been laid into the fossilized sedimentary strata of the mass marketing age. Consumers in the 21st century will have access to a proliferation of sources, over which they will exert considerable control. In this context unintegrated messages, or messages unattuned to consumer mind-sets, will have little impact and may even rebound negatively on established market share.

Second, product, brand, and corporate communication will follow the well-blazed, unrhetorical trail of politics and politicians. Sound bites of information will become the norm. Telling consumers will be replaced by far more creative forms of integrated communication attuned to a sound understanding of consumer needs, wants, and desires.

Third, the future will be about firms building real relationships. Successful marketing is always about relationships. One-to-one marketing will become far more the norm, and retention of existing customers will become the dominant paradigm in a product-, brand-, and service-saturated planet.

The fourth reason is the globalization of markets. Consumers can be subdivided, segmented, and targeted *ad nauseam*. But, they also wish to be served. Perception, for consumers, is reality. It is not enough for a company to be global in scope or scale or for that matter to develop integrated and standardized marketing communication campaigns. Instead all forms of marketing communication must be focused clearly on the dynamics of to-be-served markets, and the dynamics must be understood.

Hence with this discussion of factors bringing about change in marketing communication, together with the review of how communication works from a consumer perspective, the next chapter will look at what we consider integrated marketing communication to be from a global perspective.

CONCLUSIONS

- Homogeneous segments of demand exist within heterogeneous global markets. The global consumer has finally emerged—*but in the triad countries only.*
- The database of consumer or market information must underpin every marketing decision you make.
- To break through communication clutter, invest your brand with meaning, so much so that your basic message does not require words to be communicated.
- Meaning is in the mind of the receiver; thus you must understand the cultural framework of the customer you are trying to reach. Not doing so is courting failure.

Integrated Communication or Integrated Marketing Communication

THE CONTEXTUAL GLOBAL ENVIRONMENT

It has been only since the mid-1980s that what could be termed a *global economy* started to be differentiated clearly from all preceding stages. The world has progressed and is still progressing through a dramatic series of economic, social, and political upheavals. John Dunning, author of *Multinational Enterprises and the Global Economy*, states:

> The decision-making nexus of the [multinational enterprise] in the early 1990s has come to resemble the central nervous system of a much larger group of interdependent, but less formally governed activities, *aimed primarily at advancing the globally competitive strategy and position of the core organization*. This it does, first by efficiently combining its O-specific resources with those it acquires from other firms, second by its technology, product and *marketing* strategies, and third, by the nature of alliances it concludes with other firms. (italics added)

Dunning then cites Bartlett and Ghoshal, mentioned in Chapter 2, who suggest that for corporate success in today's global environment firms need to develop and manage a cross-border network of separate but interrelated activities. As was discussed in Chapter 2, they determine that firms require a threefold competency, which involves

1. taking full advantage of economies of scale and scope arising from global integration
2. a proper appreciation of differences in the supply capabilities and consumer needs in different countries
3. using the experience gained in global and national markets to strengthen the resource base of the firm as a whole

Dunning then astutely summarizes:

Such a balance between globalization, localization, and learning experience will clearly vary according to the nature and range of products produced, where they are produced, and firm-specific characteristics. It may also depend on the channels of knowledge and expertise within the [multinational enterprise] and the way in which decisions are taken.

Of course, not all firms are at the stage where global decisions need to be made. Firms may be located at various points on the continuum from domestic to global and may be using one or many mechanisms to communicate with those customers who could either impact corporate performance or constitute a target market. There is nothing global or domestic (or, for that matter, international or transnational) about a set of public or consumer needs or markets. Needs are there to be understood, then focused on via marketing communication activities. However, the rationale for such activities is to advance the competitive strategy and position of the core organization and to build relationships with customers. Several examples from the business and academic worlds make the point:

The international growth of the *Financial Times*—to the point that its circulation is now greater outside than inside the UK—has been driven by the same trends that have reshaped so many British businesses over the past two decades.... They include ... the rapid increase in cross-border trade and capital flows, the growing acceptance of English as the language of business, and changes in technology.

"The Global Financial Times," *Financial Times*, November 6, 1998

In the environment of the 1990s, globalization must be taken for granted. There will only be one standard for corporate success: international market share. The winning corporations will win by finding markets all over the world.

Jack Welch, CEO, General Electric, 1994, cited in Keegan and Green, 1999

In today's society, only the best companies and brands prosper. As always, there is never a single secret, or panacea, to success. Superior technology, better quality, manufacturing and merchandising efficiencies, and marketing savvy are just a few of the most significant ways in which a company and its brands may succeed. Marketing communication . . . is a critical aspect of a company's overall marketing mission and a major determinant of its success. Indeed, it has been claimed that marketing in [the next millennium] is communication and communication is marketing. The two are inseparable.

Terry Shimp, 1997

All the evidence points to a growing trend toward globalization. Success, primarily, is built on competitive performance. Competitive performance is the major function of marketing effort, and marketing is basically about creating exchanges and ultimately relationships. From an external perspective, market share (or, put another way, the satisfaction of consumer needs) is the desirable outcome. From the same perspective, consumers need to be communicated with effectively. Following Terry Shimp, it is evident that in the highly competitive global marketplace, whatever is marketed (product, service, corporation, political party, idea) also has to be communicated. The most meaningful psychological metaphor for what is to be communicated is the concept of brand.

THE MOVEMENT OF COMMUNICATION TOWARD A GLOBAL BRAND-ORIENTED APPROACH

Most people trained in the marketing discipline recognize that marketing as a practical discipline is a product of the 20th century. However, it was only late in the century that marketing was accepted as a legitimate business activity. It has been argued by Jagdish Sheth et al. (1988) that marketing rests on two pillars: a thorough understanding of consumer needs and behavior and critical analysis of opportunities for competitive advantage. Marketing is about creating satisfactory exchanges via effective and integrated communication with consumers and building relationships with customers and with other publics who could impact organizational performance (the investors, analysts, employees, pressure groups, and so on) by means of effective corporate communication. Businesses are consumer *and* profit oriented. But the marketing concept—creating exchanges that satisfy individual and organizational objectives more effectively and efficiently than the competition—has been proclaimed by Philip Kotler, a leading scholar of marketing, as not entirely appropriate in a world of environmental deterioration, over-population, hunger, poverty, and neglected social services. Thus the societal marketing concept was born—marketing in a way that preserves or enhances consumer *and* societal well-being.

This new type of societal marketing, when coupled with dynamic and irreversible changes in the global economy, means that firms have to engage in a three-pronged balancing act: company profits, consumer need satisfactions, *and* public interest. Each of these responsibilities has resonance for integrated marketing communication. Both profits and consumer want satisfactions are delivered by means of appropriate products, conveniently available, priced appropriately, and communicated relevantly. Each of the 4Ps of marketing, popularized by E. Jerome McCarthy, or the 6Ps of Philip Kotler, is the basis for effective traditional marketing strategies and tactics. Each is focused on target markets. And, in our view, all are quickly becoming the table stakes required *simply to survive*. To prosper in the 21st-century marketplace will likely require more, as we discuss later. Each is interactive and synergistic, and each plays a role in communication.

Following nearly a century of development, most marketing-oriented companies would be expected to get things right. But recently, one of the world's premier branded marketers, Procter & Gamble, discovered that it had forgotten someone—the consumer! Until 1997, P&G was making more than 55 price changes a day across 110 brands, offering more than 400 sales promotions each year, tinkering continually with package design, color, and contents. In the *Wall Street Journal Europe*, Durk Jager, P&G's president and CEO, admitted, "We were confusing [consumers]." P&G has now changed to a more concentrated, less confusing approach.

Marketing has moved from its moorings in national environments and is a global necessity. It is no longer company versus company in a domestic setting but company versus company in a global or international setting. Witness, for example, the recent rush of mergers and acquisitions by firms jockeying for global position: in oil, British Petroleum's taking over Amoco; in automobiles, Daimler's merging with Chrysler. Previous takeovers, such as BMW and Rover in the UK, have not really created economies of scale in production, nor has BMW apparently been able to take advantage of learning and experience curve effects, and there have been image problems. Daimler-Benz's reputation for engineering excellence does not square well with Chrysler's overt focus on finance and marketing. How does the drive to globalized markets affect consumers? Do consumers know of the drive for globalization? More important, do they care?

D. Kirk Davidson argued that consumers don't really care about brand product owners. We would disagree, as more and more consumers are becoming concerned about what companies that market brands actually *do*.

Meanwhile one of us (Schultz) has stated that the brand is the key to integrated marketing. The brand is the center or hub of what consumers want, need, and consider to be of value. But the brand can be a company as well as a functional or emotional benefit wrapped in appropriate packaging.

So, the brand is key. Or is it? It could be argued that in the wake of new media revolution and expansion, in the revitalized focus on target marketing, in the focus on brand/consumer dialogues, in the jockeying for global market share, and juxtaposed with the worldwide demand for marketing to *prove* its contribution, there is pressure on all firms to integrate.

Integration needs to take place on two fronts to be of value. In an age of increasing resemblance between competing brands, where price strategies and distribution channels are fairly uniform, communication is becoming the heart and soul of marketing. Many scholars have stipulated the need for *all* organizational communication to be integrated, but this argument affects not just organizational fiat but also corporate culture, strategies, and brand life cycles.

So what needs to be integrated? Undoubtedly, the brand has become or is becoming the dynamic hub around which all marketing effort and communication revolves. Consumers ultimately own all brands. Firms create brands, but consumers own brands. Firms strive to create brand identities; consumers give brands imagery. Brand images can change as fashions and life cycles change, or, put another way, as consumers change the ways they satisfy their needs. Five years ago Levi Strauss was galloping down the highway of global expansion with a pair of 501s fixed firmly in the saddle; today sales and profits are declining precipitously, and the ambitious goals of the company are turning into layoffs and factory closings. In this case, and despite the spin-off toward work clothes with its Dockers brand, Levi Strauss has encountered the downside of the fashion/casual clothing life cycle and has been supplanted (perhaps only temporarily) by newer and more fashionable icons. But for a while the Levi 501 brand was the center of worldwide profitable growth. Exhibit 4.1 indicates how and in what ways a brand can be the hub for profitable growth. The variables outside the figure are all performed by different factors which are likely to have different perceptions. However, all the factors need to be taken into consideration.

Levi Strauss is an example of a company with a corporate/product brand name. Unable to respond quickly as a result of fashion cycle changes, Levi recently encountered problems in terms of brand image, values, benefits, and barriers, and these factors have impacted both individual brand performance and overall corporate results. For many companies the brand is a twofold entity. The first entity is the brands consumers encounter. From Lysol to Armor-All, from Crest to Zest, consumers the world over know these brands. But consumers increasingly want to know more of the company

EXHIBIT 4.1 · Brand Structure

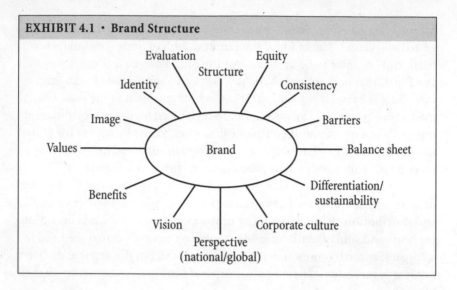

behind the brand. What does it do? What values does it personify? What personalities are running the company? If we are to talk brands, then companies have the usual choices concerning alternative branding strategies (product line branding, specific product branding, corporate branding, combination branding, private label branding, or no brand identity). From a communication perspective, and maybe from the integrated marketing approach, specific product branding (Crest, Pampers, Snickers, etc.) comes to mind. These could be integrated under the heading of what has been described as the promotional mix. But the corporation behind these brands presumably stands for an identity planned by corporate communication specialists and an image possessed by publics impacted by the corporation. This is roughly conceptualized in Exhibit 4.2.

The corporate brand is thus the central core or fulcrum that gives an overall sense of meaning, identity, strategy, and dynamic thrust to the basketful of individual brands within its portfolio. Meanwhile, individual brands, powerful corporate assets in their own right, provide exchanges that inculcate brand loyalty, provide brand equity, and immeasurably enhance and empower corporations that ostensibly "own" them. But these individual brands can be affected by consumer likes, dislikes, tastes, and perceptions. Hence the somewhat arbitrary movement away from Levi Strauss in the late 1990s. But equally, perceptions of the corporation can influence individual brand performances. However, the model is imperfect; it does not show the interactions between brands, nor does it show the interactions between individual brands and the corporation in terms of reflecting overall values associated with both.

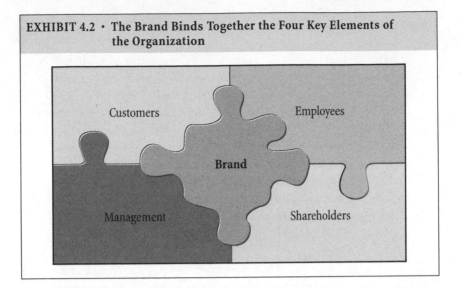

EXHIBIT 4.2 • The Brand Binds Together the Four Key Elements of the Organization

There is a brand puzzle to be solved. From an individual brand perspective, communication needs to be integrated not just at the tactical level but ultimately in terms of financial and strategic integration. This strategy of communication must be underpinned by a sound ongoing analysis of consumer behavior in terms of returns on investment by behavioral segmentation. From a corporate perspective, a similar strategy needs to be deployed to internal organizational members, suppliers, retailers, customers, and analysts. Interactions between the two different types of brand—the corporate brand and individual brands within the corporation's portfolio—have yet to be explained and/or fully analyzed.

INTEGRATED COMMUNICATION

To many managers, executives, and leading-edge managerial and marketing thinkers, globalization is already a reality. But as Theodore Levitt pointed out, the real driving force of marketing is the marketplace that is not merely national or international but is now global. But, as he noted elsewhere:

> . . . the marketplace is not autonomous. It merely reflects the results of those who act upon it: those who "buy" in it, and those who "sell" in it. They marshal materials, technologies, people, sentiment, wits, and money to their intended ends, *meeting head-on in an amalgamating and unforgiving crucible.* (italics added)

He also stated:

> The purpose of business is to get and keep a customer. Without solvent customers in some reasonable proportion, there is no business. Customers are constantly presented with lots of options to help them solve their problems. They don't buy things; they buy solutions to problems. *The surviving and thriving business is a business that constantly seeks better ways to help people solve their problems.* To create betterness requires knowledge of what customers think betterness to be. *This precedes all else in business.* The imagination that figures out what that is, imaginatively figures out what should be done, and does it with imagination and high spirits will drive the enterprise forward. (italics added)

Most of the preceding concerns *marketing* and exchanges, and we agree that the marketing/managerial imagination is what drives initial marketing impetus. But consumers do not choose just brands (usable, functional, or symbolically representative products). They also choose to support (or not) and to carry images (positive or negative) toward companies. The corporation has meaning and resonance for consumers and other publics. Corporate performance is not just a function of how well its brands are doing but also of how well the *company as brand* is doing. In our view it is insufficient to integrate all communication activities at product brand level only. All communication activities at the level of the business or corporation must be integrated as well. Moreover, interaction between the two forms of communication must take place in an ongoing, interactive manner. No walls or barriers should stand between these types of communication, for both ultimately will drive the business forward.

Corporate communication is aimed at publics via a variety of interactive tools. These include corporate advertising, corporate publicity, public affairs, government relations and lobbying activities, issues management, city and analyst relations, and corporate sponsorship. The aim of such activities is to support and underpin image and identity.

CORPORATE IMAGE

Corporate image has been described as the picture people have of a company. In other words, corporate image is "owned" by people without any conscious effort by the company concerned. Cees Van Riel (1995) described image as "the set of meanings by which an object is known and through which people describe, remember and relate to it. That is, the net result of the interaction of a person's beliefs, ideas, feelings, and impressions about an object [company]." This definition corresponds to the idea of fields of experience and memory organization packets discussed in Chapter 3. People can be employees; consumers; suppliers of material, parts, labor, or capital; customers; distributors; agents; joint venture partners; business analysts; share dealers; newspaper editors; business journalists; or pressure groups. Each will have a view, an opinion, and an image, which consciously or unconsciously sway expectations and direct choices.

Integrated communication at the corporate level implies that relationships with each of these publics or groups need to be managed in a pluralistic, interactive manner and with a long-term relationship marketing perspective in mind:

1. Integrated communication, like marketing, needs to be *managed*. It is preceded by a sound understanding of the dynamic(s) of each public. Relationships have to be *planned*, then *implemented, monitored,* and adjusted when necessary. This implies that different marketplaces may require different approaches and different strategic alliances and relationships while not losing sight of the strategic imperative for a globalized approach. Integrated communication is driven by the long term and the strategic vision. The process is not short term, or ad hoc. Reactive fire fighting may occasionally be necessary but must always return to the strategic imperative.

2. Integrated communication is not about one activity. It is diverse in nature and may involve singular or multiple deployment of elements of the corporate communication arsenal.

3. It is not oneway communication but is twoway, interactive, and aimed at mutual beneficiality. Thus it is concerned with identifying, establishing, and maintaining relationships with various publics *nationally, regionally, internationally, and globally.* These relationships presuppose regular monitoring of awareness, attitudes, and behavior inside and outside an organization. *The Economist,* as early as 1989, suggested that this means that large companies have to change the way they talk to and listen to people both inside and outside the organization.

4. Publics able to impact organizational performance are not singular (i.e., consumers) but plural. This means analyzing and adjusting corporate and marketing policies in line with public interests and with the concomitant focus on organizational survival and growth in a globalized market.

Image is too important to be left to chance. Relationships need to be built. Image can be strengthened, reinforced, or improved by organizational efforts to create and manage corporate identity.

CORPORATE IDENTITY

Corporate image can, to a degree, be seen as representative of the identity of an organization conveyed by the messages the organization communicates about itself. Thus images are the ideas that people hold about an organization, while identity is the planned or managed effort by an organization to communicate with its target groups. At best, image will be a microcosm of the attempts an organization makes to communicate its identity. Firms approach identity, or the ways of communicating with publics, in different manners. Cees Van Riel (1995), author of *Principles of Corporate Communication*, indicated at least three different strategies to approach corporate identity:

1. *Monolithic:* The whole company uses one visual style. The company can be recognized instantly, and it uses the same symbols everywhere. Such companies have usually developed as a whole entity within a relatively narrow field. Examples: Shell, Philips, IBM.

2. *Endorsed:* The subsidiary companies have their own style, but the parent company remains recognizable in the background. The different divisions can be recognized, but it is clear which is the parent company. These are diversified companies, the parts of which have retained parts of their own culture, traditions, and/or brands. Examples: General Motors, L'Oreal.

3. *Branded:* The subsidiary companies have their own style, and the parent company is not recognizable to the "uninitiated." The brands appear to have no relation to each other or to the parent company. Separation of brands from parent company limits the risk of product failure, but it also means that the brands cannot benefit from any favorable reputation that the parent company may enjoy. Examples: Unilever, Procter & Gamble.

Ultimately these identity structures (which are not mutually exclusive) are related to different types of strategy. While it is not necessary to review all types of strategy here, plainly companies not only are at different stages in terms of their development but also adopt different strategies based on the overarching organizational strategy, which itself is a function of historical development. However, it is our view that corporations are becoming more visible, more accountable, and less able to hide inside empty corporate raincoats. Corporations have to play a role, become global citizens, be seen to contribute in some way to the quality of life on this planet—in other words, go beyond quid-pro-quo exchanges. For example, what a company does in Asia-Pacific in terms of employment policy impacts corporate image around the world.

Corporate communication at its simplest is a mechanism for developing and managing a set of relationships with publics or interested parties who could affect overall performance. These relationships must be viewed in a long-term, strategic fashion. Even for those firms that maintain a branded approach, many publics are becoming more and more interested in what a company is, where it is coming from, who is managing it, whether problems of an environmental nature are created because of business processes, and how and in what ways the organization as a whole is acting as a corporate citizen. Moreover, each type of firm is involved in the process of analysis, planning, implementation, and control of corporate identity programs in various markets around the world. Images are, to a very significant degree, dependent on the meaningfulness of the identity programs deployed. And, it is relatively straightforward these days via the Internet to access positive information (via a company website), but also to gather criticisms of firms, products, and brands—at least some of the negative aspects of corporate and brand behaviors that most firms would probably like ignored. Organizational image, in our view, can act as a powerful and protective force field in containing and nurturing the basketful of brands within corporate portfolios. Expenditures in the corporate domain, however, are dwarfed by the expenditures taking place at the level of individual brands.

INTEGRATED MARKETING COMMUNICATION

Integrated marketing communication (IMC) was the major communication development in the last decade of the 20th century. Just as businesses do not spring full blown into the arena as global combatants, businesses do not suddenly decide to become integrated. More and more firms are considering communication the key competitive advantage of marketing per se, and we agree with them. Exhibit 4.3 outlines the relationship between integrated communication at the corporate level and integrated marketing communication at the level of the brand.

Most firms have raised the corporate umbrella over the brands within their portfolios. These brands are powerful strategic assets. They need to be protected, nurtured, and developed into international and, in some cases, global brands. But to consumers the only real equity of those brands is in the knowledge organization packets about the brands they use or recognize. What do consumers believe about a company, product, service, or their relationship with the brand? Put another way, what really creates and sustains brand loyalty? It is communication! Product design, packaging, brand name, pricing strategy, location, and ambience of accessibility (or distribution) are all forms of communication. From our perspective, all forms of

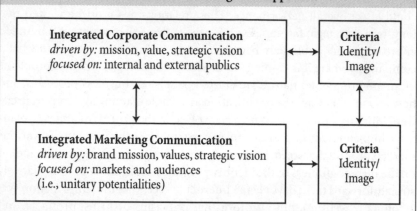

EXHIBIT 4.3 · Corporate Communication and Marketing Communication: An Integrated Approach

Integrated Corporate Communication
driven by: mission, value, strategic vision
focused on: internal and external publics

Criteria
Identity/
Image

Integrated Marketing Communication
driven by: brand mission, values, strategic vision
focused on: markets and audiences
(i.e., unitary potentialities)

Criteria
Identity/
Image

communication over which the company can exercise control or influence can be integrated. Firms do not arrive at integration overnight. Instead they progress through at least four stages, as shown in Figure 4.4.

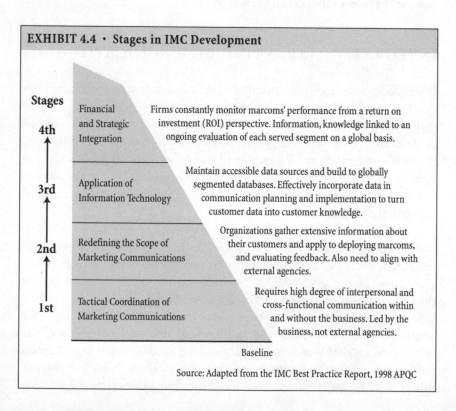

EXHIBIT 4.4 · Stages in IMC Development

Stages

4th — Financial and Strategic Integration — Firms constantly monitor marcoms' performance from a return on investment (ROI) perspective. Information, knowledge linked to an ongoing evaluation of each served segment on a global basis.

3rd — Application of Information Technology — Maintain accessible data sources and build to globally segmented databases. Effectively incorporate data in communication planning and implementation to turn customer data into customer knowledge.

2nd — Redefining the Scope of Marketing Communications — Organizations gather extensive information about their customers and apply to deploying marcoms, and evaluating feedback. Also need to align with external agencies.

1st — Tactical Coordination of Marketing Communications — Requires high degree of interpersonal and cross-functional communication within and without the business. Led by the business, not external agencies.

Baseline

Source: Adapted from the IMC Best Practice Report, 1998 APQC

Tactical Coordination

Firms at this first stage of tactical coordination focus on the idea of *one sight, one sound,* integrating promotional elements such as advertising, sales promotion, marketing public relations, direct marketing, and/or the Internet. Firms also strive to maximize consistency and synergy among all promotional mix elements and may instruct advertising agencies to maximize all potential exposures to the brand through a multiplicity of different media. Typically, and in accord with marketing communication theory, messages may vary in content, but the same core values will be depicted repeatedly. Repetition of the same promotional campaigns, however, which have been successful, say, in the United States, will undoubtedly mean problems if adopted wholesale overseas. Typically consumers may respond in different ways simply because their fields of experience differ.

Redefining the Scope of Marketing Communication

At this second stage the firm starts to adopt an outside-in (as opposed to inside-out) perspective. Typically the focus here is on the consumer's perception. Rather than simply integrating from a tactical stage 1 perspective, businesses look at *all potential contacts* a customer or consumer may have with a product, service, brand, or company. For the first time firms start to consider integrated communication from the dual perspective and potentially to align all communication with the needs of corporate publics and exchange partners.

Application of Information Technology

The third stage does not constitute the arrival and incorporation of consumer and customer data as the driving force for marketing activity. Usually this empirical data is already available inside the organization. Instead the firm starts to apply the data to identify, value, and monitor the impact of integrated communication programs to key customer target markets or segments over time.

Financial and Strategic Integration

The fourth stage constitutes the highest level of integration, where the emphasis moves to deploying both the marketing database(s) derived from stage 3, with the previous abilities derived from stage 1 and stage 2 to drive corporate and marketing strategic planning using customer information and insight. Firms in this stage will tend to reevaluate financial information infrastructures to aid development of "closed-loop" planning and evaluation to determine and measure marketing expenditures based on return on investment customer and consumer measures.

Contextual Overview

The majority of firms, whether international or global in scope or scale, are moving through these stages, though few will be at stage 4. Most multinationals will be working at stage 1 or 2, with a view considering how to integrate their large marketing databases with the customer segments or niches they are serving and the to-be-targeted marketing communication. However, overlaid on this ideal template will be firms positioned in their historical, cultural, and managerial context; likewise each brand within the corporate portfolio may be positioned nationally, internationally, regionally, or globally.

IMC DEFINED

In a study of IMC within advertising agencies in the United States, United Kingdom, Australia, New Zealand, India, and South Africa, this definition was used:

> IMC is a concept of marketing communication planning that recognizes the added value of a comprehensive plan that evaluates the strategic role of a number of communication disciplines (for example, general advertising, direct response, sales promotion, and public relations) and combines these disciplines to provide clarity, consistency, and maximum communication impact.

This early definition was based on developmental work at Northwestern University's Medill School of Journalism. For its time the definition was useful. Most ad agency practitioners in the countries mentioned agreed (*to an extent*) that this definition adequately conceptualized IMC. From this definition, in 1993 IMC was somewhat strategic in nature and tactical in implementation; in other words, it was very closely linked with stages 1 and 2 of IMC development. Some ad agencies, particularly in the United States, were starting to express some misgivings or attempting to expand the definition. At least part of the definitional process was bound up inexorably with the rapidly changing marketing communication landscape in the 1990s. IMC itself was evolving with input from academics and practitioners around the world. A more succinct definition for the 21st century is suggested:

IMC is a strategic business process used to plan, develop, execute and evaluate coordinated measurable, persuasive brand communication programs over time with consumers, customers, prospects, and other targeted, relevant external and internal audiences.

This definition first focuses on strategy—a strategy of communication that is clearly related to corporate mission, values, and needs, but relates equally to brand mission, values, and needs. At both levels executives will need to develop resonance and consonance in terms of brand identity. Simultaneously, empirical studies in relation to clearly segmented target markets and publics need to be carried out to ascertain and measure brand image. Results need to be measured in behavioral, not just attitudinal, terms. Executives need to know the return on investment from any communication activity. A strategic business process suggests an ongoing approach in what may be a global market or a national market where *for now* the global approach may be inappropriate. For each delineated audience measurable outcomes need to be specified in advance. Also crucial will be an understanding of what is persuasive. Can a persuasive message, delivered via a variety of media in one country, exert similar persuasiveness when deployed elsewhere?

CONCLUSIONS

- Whatever is marketed must also be communicated, and the brand is the best psychological vehicle for delivering meaning.
- The new concept of societal marketing means that you consider not only shareholder value but also how to enhance societal well-being.
- Corporate image is owned by people inside and outside the company, whether you consciously try to implant that image or not.
- Integrated marketing communication offers you a way to meld image and brand meaning into a unified message—but it takes strategic and financial commitment to realize the potential of IMC.

Developing Integrated Global Marketing Communication Programs

As we've discussed, developing an integrated global marketing communication (IGMC) program involves more than simply agreeing on a corporate logo or icon, a recommended corporate color, or even an advertising campaign that can be translated into a number of cultures and languages. Nor, from a corporate view, is an IGMC program simply a press release that can be edited so as to be made appropriate for various international editions of business publications and the multiple stakeholders that might see it. From a more decentralized view, IGMC is much more than determining if the communication program could or should be localized or if a full global message and image can be created and delivered. To develop a truly integrated global marketing communication program requires a number of skills, talents, and capabilities in the organization. Some of those may be present now, some may have to be learned, and still others may have to be outsourced.

CRITICAL REQUIREMENTS FOR IGMC PROGRAMS

An organization must either have or have access to nine basic elements to become a truly integrated global communicator. In reviewing these requirements, the marketing or communication manager's first comments might well be "These aren't communication issues. These are management or finance or technology or operations activities. We do only the communication here. We don't develop the strategy or run the company." For traditional managers those are legitimate concerns. For the most part marketing communication managers have dealt primarily with advertising, promotion, or merchandising content, message production, and distribution issues. Strategic concerns have generally resided elsewhere in the organization. However, IGMC must become a strategic resource of the organization, not just a functional support tool. As we argued in Chapter 1, if most organizations will have no product, price, distribution, or even people advantage in the 21st-century marketplace, then communication and ultimately brands, branding, and the resulting relationships those activities create and maintain with customers become the organization's only true competitive advantages. Thus marketing communication moves from a primarily support role to one of leadership in the organization. IGMC moves from just echoing what the product is or does to identifying customers and prospects and where the organization should invest its finite resources.

COMPETENCIES ASSOCIATED WITH MASTERING IGMC

The following are the nine key areas we believe the organization must master or at least be able to access to develop effective globally integrated marketing communication programs.

Create Global Processes and Standardization

As evident in the Dow Chemical case (Case Study 3), internal and external standardization is mandatory in a global arena. The ability to create systems and processes that can cross borders, cultures, and businesses becomes absolutely critical. Until the organization has standardized methods of operating, producing, transporting, and communicating, it will be nothing more than a group of geographically based elements struggling to find common ground with its other parts. In most cases this standardization comes about through the development of operating systems. Dow chose to initiate a totally new internal operating system. Other organizations have chosen to standardize on existing platforms. Still others are struggling to find a common solution. In no area is standardization more important than in communication. The organization simply must have ways of communicating up, down, and across to succeed. Review the requirements of an international company and worldwide knowledge transfer described in Chapter 2 as a prelude to our discussion of the IGMC process described later in this chapter.

Start with Customers, Not Products or Geographies

IGMC is founded on communicating with all internal and external customer groups. Historically most communication started with what the organization wanted to sell. The communicator's task was to find ways to deliver messages to the most likely prospects. For the most part this was an inside-out approach to marketing communication. What products are to be sold? To whom? Where should messages be directed? In what form? Through which media?

Integrated global marketing communication flips the process around. IGMC starts with the customers—who they are, what they do, what interests they have—and then works backward to design products and communication. For example, questions in an IGMC process generally start with: How does the customer or prospect behave toward our product category now? Do they use it? Have they used it? Might they use it? What information do they have about our products, services, or brands now? What would they need or like to know? How can we make that information or knowledge or material available to them? This approach puts the customer, not the marketer or the product, in the center of the system, as described in Chapter 2. Where historically the product was at the center and the system was marketer driven and currently the distributor is at the center and the system is channel driven, the 21st-century global marketplace will be interactive and customer driven.

Inherent in our approach is the need to consider all the organization's stakeholders in the marketing communication process. As noted in Chapter 4, the organization has a number of stakeholders, all of whom have an interest in the firm and can impact future success. Noncustomer stakeholders can range from government authorities to lobbyists and pressure groups. In addition, they might be employees or channel partners or distributors. All these groups may be crucial to the short- and long-term success of the organization. However, most internal and external stakeholders have a limited influence on income, affecting only the level of income flow generated from end users. The global marketing communication manager must always keep in mind that end users are the only people who generate income for the firm. They supply the dollars or pesos or yen at the top and provide the organization the resources to manage and determine the profits that are generated at the bottom. If the organization has no customers, it has no future no matter how supportive or influential the other stakeholders may be.

Identify and Value Customers and Prospects

Since customers and prospects are the key elements in the success of the organization, we must have some method of identifying and valuing these people or firms. Commonly we value customers based on the income flows they have produced in the past and their potential for the future. Further, we can value prospects based on what income flows they might create for the firm in the future. In other words, we look at customers and prospects as assets.

Our task as communicators is to manage those assets so they produce the greatest return to the company. Thus the finite resources of the organization must be directed toward the best customers or prospects either to continue current income flows or to generate new or increased income flows. It's as simple as that: the firm must direct its communication resources toward those customers and prospects most likely to pay the best returns. Inherent in this approach is the requirement that there must be some way to identify or value customers and prospects for investment. If we can't value them or estimate what return we might get from investments in them, there is no way to determine either how much we should invest in communication or how we might measure the returns. In the IGMC approach we make great use of information technology to capture and analyze vast amounts of information about customers and prospects. We will describe this process in more detail later in this chapter.

Identification of Customer and Prospect Contact Points

In today's crowded and confused marketplace it is not so much how an organization wants to communicate with customers and prospects but understanding how and where and in what ways the customer or prospect already comes into contact with the firm. For example, among present customers any type of marketing communication the organization might develop pales in comparison to the many ways in which the customer already receives volumes of information about the company, its products and services, how it views customers, how it services and supports its products, and so on. For example, a present customer interacts with the product or service in use and with the channels or systems through which it is delivered. Commonly various forms of customer service or inquiry resolution or technological support are provided. And so on. Contact points with present customers are numerous.

The same is true with prospects. They observe product or service users in the marketplace. They see product and service evaluations in the media. They listen to or ignore advocates. Undoubtedly the paid, planned, and measured communication programs the organization develops are only a part of what exists in the marketplace and to which customers and prospects alike, along with employees and stakeholders, are exposed. Thus the task of the IGMC manager is not just to prepare and deliver integrated marketing communication programs. It is also to understand how and where and in what ways customers and prospects come into contact with the brand and the organization. The task is *process*—to understand the system, not just the specific elements involved, and then to begin to *manage* global communication programs in an integrated fashion. How one organization looks at the global communication system is illustrated in Exhibit 5.1.

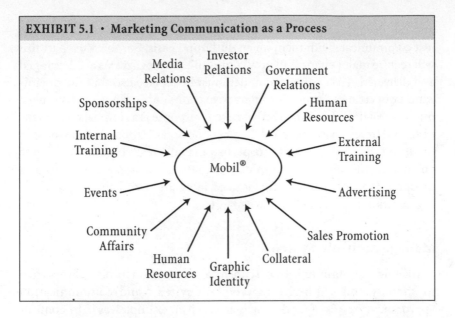

EXHIBIT 5.1 • Marketing Communication as a Process

Mobil Oil considers all the forms and ways it communicates with customers and prospects and attempts to manage all those elements as a process. In some cases Mobil controls the communication activities; in others it doesn't. The critical factor is to know and understand the system in which the organization operates and how that can impact the overall fortunes of the organization.

Align the Organization's Interactive Response Capabilities

Traditionally marketing and communication organizations have focused primarily on developing and implementing outbound communication programs. That is, the organization has decided what it wanted to do and then set about planning programs that would implement those decisions. While some attention was paid to what customers or prospects wanted or what they might need, the primary emphasis in planning was on developing persuasive messages and incentives that stated the organization's views in the most appealing and creative ways possible.

For the most part companies have had limited listening posts through which to assess customer needs or wants, relying primarily on sales force reports and formalized market research and increasingly on customer service activities and data. As a result the organization focused on outbound communication programs for selected groups that it believed had potential. (Refer back to the marketer-driven and distribution-driven marketplaces discussed in Chapter 1.) The primary focus of the organization in the

21st-century marketplace must be its ability to respond to customers, not just communicate with them on an outbound basis. For the most part this will require major changes in how communication programs are developed and delivered. The outbound model must be replaced so that the organization can create and manage interactive communication with customers, often in real time. In an interactive system response is as important as planning, and time becomes critical. Further, the organization must be focused totally on the customer and prospect so that all areas combine to provide an integrated global communication message to every customer and prospect. We will deal with this idea of integration and alignment of the organization in more detail in Chapter 6.

Manage Multiple Systems

Marketing and communication scholars and practitioners have always tried to simplify and synthesize marketplace systems and communication approaches (the 4Ps of marketing is an excellent example), as if, by controlling those elements, we could control customers and competitors. The same is true with marketing communication. We used the AIDA (attention, interest, desire, action) model, again believing if we could manage the process we could convince customers and prospects to buy. Obviously a global marketplace is far more complex and certainly not simple to summarize and synthesize. Indeed the marketing and communication manager of the 21st century must recognize that there are multiple markets, multiple marketplaces, multiple customers, multiple channels, multiple media, and so on, as illustrated in the three-marketplace scenario developed in Chapter 1 and depicted in Exhibit 5.2.

The first task of the manager will be to identify the marketplace in which the organization is operating. That, of course, will depend on the customers and prospects to be served. In many cases the manager will quickly discover that there are customers and prospects in all three of the marketplaces illustrated in Exhibit 5.2. And there may well be some in totally new and different marketplaces specific to the organization. The key challenge is to recognize the marketplaces and the various customers and then define IGMC programs to serve them. Often this analysis reveals the need for multiple marketing and communication programs. While there is commonly a need for an umbrella approach for the brand, generally specific communication programs are needed for individual markets and customers and prospects. In other words, for the most part the global marketing communication manager is involved in multiple communication programs in multiple markets for multiple customer groups. Do not confuse this multiplicity of programs with differences in geographies, languages, and cultures. Instead, recognize that the differentiation will come from different customers with

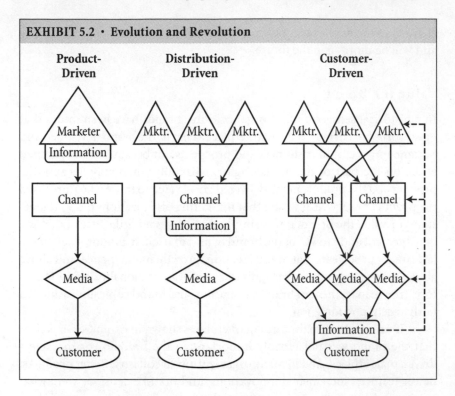

EXHIBIT 5.2 • Evolution and Revolution

different needs seeking different types of information and responses from the marketing organization. While there may well be local market requirements to deal with—language, culture, customs, and the like—it is the customer who will drive the system, not the other way around. It is this customer-based approach to marketing communication that differentiates IGMC from the traditional international or multinational programs of the past.

One of the best examples of how globalization has changed many of the traditional planning approaches in marketing communication has been the development of global media systems and brands. For example, CNN and BBC circle the globe. They can be received in most countries where television is available. Yet these organizations generally broadcast in only a single language, English. MTV is a bit different. MTV, while featuring the same artists and concepts, changes the language and some of the music to fit the local country, though the basic approach is the same. In print, *Playboy* magazine is published in multiple countries, in local languages, with local stories and personalities. But the *Playboy* concept is the same. Thus what we see today is the development of circular groups of customers and prospects around the globe. They have the same interests, purchase the same products, and are attuned to a culture and approach they have adopted no matter where they live or what language they speak. This globalization of markets is a key element in the development of marketing communication programs today and will be more so in the future.

Value the Brand

In a historical sense, for many organizations, brands have been things that have "sort of occurred" in the marketplace. That is, the brand developed and became important to customers and prospects not because of any planned effort on the part of the marketing organization but simply because the product and the product name delivered good value to those who purchased the product or service. It wasn't that marketing organizations didn't understand or value the brand, it was simply that they paid little attention to the management and growth of the brand in and of itself. It has only been in the last twenty or so years that brand creation, growth, maintenance, and above all *value* have begun to be recognized as an organizational priority. Therefore, true management of brands, branding, and brand communication is a fairly recent phenomenon.

If we refer back to the three marketplaces shown in Exhibit 5.2, it is clear that the brand was not terribly important in the product- or marketer-driven marketplace. And in many organizations it still isn't. Better products, newer features, incremental innovations, and brand extensions were what marketer-driven organizations were and still are all about. The same is true for distribution-driven marketers. The brand is a name to differentiate products and services from others in the distribution system. It was generally not a major factor in the success of the firm. It is only when all the traditional marketing activities become commodified or easily replicated that the value of the brand comes to the fore. Our argument is that in a customer-driven marketplace the brand, and the brand's relationship with customers and prospects and other shareholders, will be the primary competitive advantage organizations will have. As a result, to compete in any of the marketplaces we have described earlier, it is important to understand and manage the brand properly, including, if necessary, the dualistic approach discussed in Chapter 4.

Focus on Financial Measures

To be honest, many marketing and communication activities in the past have been weak on measurement, particularly when an attempt was made to relate marketing communication spending to financial returns. The measurement focus has traditionally been on attitudinal responses from customers—awareness, preference, intent to buy, and the like—rather than on what actually happened in terms of returns on the investments. While there are many reasons for this lack of focus on the financial aspects of marketing and communication, this myopic process does not have to continue. New technology and improved financial management mandate that marketing communication managers be able to relate their financial expenditures on marketing and communication to the financial returns received as a result of those investments. Whether this is considered accountability, stewardship, or simply ROI (return on investment), marketing communication managers must be able to relate what was spent or invested to what was received in return.

In the IGMC approach, we use financial investments and returns from customers and prospects as the basis for evaluation. Part of the difficulty in measuring the return on marketing communication investments has been a lack of precision in setting objectives. The two are intertwined; if you can't measure, you can't set realistic objectives. If you don't set objectives, you can't measure. Given that the firm has finite resources, the ability to invest those resources in activities that will generate the greatest returns is critical. Thus in the IGMC process we focus on financial objectives and use attitudinal measures to understand customer behavior and to better understand our success in the marketplace.

Create Horizontal Organizational Structures

Managers have always organized things on a vertical basis. The Romans created vertical structures with their legions. Kings created vertical structures with very defined levels of prestige and authority. Organizations have been built on vertical structures such as divisions, sectors, units, and the like. Yet the global marketplace demands *horizontal*, not vertical, structures, the ability to work across business units, the ability to cross borders and cultures. The demand today is for singular units that can access and use all the talents in the organization to focus on customer needs and wants. This demand for horizontal, not vertical, approaches is perhaps the most difficult challenge for any organization attempting to operate globally.

As you will recall from Chapter 2, most organizations are not global in their structure at all. In many cases they are not even international. Instead they are multidomestics with kingdoms and fiefdoms run by local managers spread across the globe. Yet, if you will remember our mythical case example of Marvel Products and Whiz-Bang Stores, customers today want one point of contact, one billing and delivery system, and one pricing schedule. That requires horizontal structures, not vertical ones. Global communication must cross borders, geographies, and cultures effortlessly and quickly. That means communication must move across and through and around and among groups and firms. That is horizontal organization in action. We will

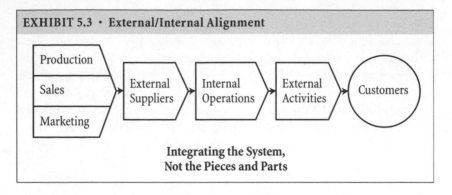

EXHIBIT 5.3 · External/Internal Alignment

Production
Sales
Marketing
→ External Suppliers → Internal Operations → External Activities → Customers

**Integrating the System,
Not the Pieces and Parts**

discuss this horizontal approach in more detail in Chapter 8. In the meantime, Exhibit 5.3 illustrates how the organization must align and integrate itself to focus on customers and prospects.

As illustrated in Exhibit 5.3, the organization must align and integrate all the various elements in the communication process. That means internal integration and organization so that marketing, sales, operations, production, and the like are all working together and focused on the customer. Similarly, external suppliers must be aligned and integrated. Internal operations, which generally include employees, channels, and support units, must be aligned as well. Likewise, external communication in the form of advertising, public relations, sales promotion, direct marketing, events, and the like must be integrated and aligned with a customer focus.

THE EIGHT-STEP INTEGRATED GLOBAL MARKETING COMMUNICATION PLANNING PROCESS

The first step in the development of an IGMC program is the planning process. We have developed this process to include and enhance the nine competencies for mastering IGMC. As we work through the process, you will be able to see how the various elements fit together and flow as a process.

The eight-step planning process discussed on the following pages has been used successfully with a number of companies around the world. It is a logical approach that leads the planner through the various steps involved in developing a successful communication program. It is not, however, a template that can be used as a fill-in-the-blanks tool. Instead it is a thinking process, a format and structure designed to lead to logical outcomes and successful programs. Some organizations may need to expand some of the steps; others may need to delete some of the activities. Much depends on the specific organization in its current contextual circumstances for which the com-

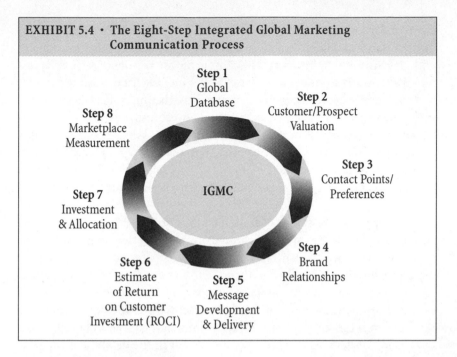

EXHIBIT 5.4 • The Eight-Step Integrated Global Marketing Communication Process

munication program is being planned. We will illustrate some of those alternatives when we explain the process in more detail in Chapter 6.

Exhibit 5.4 shows the circular nature of the IGMC planning process: working through all eight steps takes us back to step 1. Through this closed-loop planning system the learning from each step in the process and from each completed communication program is included and combined with the data previously gathered and stored and provides a basis for planning the next stage of the communication plan or the next communication program. We are continuously learning from marketplace experience. We are continuously improving and enhancing our knowledge of customers and prospects. We are constantly testing our assumptions and connecting them to marketplace reality. As we will explain in more detail in Chapter 6, the idea of a closed-loop system is an integral part of the overall IGMC process.

Step 1. Global Customer/Prospect Databases

One of the key ingredients in the IGMC approach to developing effective and efficient global marketing communication programs is substantive, continually updated knowledge about customers and prospects. That generally comes from data and information stored electronically in a customer or prospect database or in databases that the organization may maintain. While we will delve into databases in more detail in Chapter 6, the most important element for an organization to capture and be able to use in planning is information that describes or illustrates the relationship the organization has with the customer or prospect. This simple phrase *relationship with the customer or prospect* separates a database from a mailing list or various types of segmentation schemes. To plan and manage marketing and marketing communication on a global basis, the organization simply must have information on its customer relationships, whether that be sales, service, or simply contact with customers and prospects. Without this type of data, the firm must resort to practicing mass marketing on a global scale. The database is the core of any integrated global marketing communication planning process.

Most useful databases contain, at a minimum, details on past purchases by the customer or qualifications of prospects that allow them to be separated from mere suspects. Generally, most organizations will have demographic details attached to their customer's records such as location, age, sex, education, income, and the like for consumers or end users. In the business-to-business area, commonly the records will include products or services produced, number of employees, annual turnover, standard industrial code (SIC), and so on. The key ingredient in the database is the relationship the organization has developed with customers and prospects over time, reflected in data on purchases, inquiries, responses to promotions, and other behavioral data that allow the organization to determine what actions the customers or prospects have taken in the past and thus what might be expected in the future. Such longitudinal data provides the most insight for the marketing organization. If one can observe customer behavior over time, it is much easier to understand the buying strategy the customers are employing or at least the trade-offs being made in brand purchase and supplier selection.

Databases come in many forms. Ideally they are electronic so the data can be managed and analyzed by multiple people in the organization. Hard copy sales records and the like often have to suffice in less-developed economies. The key ingredient in a database is bringing all the known information and data about customers and prospects together in one easily accessible form, whether that be electronic or hard copy. It is here that most organizations have the most difficulty. In too many instances customer files are set up individually by country or, even worse, by strategic business units (SBUs) within a certain geography. Commonly, the needed data was organized to provide working knowledge for the group that initiated the database without consideration for how that data might be used by other divisions. Thus one of the major challenges for almost all organizations is simply gathering and combining the data that they currently hold on customers and prospects and putting it into some usable form that can be accessed by those needing information, no matter where they may be or how the information might be used.

In a benchmarking study conducted in the United States in 1997 on best practices in integrated marketing communication, we found that one of the major differences between best practice organizations and those seeking to improve their integrated processes was that the best practice organizations had managed to integrate their global databases while those seeking to emulate them had not. There is clear evidence that the database is the key to developing effective IGMC programs.

Step 2. Customer/Prospect Valuation

The critical nature of the global customer database becomes apparent when we consider that step 2 in the IGMC process is to value customers or prospects in some way. The reason for this valuation is simple. If we are to invest the finite resources of the organization in cultivating the best customers and prospects, we must have some way of valuing each of them as a basis for this investment process.

The best way we have found to value customers and prospects is financially, that is, by determining their purchases, or what we call "income flows." If we know the financial value of a customer or prospect, we have a solid base from which we might determine the amount we would be willing to invest to either retain, grow, or migrate that customer to other products or services in our portfolio. Likewise, if we have some idea of the financial value of a prospect, that is, how much income that person or group might generate in the future, we would have a fair idea of how much we would be willing to invest to acquire that prospect and turn him or her into a customer. Experience around the globe has shown that neither all customers nor all prospects are alike in terms of their current or future value to the firm. Therefore we convert the typical marketing and communication tasks of implanting messages or gaining awareness into solid financial decisions that allow us to differentiate one customer or group of customers from another.

Step 3. Contact Points and Preferences

Traditionally, marketing communication managers have made the decisions as to how and when and under what circumstances customers and prospects were contacted, or at least exposed to the organization's marketing messages. Thus, historically, the primary goal of the marketing communicator has been to get the messages and incentives in front of customers and prospects efficiently with only passing regard for effectiveness. As a result, various forms of efficiency measures such as CPM (cost per thousand) delivered, gross impressions, total audience, and the like have been developed. Only rarely have we developed or used effectiveness measures—cost per sale, cost per order, return on investment, or the like—except in direct selling situations. When we use financial measures to value customers and prospects, many of our traditional media and communication tools become woefully inadequate. But, there is a larger problem as well.

We are now beginning to understand that customers and prospects come in contact with the organization in a multiplicity of ways in the marketplace. Often these marketplace contacts come about with employees or channel partners or service groups or other nonmarketing people. Yet these communication or brand contacts are often much more powerful messages or relationships than those the communication manager can develop or deliver. Thus our focus in the planning process is to attempt to audit and value the various ways in which customers already come into contact with the organization. From this we can then view each of those contact points as useful methods of communicating in the future. In many cases the most powerful communication tools at the disposal of the integrated global marketing communication manager are noncontrollable but manageable communication methods both internal and external to the organization.

It is critical to determine what communication approaches customers and prospects prefer since, given the many alternatives available, we simply can't push our wishes on them. Instead we must respond to their preferences. As outlined in the Dow Chemical case (Case Study 3), it's no longer how the organization wants to communicate; it's how the customer wants to communicate that really matters in the global system. Understanding current and existing customer contact points and preferences is critical to the IGMC process.

Another important part of understanding contact points is the impact of various internal and external stakeholders. For example, an environmental group may mount a strong communication program against the practices of our brand or organization. Or it may attempt to obtain legislation that would impact or restrict the operations of the organization. The group may achieve great public awareness through the press and electronic media. Obviously the global marketing communication planner must take these activities into consideration. The same is true for other stakeholders such as the financial community, government and legislative bodies, unions, and other organized groups. While these stakeholder actions and activities may or may not be related directly to the specific audience, for whom the marketing communication program is being planned, the communication manager must factor them into the overall program to account for the impact they may have in the marketplace.

Step 4. Brand or Organization Relationships

Obviously, there are major differences in how a firm should or would communicate with a long-term, valuable customer and how it would communicate with ones with which it has had little or no relationship. That sounds obvious, but many global organizations attempt to treat all customers the same, or at least they do so in their communication activities. The common practice for many marketing communication managers is to prepare one advertisement and, using various forms of mass media, send it out to every customer, prospect, suspect, and even those who are not interested. The same is commonly done with direct mail packages, brochures, product literature, and most other forms of communication. Everyone is the same to the communication manager, so all are treated the same in the communication program. Often, this is done in the guise of efficiency, the rationale being that it is less expensive to produce one common piece of communication than to try to individualize. Unfortunately, such efficiency is not always more effective. And in the customer-driven marketplace of the 21st century it is effectiveness that will count the most.

We have different relationships with different customers and prospects. That simple fact determines and defines step 4 in the IGMC process. We simply must understand the relationship customers and prospects have with our firm to develop effective marketing communication programs. We must also understand the relationship customers believe they have with us. That is perhaps the more important point.

For the most part customers have relationships with brands; that is, they have confidence in the brand and the organization that produces it. There is a famous saying, often attributed to Jim Taylor, former marketing director of Gateway Computers: "The brand is a promise and it is a promise we must keep with customers. There is no difference between what we sell and what we are." This has never been truer than now. Customers buy brands. Customers trust brands. Customers rely on brands, but most of all customers have relationships with brands. To build effective communication programs, the marketing communication planner must know what type of relationship the customer has with the brand.

It is also important to take into account the activities of various stakeholder groups. The goals of these groups may be either to enhance or to destroy brand relationships. While they often have only an indirect impact or effect, they must be considered if an effective IGMC program is to be developed. In Chapter 6 we will outline methods for understanding customer-brand relationships and, from that, enhancing or initiating brand relationships.

Step 5. Message and Incentive Development and Delivery

One of the most dramatically different features of the IGMC process is that development of messages and incentives, generally at the heart of any marketing communication program, is fairly far down in the development process. That reflects the basic premise of IGMC: you can't develop effective messages or incentives unless and until you understand the people and organizations you are trying to communicate with. In our experience, all too often communication managers come up with a clever idea or a neat concept and then try to fit that to the audience. In other words, the creative, rather than the customers and prospects or publics for whom the communication is being designed, drives the communication. Creative is important, but it must be controlled creative that reaches and impacts customers and prospects, not creative that is simply unique and different for its own sake.

You may have noticed that we use the terms *messages* and *incentives* rather than *advertising* or *public relations* or *sales promotion*. This is intentional. In our research we have found that customers rarely differentiate among the functional areas of marketing communication. Instead they tend to roll up the functional areas into messages and incentives. In other words, customers say "This organization is trying to tell me something or to get me to remember this or that." In other words, the customer perceives that the organization is trying to deliver a message. Alternatively, customers and prospects, on viewing other types of marketing communication activities, will say, "This firm wants me to do something and is offering me an incentive to do it—a coupon or discount or a limited time offer." In this case the customer takes the information to mean that the marketer desires short-term action and is offering an incentive to encourage a favorable decision. So, to align our thinking, we have converted to customer or consumer terms. We will use messages or incentives in our planning process rather than refer to the functional activities that have gained popularity over the years.

Along with the development of messages and incentives, this step includes delivery systems. Historically, we have thought of delivery systems as being forms of media—print or broadcast, in-store or through the mail, and so forth. The broader view, that delivery systems include whenever and wherever a customer or prospect comes into contact with the brand or the organization, gives us a new view of how we might communicate with our audiences. In truth the concept of delivery systems opens up totally new forms of communication for the IGMC planner. It also removes many of the restrictions and constraints that previously existed. With this new freedom for the planner, however, comes accountability. That is, if new and unique forms of delivery are to be used, there must be methods and ways of measuring the impact and effect of those delivery systems so they can be compared with existing media forms. Delivery systems may be more important in the 21st-century marketplace than messages or incentives. If the message or incentive can't be delivered to the intended customer or prospect, it really doesn't matter what the message or incentive is or was. Thus delivery systems have become extremely important and will become even more so in our view in the years ahead.

Obviously one of the major decisions at this point will be whether or not the marketing communication program should be local, regional, or global. We will discuss the alternatives in the next chapter and provide some guidelines for what really determines how the particular marketing communication program should be executed. Those decisions will have a great deal to do with the level of investment we make in the IGMC program and how we allocate our finite resources.

Step 6. Estimate of Return on Customer Investment (ROCI)

With a thorough knowledge of customers and prospects, their knowledge and understanding of our firm and our brands, and their relationship with them and to us, we now should be able to develop appropriate messages and incentives and find ways to deliver them to relevant customers and prospects. The next logical step is to estimate what type of return or response we might generate from our marketing activities. In the IGMC process, we call this *return on customer investment (ROCI)*, not the more familiar *return on investment (ROI)*. While the differentiation may sound like nitpicking, there are sound reasons for speaking of ROCI rather than ROI.

Most organizations get absolutely nothing back from their advertising investments. That is, no return is given for their level of spending. Media groups do not refund or rebate amounts to the organization for the investment. Nor does the postal service give a refund for properly using its facilities. Income from marketing communication comes not from doing the activities or events or even doing them well. The only return an organization gets from its communication activities is from customers and prospects. They are the ones who respond to the communication programs by purchasing the firm's goods or services, thereby producing income. Therefore our approach is to attempt to estimate what type of return we might get from investing in various customers or customer groups. Obviously, the better the customers or prospects we choose to invest in, the better our returns should be.

One of the key ingredients necessary to estimate any type of return from a customer is knowledge of the current value of that customer. In other words, we must know what the customer is worth now to be able to estimate what we might get back from any level of investment in the future. Our initial information will come from step 2, where we estimated the current and potential value of the customer. By knowing that value and what our investment in messages and incentives might be, we can begin to estimate what type of return we might generate. Clearly, in planning an IGMC program, we will rely on estimates of returns—that is, based on experience or research or management knowledge, what we reasonably assume might come back. Once the program is in the marketplace, however, if we have set up the necessary closed-loop systems, we should be able to measure the actual results of our investments. Thus we start with estimates and convert those into actual returns as we capture marketplace results. In Chapter 6 we will show how this might be done.

This initial estimating activity is critically important to the IGMC process. We generally have before us a wide variety of activities and alternative messages and communication programs. Only by estimating in advance can we determine which might be most valuable or return the greatest result to the organization. It is this testing process that leads to step 7, investment and allocation.

It is in this step and the next that we first meet the question of time frames on returns. If we invest our resources now, when can we expect to see a return on those customers against whom we have invested? Would our returns be short term, within the current fiscal year of the organization, or would we expect to get our returns over several accounting periods or perhaps several fiscal years? This is a major decision for most organizations and has a great deal to do with the investment of finite corporate resources.

Step 7. Investment and Allocation

The next step in the IGMC process is the actual determination of the financial investment we plan to make in customers and prospects through various forms of IGMC programs. This is primarily a process of matching up costs of various marketing communication activities and testing them against estimated returns. Here a great deal of judgment is needed along with the information and material that is contained in our databases and our actual marketplace experience. For example, we may know we need to deliver messages to a specific group. At this point the question becomes: should this be done through media advertising, through direct marketing approaches, or would it be most effective through in-store point-of-purchase? Here is where the knowledge of the marketing communication manager comes into play. While there might be equally relevant returns to the firm from any of these investments, the question is what will provide the best returns on the investment. Thus allocation of resources to messages and incentives is one of testing and evaluation of alternatives both by the communication manager prior to the investment and through actual marketplace results, as we will see in step 8.

The critical step in most investment and allocation decisions is to take a zero-based budgeting approach. There should be no preconceived conditions or preset media or delivery choices. Each decision should be made independently, allowing for interaction among the various programs being planned and executed. Inherent in this approach is the idea of media neutrality: decisions will be based on what will provide the best return to the organization, not on which medium is most attractive to the planner or what might be considered the "sexiest" allocation decision. We are dealing with the finite resources of the organization and must recognize that we are investing our resources in developing the best customers and prospects in hopes of the greatest returns. After all, that is why we have gone through this entire process in the first place.

Step 8. Marketplace Measurement

Once the investment and allocation decisions have been made, the final step is to set up systems of measurement to determine what really happened in the marketplace. Of course, most of those decisions—what customers, what messages, what investments, and the like—were made earlier in our eight-step process. The marketplace results, however, are what actually happened, what the organization got back for its investment in various customers, and how long it took to achieve those returns. We will spend considerable time on this marketplace measurement step in Chapters 9 and 10, but for now it must be recognized that this is the actual summation of the marketing communication program, forming the basis for all our evaluations.

Of critical importance here is the understanding that while the marketplace measurement really sums up the results of our IGMC program, that is not the end of the process. In fact it is really the beginning. We will input the marketplace results of our global marketing communication programs into our customer/prospect database. The data enhanced by our results will provide the base from which we can start the process all over again. It is this closed-loop, circular system that really differentiates the IGMC approach from other, generally ad hoc approaches. Only by using actual marketplace results as the basis for our next planning cycle can we truly become a learning organization. Knowing what worked and what didn't work, knowing what performed up to expectations and what didn't enables us to become better, more effective integrated global marketing communication managers. We can't succeed unless we can close the loop.

CONCLUSIONS

- Internal and external standardization is mandatory in the global arena.
- It is critical to identify and assign value to customers to assess the worth of your communication efforts.
- Horizontal organizational structures will triumph in the 21st century. Vertical ones will struggle or perish.

Implementing the IGMC Strategy

Using the overview from Chapter 5 on the process for developing an integrated global marketing communication (IGMC) strategy, we can now begin to "put some meat on the bones" of the eight-step process. In this chapter we will work through the process using a template that provides the detail necessary to develop an effective strategy and, more important, a method of generating all the material needed to implement a specific plan.

Exhibit 6.1 illustrates the eight-step IGMC process, recast as a flowchart that provides a step-by-step methodology for developing an effective and market efficient communication approach. We have found this methodology can be adapted for use by most marketing organizations.

STEP 1. GLOBAL DATABASES FOR DEVELOPING
CUSTOMER DEFINITIONS

As discussed in Chapter 5, any useful and usable IGMC program must start with a basic understanding and identification of customers and prospects. Without this information the communication planner is simply shooting in the dark, developing messages or incentives, buying and delivering media with little or no understanding of who he or she is talking to, what to say, or how to know what results are being obtained. The customer/prospect database provides the underpinning base and structure for the development of an integrated communication program.

Data is almost everywhere. Therefore, in our experience almost every organization has some type of database, whether it be a formal, organized

EXHIBIT 6.1 • The IGMC Eight-Step Planning Process

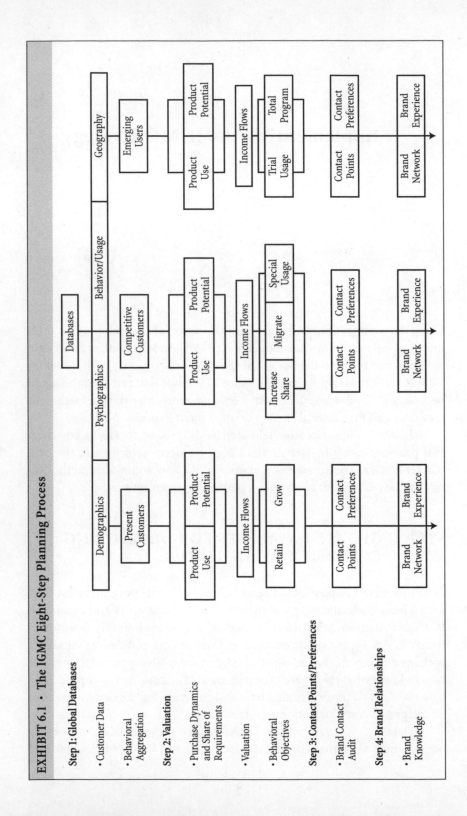

Step 1: Global Databases

- Customer Data
- Behavioral Aggregation

Step 2: Valuation

- Purchase Dynamics and Share of Requirements
- Valuation
- Behavioral Objectives

Step 3: Contact Points/Preferences

- Brand Contact Audit

Step 4: Brand Relationships

- Brand Knowledge

EXHIBIT 6.1 · The IGMC Eight-Step Planning Process (continued)

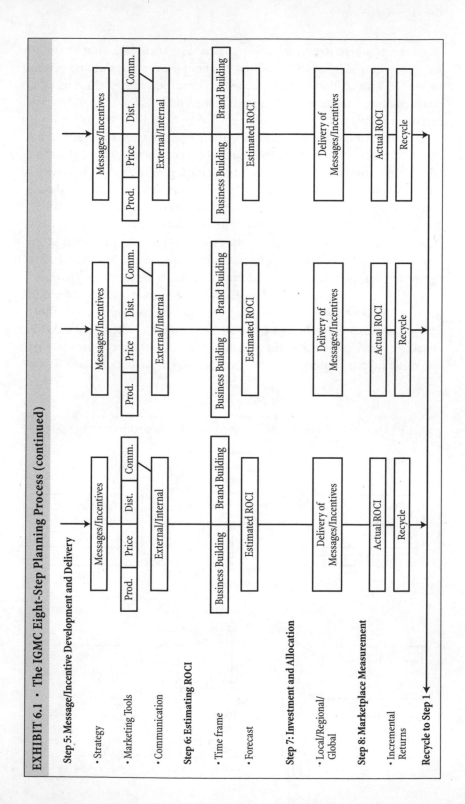

electronic resource structured and managed as a corporate asset or simply an aggregation of bits and pieces of data about the relationship the organization has with customers and prospects. The critical ingredient is whether the marketing and communication managers have access to that data and can use it for planning purposes.

In spite of many protestations, we have found almost all organizations have all the customer, market, and channel data inside the organization that they need to develop effective communication programs. So the problem isn't data; it's organization. Thus today's challenge is to organize the data in some way so that it provides useful and usable information, not simply customer records or lists or files of data. The key to 21st-century data and database management is bringing all the relevant data together so that the organization truly knows and understands its customers. Exhibit 6.2 illustrates some of the areas where customer data might be found in a firm.

As shown in Exhibit 6.2, data exists in the marketing department, in sales, in customer service, in technology support, in research—in short, everywhere. Unless it is brought together, however, it is often useless. While marketing and communication managers generally have only marginal responsibility for the development, structure, and use of organizational data-

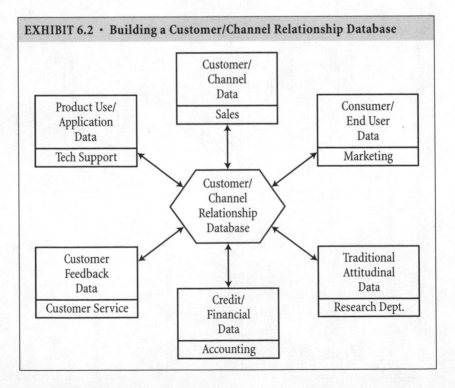

EXHIBIT 6.2 · Building a Customer/Channel Relationship Database

bases, they are often the prime beneficiaries. Therefore communication managers must be at least knowledgeable about data, data handling, and data access. Indeed, in the Best Practices IMC study mentioned earlier, one of the primary differences in leading firms was that they had created global, integrated customer databases and made them available to marketing and communication managers around the world. The "wannabe" firms were still struggling with data that was held or managed by individual units, geographies, SBUs, or the like.

In our research and consulting work we have found three major issues that most organizations face when they attempt to develop a customer marketing and communication database: (1) level of data needed and costs of capture and maintenance, (2) types of data needed for marketing and communication planning, and (3) methods used to analyze and understand the data. Since marketing and communication people generally are data users, rather than data developers or managers, we will discuss each of these three issues from a marketing and communication standpoint, not a technical one. This is done to provide background on the type of database the organization likely will need for marketing and communication planning, implementation, and measurement.

Level of Data Needed and Database Costs

In too many instances organizations have not put much time into planning or developing a database. Generally we see two extremes. One is where the firm or organization takes what is available or easy to obtain and then attempts to massage and manipulate that data into something usable. The other extreme is to attempt to capture, store, and manage everything the firm can get its hands on and then try to make some sense out of it. Neither is generally practical or useful from a management standpoint.

The best approach to developing and using a marketing and communication database is (1) to understand what the data will be used for, (2) to understand how it will be used to develop communication programs, and (3), then to match up the costs with the needs and benefits. Exhibit 6.3 shows the relationship.

The two axes of the chart in Exhibit 6.3 are "Customer Value" and "Sophistication of Database Technology," each progressing from low to high. At the low end, if customer value is low, and the relationship consists primarily of mailing unsolicited promotional material, database investment can be relatively modest. As customer value increases, and the need to communicate with customers and prospects develops into dialogue and ultimately to personal service, the database requirements will be relatively high. Costs increase as the value rises as well, since these communication programs

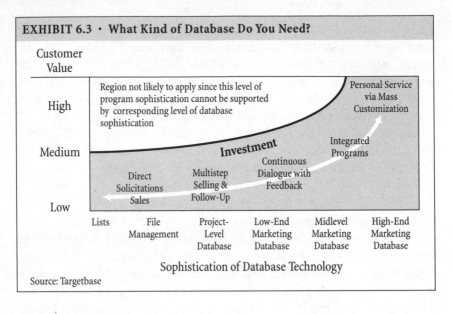

EXHIBIT 6.3 · What Kind of Database Do You Need?

Customer Value

High — Region not likely to apply since this level of program sophistication cannot be supported by corresponding level of database sophistication — Personal Service via Mass Customization

Medium — *Investment* — Integrated Programs

Continuous Dialogue with Feedback

Direct Solicitations Sales — Multistep Selling & Follow-Up

Low

Lists — File Management — Project-Level Database — Low-End Marketing Database — Midlevel Marketing Database — High-End Marketing Database

Sophistication of Database Technology

Source: Targetbase

require fairly sophisticated methods of handling inputs and outputs. From an internal planning standpoint, the chart in Exhibit 6.3 can be helpful in explaining the level of detail needed in your database to the technology managers responsible for actually managing and developing the activity.

Types of Data Needed

The data types listed in Exhibit 6.1 are:

• Demographics: hard facts about a consumer such as age, sex, income, and education; similar information about business-to-business customers such as the SIC code for type of business, number of employees, annual turnover, geography served, and the like.

• Psychographics: lifestyle aspects of the consumer such as hobbies, interests, activities, and so on. In business situations these generally include how the organization buys, its level of commitment to suppliers, and the like.

• Behavior/Usage: This is by far the most important information an organization can have about its customers, whether they be consumer or business to business. The real value of customers or prospects is in what they do, not in how they feel or where they are located or even the hard facts about them. Behaviors generally equate to sales, and sales at a profit are the ultimate goal of any IGMC program at any level. Building sustainable relationships that underpin ongoing profitable performance is generally the goal at the corporate level. We will say a great deal more about behavior in the next sections, but it is the ability to observe and understand customer, prospect, and publics behaviors that is critical in the global marketing and communication arena.

• Geography: a critical element in any global marketing communication analysis that commonly influences the types of products people use; whether they congregate in towns, villages, or cities; how laws and commerce have developed; and so on. For some firms this involves where products or services are distributed and the like.

Analyzing and Understanding the Data

Most markets are typically analyzed through some type of segmentation process—that is, breaking the general market down into smaller groups so that marketing and communication programs can be directed at them. Often marketing managers spend great amounts of time and money trying to understand and explain how markets are organized and what the specific groups in those segments do and how they respond to marketing and communication programs. In the IGMC approach we do not use segmentation. Instead we base our understanding of the market on *aggregation*, or bringing together similarly behaving customers and prospects. In other words, we aggregate naturally occurring groups of consumers and customers based on how they behave in the marketplace. Exhibit 6.4 illustrates the difference between the two approaches.

The premise behind aggregation is that behaviors are the most important variable in understanding customers and prospects. What people or firms do reflects how they feel, how they prioritize their time and money, and how they manage their lives and businesses. We have found these to be much better predictors of future customer behavior than traditional demographic,

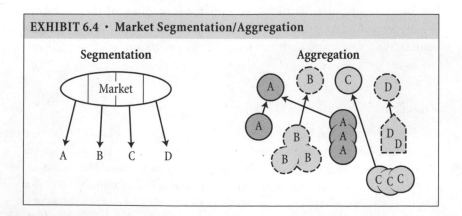

EXHIBIT 6.4 · Market Segmentation/Aggregation

geographic, or even psychographic data. This type of behavioral data is critical in new and emerging countries where behavioral observations may be more plentiful and easier to come by than the demographic data found in more developed marketplaces. This aggregation approach forms the basis for our analysis of customers and prospects.

Behavioral Aggregation of Customers

As shown in Exhibit 6.1, the first real activity in the IGMC process is to identify various types of customer or prospect groups for marketing and communication purposes. Characteristics of these groups are generally aggregated from behavioral data. In the flowchart we show three groups: present customers, competitive customers, and emerging users. While these are merely placeholders to illustrate the process, these are common groups aggregated in global marketing communication plans since these groups generally require different types of communication. Certainly you would not say the same things to your present customers as you would to those you are trying to lure away from the competition. Emerging users normally have totally different needs and requirements for information about your products and services. While we use these three groupings primarily as illustrations of the process, we will also use them in developing the balance of the IGMC program. In the development of your IGMC program, you may want to expand these classifications based on your specific business.

   Let's examine the rationale behind the behavioral classifications of present, competitive, and new users. In most categories there are very few "loyal to a single brand" customers. That is, most of our customers are also our competitor's customers. We use the term *present customers* simply to indicate that these people or firms generally buy more from us than they do from our competitors. Our rule of thumb is if the customer buys 60 percent or more of his or her product category requirements from us, we call them our present customers. If they buy 60 percent or more of their category requirements from our competitors, we consider them to be competitive customers. We'll deal more with this identification of customers and their values in the next step.

The True Value of the Database

To this point the database has appeared somewhat mechanical, that is, a collection of bits and pieces of data about customers and prospects that we are trying to weave into a pattern that will help us understand the multitude of cultures, societies, languages, customs, and beliefs that make up a global marketplace. As we have said on several occasions, the real purpose of a database is to enable the organization to understand its current relationship with customers and to develop relationships with prospects and influential publics. In truth, however, the database has an even more important function. That is, the information contained in the database, if used properly, should allow us as marketers and communicators to *become more relevant* to those customers, prospects, and publics. For the most part marketing and communication in today's global marketplace fail not because the messages and incentives aren't creative or clever or well produced. They fail because they are irrelevant to customers and prospects, unrelated to their needs and concerns. Irrelevant messages are the result of the organization not recognizing, understanding, or focusing on the needs and concerns of customers and prospects in markets and areas different from where the marketing communicator lives or works. The worst sin, and the greatest waste of marketing communication resources today, is being irrelevant. With a solid database of information and an understanding of customers and prospects around the world, relevance should be the first and most critical task for marketing communicators to accomplish.

While many other issues are involved in creating and maintaining a database, the preceding section should give global marketing and communication managers a clear enough understanding of the use and needs of a database to be able to discuss the subject intelligently with the technology experts who actually operate the database.

STEP 2. VALUING CUSTOMERS AND PROSPECTS

In our approach to customer and prospect valuation, we deal primarily with the most important return to the organization—sales and, ultimately, profits. That is, we try to identify those customers who are the most financially valuable to the organization today and those that might be worth the most to the firm tomorrow. Thus we focus on both short-term and long-term returns to the organization. The difference between these two groups, their potential returns, and the time frame of those returns will become important when we start to measure the returns on our marketing and communication investments. Thus our marketing communication approach is based on a financial model; that is, how much to invest, against whom, and with what expected return.

The General Approach to Customer Valuation

As shown in Exhibit 6.5, the basic approach to valuing customers is based on four elements. First, what is the total penetration in the product category?

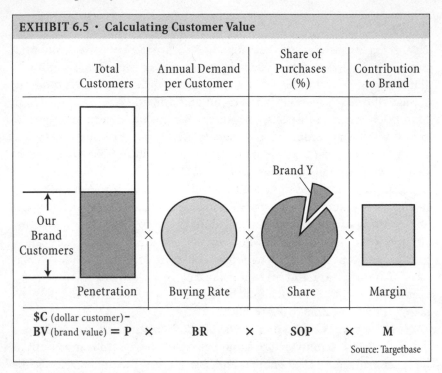

EXHIBIT 6.5 · Calculating Customer Value

	Total Customers	Annual Demand per Customer	Share of Purchases (%)	Contribution to Brand

Our Brand Customers

Brand Y

| Penetration | Buying Rate | Share | Margin |

$C (dollar customer) –
BV (brand value) = P × BR × SOP × M

Source: Targetbase

That is, how many customers consume our particular product or service or how many businesses purchase our product or service? In our earlier example shown in the database section, this figure would represent the aggregated total of all customers who purchase in a product category in which we are interested—people who eat hamburgers at fast-food restaurants, companies who buy ethyl chloride, fraternal groups who attend rock concerts, and so on. In other words, they have demonstrated some type of behavioral purchase or use in our product category.

Among that group of users, our first interest is how many of the total consumers in that product category purchase our brand or brands. In other words, what share of total consumers in the category do we have? Once we know that, we need to know the buying rate of those customers compared to the rate of the total market. Are our customers heavier or lighter buyers or users than our competitor's customers? That gives us an understanding of how our customers fit into the overall product category.

Once we have established the buying rate of our customers, the next step is to determine what share of their total category requirements their purchases of our brand represent. What share of their purchases do we enjoy compared to our competitors? This share of requirements or purchases (SOP) percentage is important, for it gives us some idea of the revenue potential represented by each customer now and into the future. Among some customers, we will have a high share of purchases or requirements, meaning there is little opportunity for growth. Among others, a low SOP often indicates substantial potential for the future.

Finally, we need to develop a measure of margin contribution for each customer. Not all customers are equally profitable. Some buy large amounts of our products; others buy only a few. Some customers require a great deal of service; others require a minimal amount. Some customers buy at full price; others buy only during promotions or when the product or service is on sale. Thus this contribution margin figure is critical if we are to evaluate the actual profitability of customers and customer groups and not just total sales and volume.

The Three Elements in Valuing Customers and Prospects

As shown in step 2 of Exhibit 6.6 (enlarged from Exhibit 6.1), there are three elements in valuing customers and prospects: (1) purchase dynamics and share of purchases or requirements, (2) valuation, and (3) behavioral objectives.

Product-Use/Product Potential. The first step toward understanding the value of customers is to understand their level of use of our products or services. What is the total number of customers who buy from us, and what is their buying rate? (See Exhibit 6.5.) This yields our total current volume. The critical question, however, is what potential, or maximum amount of their requirements, we might capture. From some customers, gaining this additional business will be easy; from others, difficult. Thus our estimate of total potential must be based on some solid evidence that we can capture additional sales from customers rather than just some "hoped for" increase.

This analysis must be done not only for present customers but also for competitive customers and emerging users. Based on our template from Exhibit 6.1, that would mean at least three separate analyses and perhaps more, depending on how customers have been aggregated from the behavioral database. Again, recall that we are dealing only with volume. We have not yet converted this volume into dollars or other currency.

Income Flows. Calculating income flows for each group simply means including the additional calculations from our general model, that is, product margin. That will give us the current total value of each customer. From that we can also estimate or calculate their potential future dollar value. That will provide a basis for setting the behavioral objectives that are the third element in valuation. First, however, we must deal with what the real value of a customer or prospect might be.

Customers generate current income for the firm through their purchases and other dealings with the company. They also represent future potential in terms of continuing or increased purchases. Prospects represent future potential. But customers and prospects come with costs attached. Thus we must balance income potential with costs to determine the true value of a customer or prospect. We do that by estimating the value of a customer or prospect at the contribution margin (or CM) line. That means we take gross sales and then deduct various costs of doing business, such as cost of the product or service, general overheads, service support, ongoing costs, and other relevant expenses. Working at the CM line, we are able to understand how valuable customers are in terms of their purchase volume, as well as the costs to serve them that together yield the net returns to the company or brand. In our experience valuing customers or prospects at any level other than the contribution margin line is generally misleading. Often the customers or prospects that represent large sales in units and dollar volume are expensive to do business with because of the prices they are paying, the cost to service them, and the like. Therefore these high-yield customers are sometimes substantially less profitable than they would appear when viewed simply in terms of their gross unit total purchases.

Using the contribution margin, we can now generate what we call *income flows* at the contribution margin line. We calculate income flows from activities with each customer or with aggregated customer groups that allow us to rank customers in terms of their current income flow to the firm or their potential future income flows. This analysis enables us to determine the next stage of the process, the setting of behavioral objectives.

Behavioral Objectives. Behavioral objectives are the most critical element for the IGMC planner, for they define what is to be accomplished with the marketing communication program. That is, if the behavioral objective is to retain the present income flow from a customer, then the communication program must be focused on that goal. So, we are setting communication objectives that will be measured by behavioral results. While this will be a substantial change for many communication managers, it is necessary to assure that we are properly investing our finite resources to generate the greatest returns on those investments.

In the chart in Exhibit 6.6, we show only two alternatives for present customers, three for competitive users, and two for emerging users. Of course, there may well be more objectives for each of these groups, depending on how customer groups have been aggregated. These, however, generally represent the most common behavioral goals.

For example, with present customers our primary goal is to retain their present income flows or to grow them in some way. Of course, if we

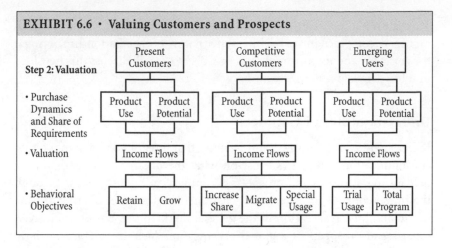

EXHIBIT 6.6 · Valuing Customers and Prospects

have a portfolio of products or services, it might be possible to migrate customers to more useful and perhaps more lucrative products and services than those they are purchasing now.

For competitive customers we will illustrate three behavioral objectives, although there could logically be more. Competitive users might well be purchasing our products or services as a part of their total purchases in the category, and we would normally be pleased with the result if we could convince them to increase our share of their purchases or requirements. Alternatively, we might attempt to get some competitive users to migrate to some of our products or services. Similarly, we might convince competitive customers to use our products or services on special occasions, as a possible prelude to making a total switch to our brand. The behavioral objectives for emerging users follow the same line of thought.

Now that our behavioral objectives have been set, we are ready to develop the marketing communication programs that will help achieve those goals. Those start with step 3—contact points/preferences.

STEP 3. CONTACT POINTS/PREFERENCES

Step 3 in our process chart lists two areas for planning: contact points and contact preferences. Contact points are all the ways customers and prospects come into contact with our organization, the brand, channel members, or any other persons or activities that are related directly to the brand and that can be or are used to influence either present or future consideration of the brand. Contact preferences are the ways customers and prospects would prefer to receive information or material from the company or the brand.

This is probably a relatively new concept for marketing communication managers, for it recognizes the interactive nature of the relationship between the company and its customers and prospects. We will discuss this new idea in more detail later in this section.

Understand Brand Contacts

Increasingly we are coming to understand that integrated global marketing communication is based not just on what the organization sends out or delivers to customers and prospects. Communication also occurs through the brand contacts or experiences customers and prospects have with the brand and the organization in the general marketplace. For example, customers and prospects of a global organization such as McDonald's have numerous experiences and brand contacts with the fast-food chain as a result of doing business with it. These consumer sources of information include news stories, signage, product, personal experience, advertising, word of mouth, the Ronald McDonald House, characters and playgrounds, employees, and even litter in the street.

Paid or controllable media messages or incentives make up only a small portion of the messages and contacts customers and prospects alike have with McDonald's. In truth, it is the total sum of the brand contacts a customer or prospect has over time that determines the consumer's response to planned and controlled communication programs. Therefore, to plan effective programs the communication manager must have some idea of the totality of contact points that currently exist in the marketplace. The goal of an IGMC program is not just to manage the contacts but to manage the process. Understanding the venues in which customers and prospects come into contact with the brand is one of the key steps.

One of the best ways to understand brand contacts is through a *brand contact audit*, an analysis by the marketing and communication group intended to identify all the ways in which the organization touches customers and prospects. This can be a formal or an informal process, in which representatives from the various areas of the firm list how and when and in what ways they come into contact with customers and prospects. For example, one of our IMC Best Practice organizations, Attorney's Title Insurance Company, conducted a brand contact audit with customers and prospects. It found more than 200 ways in which it came into contact with its customers and prospects in the normal course of doing business. These ranged from billing statements to telephone inquiries to electronic information downloads to speeches at local business club luncheons. All of these were in addition to the planned marketing communication programs.

A standardized chart often used to assist in the identification of brand contacts by an organization is provided in Exhibit 6.7. As shown, the ques-

EXHIBIT 6.7 · **Brand Contact Audit**

Target Segment:_____

Contact Points	Expectation at Each	Experience at Each	Message Sent	Positive or Negative	Importance of Contact	Target for Improvement

tions about the brand contacts include where the contact occurred, what the customer or prospect's expectation was at that time, and how that contact might be improved. This basic approach to understanding when and where and how customers already experience the brand is particularly important in a global program. Often we have found that contacts assumed to be positive were not positive at all. Knowing the types of existing brand contacts will do much to assist the communication planner in developing effective programs, especially in foreign cultures.

Contact Preferences

You will recall that the emergence of information technology has created an interactive marketplace, moving away from the traditional outbound approaches of the past. Thus in the area of contact points/preferences we must also learn and understand how customers want to communicate with us and how they want to access information from us. Recall our earlier discussion of the shift of marketplace power and control in the 21st-century marketplace.

To learn how customers want to communicate, we use a simple process: we ask them. We ask them how they would like to receive information, materials, or background on our products and services. And then we try to comply with their wishes. Exhibit 6.8 illustrates what we call a *back-flow communication model*.

As Exhibit 6.8 shows, the process is quite simple. Surveys, questionnaires, or interviews are conducted with customers and prospects. We ask them to rate the various ways they would like to receive information from

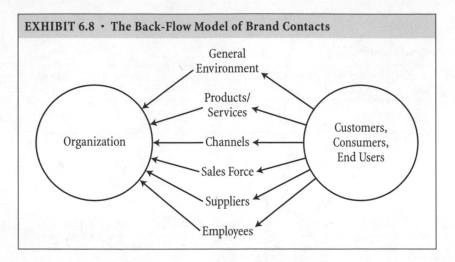

EXHIBIT 6.8 · **The Back-Flow Model of Brand Contacts**

our company about products, services, offers, promotions, and the like. Once we have that data, we connect it to the customers and attempt to use their preferences when we want to communicate with them. In many instances, because there are multiple alternative ways for customers to access information from us or for us to communicate with them, we ask them to rate the types of communication that they prefer in some sort of preagreed order. This gives us, as communicators, a broader range of choices but still stays within the preferences of our customers and prospects.

Often, when this type of back-flow model approach is suggested to marketing and communication managers, they reject the idea. "What if they say 'None of the above'? What if they don't want to hear from us at all?" In this case the organization has learned something important—that previous marketing and communication programs have not been very relevant to the people to whom they were directed. If you conduct a back-flow research project and customers and prospects tell you they don't want to hear from you in any manner or mode, don't keep using those types of programs in the future. They simply won't work no matter how much you invest in them.

Once we know customer contact points and customer contact preferences, we're ready to move to step 4—brand relationships.

STEP 4. BRAND RELATIONSHIPS

As has been discussed throughout this text, the brand increasingly will be one of the most valuable assets the organization controls. Given the lack of other sustainable competitive advantages, the brand becomes the primary relationship vehicle between the organization and its customers and prospects. This makes brand knowledge, or the understanding of current brand meanings by customers and prospects, most important in identifying and developing new brand communication programs in either local or global marketing situations.

As you will recall from Chapter 3, our definition of a brand is based primarily on the idea that it is the relationship between the buyer and seller. Relationships have history, meaning, shared understandings, and prospects for the future. All four of these elements are important in understanding the relationship a customer has formed with the brand and how that relationship might be improved, enhanced, or even changed if necessary. Notice we said the relationship the customer forms with the brand, not the relationship the brand forms with the customer. While there is little question that both parties must be involved to assure mutual benefit, we strongly believe it is the customer who decides to create a relationship with a brand, not the other way around. Customers will have a broad array of choices of products and services from all around the world. It will be the customer who picks and chooses which brands to use and how to relate to those brands. While the marketing communication activities of the organization will have much to do with the development and maintenance of brand relationships, the customer or prospect will drive them.

Part of this view comes from the increasing understanding of how brands are developed and created. While the firm owns the elements of the brand—the product or service, the icons, the symbols, the messages, and the colors—the consumer assembles them into a whole and develops the brand meaning for himself or herself. Thus, while Coca-Cola uses many of the same elements in marketing, communication, packaging, and messaging, every consumer, no matter where located, assembles those elements to create the Coca-Cola brand, as illustrated in Exhibit 6.9.

EXHIBIT 6.9 · The Consumer Builds the Brand in Memory

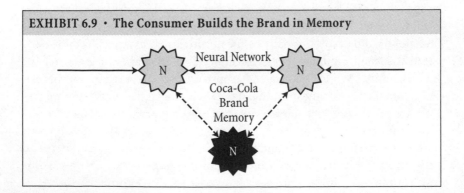

As shown in Exhibit 6.9, the mind is made up of unknown quantities of what are called *nodes* where memory is stored. Neurons or electrical impulses flow through and connect these nodes. When two neurons meet or collide, they form a loop, or another node. Thus memory is formed when the brain takes two known elements, puts them together, and creates a third or a new relationship. For example, thirst and liquids occur as separate elements in the brain. When we bring them together with the elements and symbols of Coca-Cola, a third or brand relationship is formed. Every person who connects thirst and liquids and Coca-Cola will not create the same image of Coca-Cola. Each person uniquely creates the brand for himself or herself. So, while Coca-Cola and thirst and liquids are all basic relationships, it is the other personal elements that the consumer adds to the mix that really create the brand and the relationship.

All of this is what we have labeled "Brand Network" in the process chart (Exhibit 6.1). From an IGMC view, for Coca-Cola, there are literally billions of brand networks in the world. Everyone who knows Coca-Cola has put the elements together differently, creating a unique view of Coca-Cola and his or her own relationship to the product.

Does this description make the management of brand networks sound like a hopeless task, with millions or sometimes billions of customers all over the world, each with a unique view of the brand and its relationship to her or him or the firm? How can any company or firm possibly understand these relationships or meanings? Fortunately, humans, simply to survive all the activities, impressions, meanings, and messages that impact them daily, have learned to do two things. One survival technique is to screen out or focus on the things that are important. The second technique is to group things together. We operate in the world using chunks of information or relationships that allow us to operate easily and quickly. The same is true of a brand. Customers connect certain ideas or concepts to a brand. One such brand is illustrated in Exhibit 6.10.

Over the last fifteen years, we have used the brand symbol for Volkswagen in seminars and conferences all over the world and asked participants what it means. In almost every country we get the same answers: "Bug" or "Beetle" or "small car." In many of the countries Volkswagen has not marketed the small, rounded Beetle automobile in a number of years. Yet the image endures. While Volkswagen has introduced a new version of this car, for a number of years the meaning of the Volkswagen name and symbol created images of a product that was not available or, worse yet, that didn't really represent what the organization was trying to communicate to its customers and prospects. It is critical to understand the brand networks customers and prospects have created for your brand before trying to develop brand communication programs to enhance, change, or reinforce those networks.

EXHIBIT 6.10 • The Volkswagen Example: An Embedded Brand Symbol

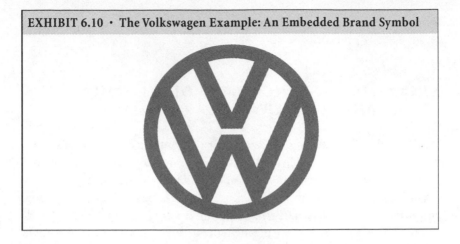

Fortunately, a number of research techniques are available today to help communication managers identify current brand networks among consumers and prospects. These techniques commonly fall under the heading of attitudinal research and have to do with the awareness, knowledge, and feelings that customers and prospects have about brands and organizations. Since this is not a research text, we leave the identification of these methodologies to the research manager. Certainly there are enough techniques that one or several can provide the necessary information.

Inherent in the question of brand networks is how those networks were created. What type of brand experience did the customer or prospect have that encouraged him or her to create the brand network currently used? The form and strength of the customer's brand experiences have much to do with the ability of marketing communication either to change or to enhance the customer's brand network. For example, if a customer has tried a brand and had a bad experience with it, marketing communication, no matter how interesting or entertaining or relevant, will not likely have much impact on that customer's view of the brand. If, however, the experience of the customer comes primarily from forms of competitive marketing communication or marketplace hearsay or other, less intensely personal sources, it may be possible for marketing communication to provide new or more relevant information about the product or service that might encourage trial. Similarly, if the customer or consumer has had a good experience with the brand and has simply not used it in some time, marketing communication can bring him or her back into the marketplace or perhaps change the perception of how the brand can or should or might be used. Only by knowing the brand relationship that exists—that is, the brand knowledge that comes from the previously developed brand network brought about by the brand experience—can the marketing communication manager develop an effective message or incentive.

STEP 5. MESSAGE/INCENTIVE DEVELOPMENT AND DELIVERY

Traditionally the heart of any marketing or communication program has been the message to be delivered to the customers and prospects. We have seen the almost maniacal emphasis on "creativity" among message delivery organizations such as advertising agencies. Messages will continue to be important in the global marketplace, but they vary in importance depending on the type of marketplace in which the organization operates. As shown in Chapters 1 and 2, and as the basis for the development of marketing communication messages and strategies, the three basic types of marketers are reviewed here and illustrated again in Exhibit 6.11.

There are three types of marketers in the world today. The product-driven marketer focuses on product superiority and continuous product improvement. The distribution-driven marketer focuses on better and more

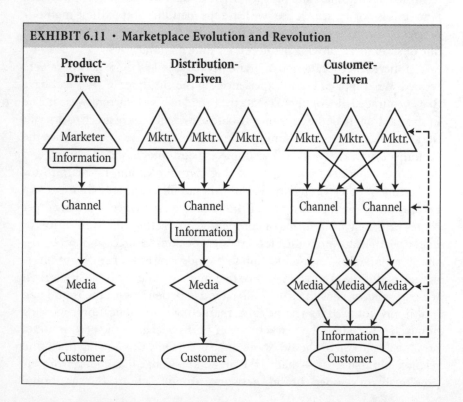

EXHIBIT 6.11 · Marketplace Evolution and Revolution

relevant channels and product/service sourcing and delivery. The customer-driven marketer focuses on understanding customers and prospects and answering their needs and desires.

For the product-driven marketer the message has high importance, since emphasis is on differentiating the product from its competitors. Commonly these organizations consider anyone who could be interested in their product or service a customer or prospect. Distribution-driven marketers often focus on a semi–mass marketing approach. They want to inform all relevant customers and prospects about the ease of acquisition or customer service provided with their products or services. While message distribution is an important part of that strategy, it is still the message of availability or ease of acquisition that is important.

For the customer-driven marketer the message itself is often secondary to the message or incentive delivery system. If the marketer knows its customers and prospects well, especially the ways in which they prefer to acquire information from the organization, the distribution of messages is often the most important factor in the process. In a complex and increasingly cluttered media and message delivery world, if the marketer can't get the message to the customer, it really makes little difference what the message is or says. Message delivery thus becomes the key issue in the 21st-century marketing communication structure.

Media Selection

This first decision regarding a media or distribution system creates many challenges for the communication planner. When message decisions come first, they drive the form or context in which the message is developed. For example, in sophisticated media markets such as North America and Europe, many consumer-marketing managers automatically think first about delivering messages through the television medium. Television works well in those markets, but not so well in areas where television broadcasts are limited or where large segments of the population have limited access to television. Often these communication planners rely on radio or exhibits or even street corner peddlers to distribute brand information. Therefore it is important for the global marketing communication manager to consider how messages can be delivered before thinking about the messages themselves. In this book we start with the customer or prospect and work back to the organization. This naturally puts delivery ahead of or at least on a par with the message.

If delivery is to be a key element, the question thus becomes how those delivery decisions are made. Traditionally marketing communication managers have chosen delivery systems on the basis of the message content or the cost of delivery. Those concerns still drive the forms in which communication appears. For example, some products or services need to be demonstrated. That requires certain types of media. Or maybe an incentive needs to be delivered at a specific time. That generally drives the use of newspapers or in-store promotions. In our IGMC approach, the issues are more generalized, for we recognize that all media are not available in all markets around the globe. Thus we use two different planning considerations in making our delivery decisions—relevance and receptivity.

Relevance. Relevance simply means determining when the message might be most relevant to the customers: When do they use the service? When do they make purchase decisions? Or at what point are they considering what they have done in the past with a thought of changing? When the customer wants to buy or consider becomes the guiding principle.

Receptivity. The second element is receptivity. When would the customer or prospect be most receptive to the message or incentive? Again, the decision is not when we as the marketing communication organization want to deliver it but when the customer or prospect would most like to receive it. This is related directly to our discussion in step 3 of brand contact preferences.

The general principles of relevance and receptivity are illustrated in Exhibit 6.12.

We have cross-linked the decisions about relevance and receptivity with messages and incentives in our process chart because the two elements generally have separate realms of interest for the customer or prospect. As shown in Exhibit 6.12 the decision process starts with the relevance and receptivity of either a message or an incentive and then proceeds to identify the various alternative delivery systems that might be employed. The illustration shows examples of traditional media, channels, and social systems. The communication planner will need to review the alternative delivery systems that might be available for each communication program. This is sure to differ by market and geography. Thus, in the IGMC process, the delivery of a message or an incentive on behalf of the product or service often drives the content of the message rather than the other way around.

At this point you may well ask, "What are these messages and incentives that are being referred to? How do they fit into the process?"

Messages or Incentives?

In our experience customers and prospects, certainly those in many of the less-developed areas of the world, have little knowledge of or regard for the various approaches to marketing communication that practitioners have

EXHIBIT 6.12 · Relevance and Receptivity

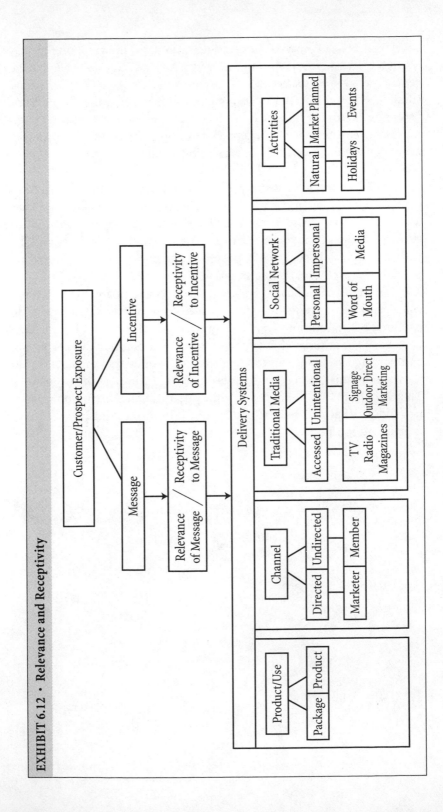

developed. Instead most consumers aggregate all the information they have about a brand or company and put it into a single, cohesive element they generally refer to as "the brand" or "the company." This consolidation process (described in some detail in steps 3 and 4), simply means that the customer takes all of his or her information and material about the brand and puts it into a convenient node or concept. For example, the customer or prospect generally consolidates all the information about a brand or company as shown in Exhibit 6.13.

As illustrated, the consumer or user or prospect puts all his or her brand experiences together and summarizes them as "That's Shell Oil," or "That's McDonald's," or "That's Mercedes." They don't differentiate between the various activities or actions or elements of the brand or organization. Thus we believe a consolidated view of the brand and organization is in order, particularly in a global marketing situation.

From this consolidated view of the brand or company comes our next concept. That is, we have found that most customers and prospects don't differentiate between various types of communication. For example, consumers don't say "The advertising is good but the sales promotion doesn't support and reinforce the brand image being created!" Nor do they evaluate the various promotional approaches such as direct marketing and public relations. Those are forms and functions that the organization and the communication industry have created and that have little or no meaning or value to customers and prospects.

EXHIBIT 6.13 • How Customers Receive Marketing Communications

Therefore we consider all forms of marketing communication to be either messages or incentives. Messages are things the marketing organization wants the customers or prospects to remember and store away in their heads. Incentives, however, are those things being offered to spur immediate action. Simply put, messages are things for the head, incentives for the hand. Thus we avoid the internal power struggles over how budgets are developed and whether advertising is being increased or direct marketing being reduced. We focus on how customers and prospects consider our marketing communication materials, that is, as messages or incentives.

If we start to use the concepts of messages and incentives, we can devise a different method of developing communication approaches. The initial stages of our planning matrix are shown in Exhibit 6.14.

In truth, what we have done is simplify the communication planning process. Most marketing communication managers, if they have some knowledge of customers or prospects, know whether they want to deliver messages—things they want the customer or prospect to remember and that they want to affect their behavior now or in the future—or incentives designed mainly to immediately change those behaviors. Thus our planning of messages or incentives ties back to the behavioral objectives discussed in step 2.

We should note here that in actual practice the line between messages and incentives is not quite so clearly defined. Often messages and incentives will be combined or coordinated or delivered together. We separate them here to make the point that one of the primary decisions an IGMC planner must make is to determine whether the results of the communication program will be determined by short-term results, commonly attributed to the delivery of an incentive, or long-term, more often related to message response. This

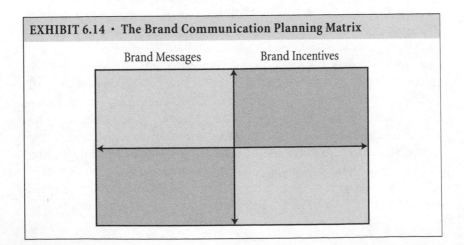

EXHIBIT 6.14 · The Brand Communication Planning Matrix

Brand Messages   Brand Incentives

differentiation will become clearer when we move to the measurement or evaluation of the results of the IGMC program.

The decision to deliver a message or an incentive has a major impact on all marketing activities, particularly the use of traditional marketing tools. Obviously, if the decision is made to deliver an incentive to customers or prospects, the so-called marketing mix must be developed to support that incentive decision. An incentive generally has something to do with some type of adjustment of the price-value relationship—a price cut, the offering of an extra amount of the product, a two-for-one combination, or a short-term promotion with an ending date for example. These types of incentives must be delivered in some way in terms of product or place (distribution) and so on. The same is true of a pricing decision. While we will not delve into the specifics of marketing mix management here, it should be clear that communication and the actual marketing mix elements must be coordinated to assure marketplace success.

Coordination

In the final stage of step 5 we focus on how to involve and unite all the internal and external parts of the organization that come into contact, either directly or indirectly, with customers and prospects. It is vital that these stakeholders understand the messages or incentives to be developed and be able to expand the reach and value of their marketing communication programs. The challenge is that, in most cases, internal communication falls outside the purview of the communication planner. It is often the responsibility of the human resources, employee benefits, corporate communication, or public relations departments. The marketing communication manager must work closely with these groups to make sure that all internal audiences are involved and supportive of the marketing communication programs being delivered to external audiences. Without internal support the marketing communication program is doomed to failure. This is particularly true of a global program. In many cases global programs are planned in a central location, and only a synchronized effort can sustain the communication across different languages, cultures, and geographies. Getting all parts of the organization focused on the external marketing communication program is one of the most important tasks for the IGMC planner. Indeed research by one of our colleagues has shown that up to 40 percent of an organization's marketing and communication budget may be wasted or misused if the internal support does not follow and support external communication activities.

The alignment of the organization behind the marketing communication program is illustrated in Exhibit 6.15. As shown, the entire process of

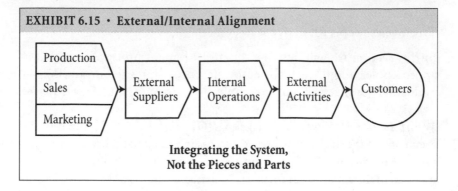

EXHIBIT 6.15 • **External/Internal Alignment**

Production
Sales
Marketing

External Suppliers

Internal Operations

External Activities

Customers

**Integrating the System,
Not the Pieces and Parts**

IGMC focuses on the customer. Internal groups such as sales, marketing, and production must also be focused on the customer. External suppliers must be aligned to support the organization's communication programs. The same is true for internal operations, from production to shipping to customer service. Everything and everyone must be focused on the end customer if the IGMC program is to succeed.

STEP 6. ESTIMATING ROCI

Estimating returns on customer investment (ROCI) may be a relatively new concept for many communication planners, so we will explain and illustrate it first. More will follow in Chapter 10 as we detail the measurement approaches that are used in the IGMC planning process.

Historically measurement of brand or marketing communication has focused on the delivery of communication activities. Were the messages sent out or delivered by the media organization, and were they received and remembered by the intended audience? By measuring only message development and delivery—the "output" of the communication group—and not marketplace results, it has been difficult to measure the actual "outcomes" of marketing communication programs.

In today's global marketplace, establishing the financial impact of marketing communication programs is mandatory. Almost every other functional group in the organization can either estimate or measure the returns on its investments. The inability of communication groups to tie financial expenditures to financial returns makes the entire process suspect. The use of surrogate measures such as awareness, attitude change, intent to buy, and other "soft" measures simply is no longer acceptable in most marketing organizations today.

The Measurement Process

In this section we will describe the measurement process in the IGMC approach, leaving the actual step-by-step procedures for measuring and evaluating the effects of our communication programs for Chapter 10.

What Is the Difference Between ROI and ROCI? In the business arena one of the major measures of success is a financial calculation, return on investment, or ROI. ROI is simply the relationship between what was invested in the activity and what was returned to the organization as a result of that expenditure. Expressed as a ratio, ROI is a common measure in all types of financial transactions. For years marketing and communication managers have tried to measure the return on their marketing and communication investments using ROI with little or no success. This measure eluded managers for many reasons, chief among them being the complicated nature of most marketing systems with uncontrollable variables and the long-term diffusion of messages making it difficult to know who received the communication. As a result, starting in the early 1960s, marketing and communication managers moved away from attempting to measure financial effects and began measuring the communication effects, that is, changes in awareness, attitudes, knowledge, and so on, based on the "Hierarchy of Effects" models that hypothesized that consumers or prospects pass through several stages of attitudinal change on the way to purchase behavior. Therefore, emphasis moved from measurement of the end result to measurement of movement in the hypothesized process.

By attempting to measure the interim steps on the way to purchase and relating them to marketing and communication investments, managers hoped that some type of relationship would emerge that was equivalent in relevance to ROI.

In most attempts to establish a communication ROI measure, focus has been placed on the delivery system. For example, "We bought so much television time [or magazine pages]; what did the organization get back from that investment?" Trying to measure the delivery systems instead of the impact of the communication program on customers or prospects makes it easy to understand why marketing and communication measurement has been so difficult.

In the IGMC process we focus on the things that can return dollars to the organization—customers. And we measure the returns from those customers based on the marketing or communication investments we make in them. For example, television advertising is simply a delivery system by which messages or incentives are delivered to customers and prospects. We

are, in effect, making an investment in those customers by purchasing television time to expose our message or encourage them to accept our incentive. Therefore measurement of IGMC returns should be made on the basis
of what customers returned, not what the delivery systems return. Delivery
systems can't provide any return. Only customers can. Therefore, we measure return on customer investment or ROCI, not ROI.

The Importance of Measurement Time Frames. Marketing and communication managers, because they have been focused on the development
and delivery of messages, have tended to view the returns on their efforts in
terms of when the communication program was originated and when
responses occurred. Thus the argument has traditionally raged in the organization as to whether or not the communication program was working.
Financial and management people, wanting the measurement of hard
returns, opted for a clear-cut, short-term decision. Communication people
argued that their programs took time and therefore often couldn't be measured in the short term. These differing views on what time frame communication programs could or should be measured in have caused considerable
difficulty in many organizations. The difficulty of relating communication
programs to the fiscal or financial year of the organization has often been
the chief culprit.

In truth the only time frame that matters to an organization is the fiscal time frame. Company books are opened on a certain date and closed on
a certain date. The importance and value of the organization to managers,
shareholders, and the business community is what occurs during that time
period. Therefore, in the IGMC process, we use the financial time frames that
drive the organization and its management, not the communication time
frames that marketing and communication managers have traditionally
relied on. The adoption of the organization's financial time frame allows us
to complete our communication planning matrix.

Completing the Communication Planning Matrix. In step 5, message and incentive development and delivery, we presented the first stage of
the communication planning matrix. As you'll recall, we separated our marketing and communication programs into messages and incentives. Using
the financial time frames of the organization as the y-axis, we can now complete that matrix, as shown in Exhibit 6.16.

This system places the two types of communication delivered in a time
frame in which we expect consumers to respond. Short-term returns are
those that will be returned to the organization in the current fiscal year. Long-
term returns will come back over several fiscal years. The goal, of course, is

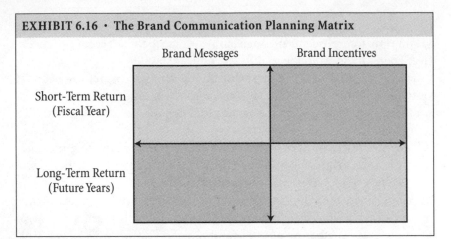

EXHIBIT 6.16 · The Brand Communication Planning Matrix

to get to some type of financial measurement of the return on our financial investments in various customers, consumers, and firms and then have a way to determine what we got back.

Separating Short-Term and Long-Term Returns. Using the communication planning matrix with its short-term and long-term time frames, the matrix provides us with a clearly defined approach to communication planning based on customer or consumer response (ROCI). To put the entire process into communication management terms, we will define short-term responses as business building and long-term responses as brand building. With these two terms defined, we can move forward to measuring the short-term and long-term financial returns on our marketing communication investments.

Estimating Returns

At this stage there is only one more activity in step 6, estimating the return we might expect to receive on the investments we are making in our customers and prospects. While that is a critical ingredient in any type of measurement system, we will leave that until Chapter 10, when we will describe the process in more detail. For the moment, recall that we have valued customers and prospects as income flows to the organization. Thus we know the current value of each customer or group of customers or can estimate with some accuracy the value of various prospects or groups of prospects. If we put that value into some type of income flow, we should be able to estimate the change in the income flow that our marketing communication program might create. Interestingly, in some cases, our marketing communication program might be designed simply to maintain or continue the income flow from a customer or group of customers. Thus our estimate revolves around what it would be worth to the organization to maintain a set of income flows. (Recall our discussion of behavioral objectives in step 2 of the process.) In other cases, the estimate is based on what it would be worth to generate new flows of income from new customers or increased flows of income from present or competitive customers. Through this methodology we can determine current value and make educated investment decisions in customers and prospects that can then be translated into marketing communication investment programs.

The final two steps in the eight-step planning process are basic but important, for they really start to deal with the critical measurement ingredients of a global marketing communication program—implementation and measurement.

STEP 7. INVESTMENT AND ALLOCATION

At this point, the planner should be ready to execute the IGMC program in the marketplace. That is what step 7 is all about.

To this point, we have not discussed the most common question in every global marketing communication planning approach: should the communication program be developed locally, or is there a reason or opportunity to develop a truly global marketing communication program? Most global marketing communication questions start here. In our process we end here, and for a very good reason.

In the IGMC approach we start with customers and prospects, not markets and countries. When we start with customers, particularly when we aggregate them rather than segment them, it becomes clear very quickly whether or not there is enough commonality to combine various customer groups when we start to cross borders and cultures. Thus the aggregation of people or firms who behave in certain ways gives them a commonality that tends to make global communication practical and possible. True, there may need to be changes in language or illustrations, but basically it is *behavior* we are trying to influence, and behaviors tend to be driven by common, underlying decisions people or firms make. Research suggests that there are horizontal bands of similar customers and prospects around the world. For example, there are MTV people around the world. These are people who like the same music and food, dress pretty much the same, and have the same cultural idols. In short they behave the same whether they are in Bangkok, Manchester, Tampa, or Buenos Aires. The same is true for international businesspeople. They fly the same planes, stay at the same hotels, dress the same, and focus on the same economic issues even though they may originate from Tokyo, New Delhi, New York, or São Paulo, and their native languages may well be German, Spanish, Cantonese, or English. They are generally the same in terms of their needs and requirements and how a marketing organization might communicate with them.

The real question for the global marketing communication planner is the commonality among the groups of customers or prospects that are to be served. In Appendix 2 the Oral-B case in India illustrates how starting with customers, rather than with products or services, simplifies the marketing communication decisions even in a single country. While the Oral-B approach had worked very well in North America and Europe, the dramatically different way in which Indians behave toward oral hygiene and dentists quickly showed that the previously developed "global approach" needed to be adapted and adjusted to succeed in India.

Inherent in step 7 is the need to build on previous decisions. For example, we will need to use the valuation of the various customer groups from step 2 to determine how much we would be willing to invest in an IGMC program. That, of course, will depend on the present value of customers and what their potential for future returns might be. We will need to use the information from step 5 to decide on whether we need to deliver messages or incentives. Likewise, we will need to use the information also from step 5 on when the messages or incentives might be most relevant to the customers and prospects we have selected.

STEP 8. MARKETPLACE MEASUREMENT

In most marketing communication processes, once the planning and development have been done and the program is placed in the market, the communication manager believes the job has been done. True, there are some details to address, but for the most part the manager's job is over until the next program is developed and executed. In the IGMC approach the job is just starting. The measurement of results and the interpretation of those results are the most critical elements in the process. It is here that the actual learning for the organization occurs. It is also here that the determination is made about whether or not all the preceding steps have been developed accurately and returns generated. The process chart in Exhibit 6.1 lists two items, actual ROCI and recycle.

Actual ROCI

In step 6 the communication manager estimated the return on proposed customer investments. In this step we measure actual marketplace results and compare them to the estimates. That tells the manager how effective her planning has been. Remember, in all cases we are measuring returns through income flows. In step 6 we estimated what level of income flow our program might generate. Here we measure any changes in the actual results of the program. Of course to do that we need methods to capture current income flows so we can then measure compared to past income flows to find the differences.

In some cases we may not be able to measure immediate income flow changes, which is why we divide our communication investments into business building and brand building. We will deal with how these measures can actually be conducted in Chapter 10. For the moment, however, recognize that the ability to measure our estimated ROCI compared to what was actually achieved is one of the key features of the IGMC process.

Recycle

This final step in the process is exactly what it says. We take the results we achieved in the marketplace from our communication program and, after evaluation, add them to our database, ideally connecting the results to each individual customer. If that is not possible, we then link them to each customer group. It is this ability to test and measure that really differentiates the IGMC process from others. By taking results from current programs and using them as input to the database, we have created a closed-loop system that allows the organization continuously to learn and improve on previous results. The concept of a closed-loop system is illustrated in Exhibit 6.17.

The key element in an IGMC process is the ability to learn from experience. As illustrated in Exhibit 6.17, we generally start with some information about the customers and prospects with whom we want to communicate. We should have some way to value those customers or estimate the value of a prospect (see step 2). Knowing the value of a customer— that is, the income flow the customer represents—we can then make a managerially relevant decision on what we would be willing to invest in marketing communication to these customers with some idea of the expected return.

Once we have made our communication investment, we can measure the results; that is, we can look at a continuation or increase in the income flow to the organization. That can be evaluated against the cost of generating .

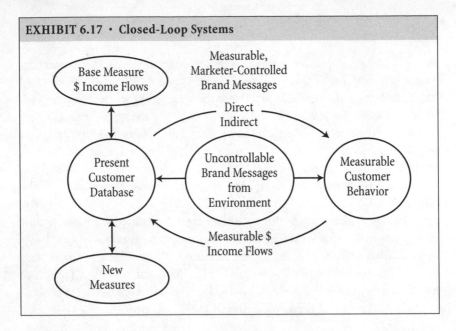

EXHIBIT 6.17 · Closed-Loop Systems

that income flow. Those results are then put back into the database and attached to the customer, creating our closed-loop system.

CONCLUSIONS

- You probably have all the data you need. The skill is in how you organize it and make it useful.
- The highest-volume customer is not always the most profitable customer.
- Your company communicates with everything it does. Make sure you know what your company's actions are saying.
- You don't own your brands; your customers do.

From Strategy to Creative Execution: Capturing the Imagination of Consumers and Publics

In Chapters 5 and 6 we discussed developing integrated global marketing communication (IGMC) strategies and then implementing those as IGMC programs. To develop a strategy and then create communication messages and incentives requires all of the nine competencies for mastering IGMC as well as a comprehensive understanding of the eight-step IGMC planning process. The IGMC process is not simply a template you can use to develop and implement programs. Instead, it is more concerned with logical, *customer-driven* processes that lead to sustainable and successful outcomes.

STRATEGIC THINKING IN THE IGMC MODE

There is nothing new about strategy, which is defined as "the art of the general." Just as an army general must work with his resources under conditions of risk and uncertainty, so must corporate executives, marketing managers, and brand managers decide how best to marshal limited marketing resources to achieve satisfactory exchanges that help grow brands. And the environment for armies and businesses is similar, for the opposing forces or competitors will develop counterstrategies.

From a corporate and brand perspective the field of action is not just the United States, United Kingdom, or Japan, but increasingly the entire world. Entering and competing in that global marketplace is not an easy task (see Case Study 1, British Telecom). From an IGMC perspective, introducing IGMC is no easy task either; it implies change, potentially knocking down or reshaping sacred marketing shibboleths (like the hierarchy of effect models or concept of mass marketing) that have held sway for nearly half a century.

When communicating with any public, the same strategy cannot be deployed to all potential customers or prospects. In other words, strategy itself is a pluralistic concept. Strategic outcomes are, however, extremely general in nature. There is, for example, the product life cycle strategy, which suggests the most appropriate strategies to be taken at each stage of the life cycle, if you can identify the stages your product is in. Then there is the Boston box, the famous four-cell matrix that suggests what to do for businesses or products if they fall within high-/low-growth competitive scenarios. A final example—though there are many others—is the GE McKinsey business screen, which suggests what to do if your strategic business unit falls into any cell of a nine-cell matrix based on market attractiveness and business strength.

The problem with these models or processes is that the strategies they suggest are incomplete; they are not prescriptive but descriptive. If taken as the former, they can spell disaster for a company or brand. For example, most businesses are located in low-growth/low–market-share positions, against highly entrenched competitors. The strategic prescription for these "dog" businesses is to divest them or milk them for cash. Plainly such strategies can be a recipe for disaster. Many so-called dog businesses are successful in returns of profitability simply because of the skills or strategies employed by the managers of the business. While this is illustrative only, many businesses still develop their marketing communication strategy on the basis of mass market techniques. The international marketing communication literature is littered with examples of mass marketing techniques or campaigns developed in one country that have been misapplied in new or different contexts that were not configured culturally to receive them or relevant to the intended audience. That is not to say that campaigns cannot be developed and used on a country-by-country basis. They can, but only where a clear understanding of market dynamics precedes campaign implementation and allows standardization.

And yet, in country after country, year after year, the same banal, unappealing, unexciting messages are deployed through broadcast and broadscale media. They are not consumer oriented or even geographically oriented but company oriented. Instead of building brands or even companies, they tend to switch consumers and potential customers off. Instead of reinforcing, rebuilding, or strengthening memory organization packets, such campaigns and messages do not pass the second stage of information processing, attention. What's important is not what the product/brand means to the company but what the product/brand means to the consumer.

Thus our strategic thinking, the IGMC mode of thought, involves developing or understanding the mind-set or behavior of our target markets. Such understanding is based on tracking customer income flows and seeing the product, brand, or communication from their perspective. Invariably this way of seeing will depend on the quality of material in the database concerning customers and their needs. Increasingly we are discovering that most of the clients we deal with and service are adding qualitative data (usually based on focus group, panel, or survey data) to try to establish levels of customer motivation and need to the high levels of quantitative data already available.

CUSTOMER AND CONSUMER MIND-SETS AND THE STRATEGIC IMPERATIVE

Customers want to be taken seriously, to be valued. That implies that they are seeking relationships. What companies can do is find out as much as possible about each customer or market and then craft marketing communication to appeal to clearly identifiable needs that in turn leads to behavioral outcomes. Today's computerized technologies and market research techniques, if used wisely, allow customers to be known and appealed to directly. Therefore, no single strategy can be deployed to all potential or existent customers.

If we combine customer mind-sets with the previous consideration of strategic thinking, the outcomes may resemble the nexus of marketing strategy as developed by William Cohen and illustrated in Exhibit 7.1. Working through this diagram means reorienting toward customers, consumers, and publics and adopting a mode of strategic thinking that requires every strategy to be associated with the ten elements listed.

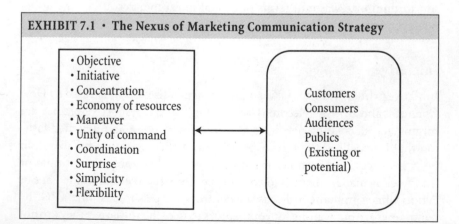

EXHIBIT 7.1 • **The Nexus of Marketing Communication Strategy**

- Objective
- Initiative
- Concentration
- Economy of resources
- Maneuver
- Unity of command
- Coordination
- Surprise
- Simplicity
- Flexibility

Customers
Consumers
Audiences
Publics
(Existing or
potential)

Objective

Every communication strategy, whether aimed at existing or prospective customers, must have an objective that can generally be interpreted as the achievement of a substantive goal. For example, the case material on the De Beers "Shadows" campaign (in Case Study 2) developed in conjunction with J. Walter Thompson had the following objectives:

1. to protect sales related to "core occasions" business segments in face of a deepening worldwide recession
2. to manage effectively esteem/value perceptions of diamonds around the world
3. to strengthen diamond jewelry's position as the ultimate gift of love
4. to translate those positive attitudes into purchase behavior

Note that this approach was spearheaded by advertising but clearly targeted at prespecified business segments. A proposed global campaign can be spearheaded by advertising or for that matter by direct mail, public relations, personal selling, or the Internet. Integration of various promotional tools for one-sight, one-sound messages is only the first stage of IGMC.

Does the strategy drive objectives, or do objectives drive the strategy? The answer is that the two are inextricably interrelated and closely juxtaposed to company needs in relation to an understanding of marketplace dynamics and behavior. The objective, at any organizational level, has to be communicated clearly to marketers, distributors, and agencies—all those persons or organizations involved in accomplishment. The driving force behind IGMC is the corporation that has previously mined the database. Those involved in implementation must clearly understand this and work in unison to minimize waste in terms of capital and other resources, including management time.

Initiative

Initiative primarily means taking a proactive position. As illustrated by Dow Chemical and British Telecom (Case Studies 3 and 1, respectively), they are forging ahead, creating new ways of communicating in an integrated fashion that is beneficial to both corporation and clients around the world. In both instances, and in other examples cited in this book, the attitude or mind-set of management is to control the time, the place, and the pace of action while simultaneously passing control of access to customers. IGMC companies are not waiting for competitors to take the initiative; they are not waiting to retaliate for offensive attacks. Instead they are assessing the ways they do things, changing what can be changed, adapting, altering, and flexing in new ways to meet the needs of today's and tomorrow's customers.

Concentration

This principle allocates marketing and corporate communication resources to achieve exchanges at the decisive point. It means concentrating marketing and corporate communication resources where they will achieve the greatest potential return on investment. From a longer-term brand-building perspective, corporations need to build corporate image (via corporate identity programs) to amortize costs effectively across the entire brand portfolio.

Economy of Resources

Recent years have seen the wave of takeovers, amalgamations, and mergers of the early 1990s reined back in favor of concentrating on core businesses. No firm or brand can be successful in all fields of endeavor, as Coca-Cola found out when it took over one of the world's largest wine manufacturers in the 1980s. Marketing wine is simply not the same as marketing cola. BMW's trumpeted takeover of Rover Cars in the early 1990s has resulted in unfavorable comparison of corporate and brand imagery and identity. In 1999 the only way to keep Rover Cars (UK) afloat was through a proposed £200 million loan from the British government. Throughout the world marketing organizations are being squeezed, becoming flatter, more horizontal. Put another way, fewer resources are being allocated to maintain market performance. It is the marketing executive's job to concentrate resources in the most appropriate ways—to clearly defined segments, groups of customers, and consumers, even individuals. Clearly whatever creates exchanges and builds brands will gain marketing communication resource allocation—but return on investment will have to be shown as well. Hence our argument for IGMC and IGMC measurement as opposed to the hit-and-miss approaches currently being used. Adopting IGMC, at least at the customer mind-set level, is essential, for few resources, if any, will be allocated for secondary efforts.

Maneuver

Maneuver implies a willingness to change, to alter, to adapt where and when necessary, especially in the marketing and corporate communication arena. The IGMC approach can be applied anywhere in the world, but it relies or depends on a sound understanding of the dynamics of served customers or markets. And in the global marketplace, these dynamics may vary on a market-by-market basis. They may, for example, differentiate on a geographic, economic, political, or social and cultural basis. There is no doubt that great campaigns can and do cross geographic boundaries, but can they cross psychographic and cultural boundaries as well? The number 4, for example, is regarded as unlucky in Hong Kong; two 4s extremely unlucky. These factors were not considered to be important by Volvo, but the Volvo 440, despite extensive promotional effort, did not sell well in Hong Kong. When Lancia launched its "Dedra" car in the United Kingdom, it was asked, Did they not consider that a car name containing the word *dead* might have unfortunate connotations? Their response was that the word *dedra* was associated with speed and panache. Again, sales were dismal. Kellogg's transplanted ad for Cornflakes featuring foot-stompin', banjo-strummin' hillbillies, developed for the American market, found little resonance of a positive nature elsewhere, even in cultures similar to that of the United States.

Unity of Command

For every campaign, based on the IGMC process, there has to be one overall leader or locus of control. At the marketing level this could be the product or brand manager; at SBU level the marketing director; at corporate level the marketing executive working closely with the person or team responsible for corporate communication. Alternatively, control can be delegated (but not abdicated) to responsible executives in advertising or other agencies or even to an executive in an integrated agency. Our experience indicates that the best examples of delegation of IGMC programs to agencies occurs only where there is a long-standing relationship of trust between client and agency. Where the relationship is short term, generally the locus of control is with the client. Where there is more than one locus of control or command, deployment of resource allocation in an integrated approach tends to be dispersed and less effective than if such command is unified under one marketing communication leader.

Coordination

Coordination supports and sustains unity of command, resource concentration, maneuver, and initiative. All marketing communication efforts must be fully coordinated to achieve organizational objectives. Thus from a global perspective all geographic units, if not using the same message, would still communicate the same *values*. Geographic units, communication tasks, the IGMC planning process, implementation, and evaluation are made similar if not identical; and behavioral and attitudinal outcomes are made available to all who need to know. Such coordination reduces the potential for other geographic units to operate in a solitary manner.

Surprise

Often this is the key to competitive advantage. Web retailer Amazon.com generated much of its brand momentum by using the proceeds from its public share offer to aggressively extend the company's customer base and brand image. It is not just as an on-line retailer of books that Amazon.com has generated surprise. It has transformed marketing communication into an integrated process. Amazon.com features a user-friendly browse and search facility by author, subject, or ISBN; Web-based credit card payment; direct shipping to clients; a book review section; a readers' comments section; and an ongoing automated search agent titled *Eyes*. No wonder traditional book retailers are casting envious eyes at Amazon's performance. Amazon.com simply acted with surprise, speed, concentration of resource, audacity, and creativity to come up with a global business in an old business sector but one with new dynamics emerging in the high-growth technological sector. It compensated for inferior resources (unknown brand name, no retail distribution, no mass advertising). It has made the Internet work for it, but its approach is consumer driven and consumer oriented. Amazon's goal of building a successful global book business and significant market share has been accomplished even while staid competitors are considering how and in what ways to access the new medium.

Simplicity

Simple direct marketing communication that promises and delivers significant benefits is always best. Someone once said, "We succeed according to the simplicity of our efforts." One example of simplicity was the 1994 launch of the "Orange" mobile phone in Great Britain. Owned by Hutchison Telecom, which had previously failed with "Rabbit," the Orange team developed an integrated proposition announcing the advent of "wire-free communication." One hallmark of this program was the heavy degree of dependence on integrated marketing communication necessitated by the small size of the in-house marketing team at Hutchison. Wolf Olins, a major international agency headquartered in London, created and has continued to develop and supervise Orange's corporate identity. WCRS, a major UK-based advertising agency, is responsible for all above-the-line advertising and helps coordinate activity with other agencies as new campaigns are launched. Dutton Merrifield (UK) ensures that all copy and terms are consistent and provides customer communication leaflets such as bill inserts.

Option One provides point-of-sale, and until recently WWAV (UK) worked on direct marketing.

All activities are managed between the agencies and the Orange campaign and design team. Postlaunch, the Orange team, based on clear market evidence, developed a multimedia mix to ensure synergy across all sectors. While new companies are renowned for innovation, Orange has succeeded in a marketplace where it was the latest entrant in 1994. It is its view that the integrated marketing communication approach, in which images of mobile phones are noticeably absent, has proved to be a significant key to success, moreover a key that is being replicated in other international markets, most recently Israel, to the chagrin of already established competitors. Again, the integrated approach, while innovative in 1994, was not unknown to competitors. The purpose, however, of market penetration and presence was fulfilled.

In the international marketplace simplicity of effort in marketing communication is even more desirable. But, this does not mean wholesale replication of whatever worked elsewhere. Introducing ready-packaged marketing communication programs may work only where no creative alternative based on underlying customer dynamics is readily available. Simplicity also needs to be allied closely to flexibility.

Flexibility

As we have implied throughout this book, customers, existent and prospective, are not one and the same. There is no mass market assiduously consuming soap operas and advertisements. Flexibility is necessary at the planning and implementation stages of IGMC. Core values associated with the brand or corporation stand at the center of the IGMC process. The vehicle for delivery of these values is the message. Messages and media may change, but the values, so long as they reflect deeply felt consumer needs, remain the same. However, radical changes in these values need to be watched for, and adaptations made. For example, Levi Strauss grew rapidly from 1985 to 1995 but then failed to adapt to major changes in customer values in the late 1990s; hence its sudden downhill plunge. Throughout its period of success every campaign depicted the same inherent core values, while the messages changed significantly. The major changes in the mid- to late 1990s have been the advent of new designer label jeans and a general worldwide decline in the market for traditional Western-style blue jeans. Such trends effectively disabled Levis as the fashion wave of 501s crashed on the rocky shore of consumer demand and value changes.

Flexibility is also suggestive of managerial mind-sets. Most so-called global communication programs are global only from a managerial perspective. This is perhaps one major reason why so many of them perform badly when facing different consumer mind-sets. Flexibility implies a willingness to change, to adapt marketing communication programs in the light of behavioral evidence from the marketplace.

COMMUNICATION STRATEGY: THE NEED FOR ORGANIZATIONAL REENGINEERING

The drive for comprehension of consumer mind-sets, coupled with the strategic imperative, means that corporations that wish to compete in the global marketplaces of today and tomorrow will almost inevitably need to undergo a process analogous to organizational reengineering. As we have seen in Chapters 3 and 4, changes taking place in the communication environment mean that all companies everywhere need to radically rethink marketing activity. As early as 1991 the argument was already being made that technology was creating feedback loops connecting customers and companies, which in turn created opportunity for firms to act more quickly in response to dynamic response patterns. Exhibit 7.2 indicates that global/multinational firms can now potentially use IGMC to further synergize marketing strategy and tactics. This potential depends on several factors.

- the domestic, international, and global environment
- the stages of life cycle in which brands are positioned on a country-by-country basis and the extent to which such brands are directed globally
- the corporate culture with respect to globalization or IGMC processes
- the extent to which IGMC prevails in each contextual environment

Reality for many corporations lies along a continuum of global and communication possibilities, as shown in Exhibit 7.3. Few corporations would disagree with continuum A in Exhibit 7.3. Likewise, few firms would argue that their communication programs are unintegrated from a domestic or global perspective. But, as we have argued in Chapters 2 and 3, integration goes beyond making communication look or sound the same. As a pencil-and-paper experiment you may like to indicate where on continuum A your company is positioned in relation to integration (following a brief review of Exhibit 4.3). We also expect that relatively few firms, probably with narrow product or service lines or in business-to-business sectors or OEM

EXHIBIT 7.2 · Global Developments and IGMC

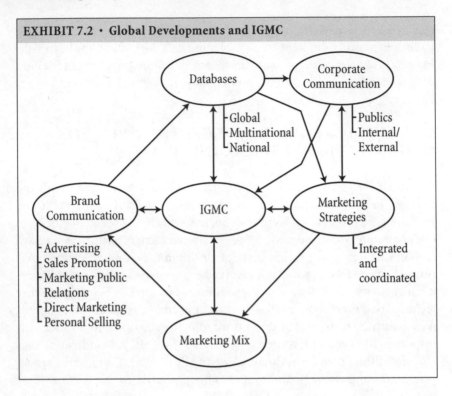

(original equipment manufacturers)—Dow Chemical, Coca-Cola, Levi Strauss, Oxford Instruments, De Beers—would be positioned to the far right. Firms such as McDonald's Corporation, while coherently integrated as a global brand in its own right, has nonetheless chosen to follow a quasi-domestic orientation in terms of communication via its policy of selecting and briefing of agency personnel on a local basis. For example, Leo Burnett, a major international advertising agency with headquarters in Chicago, London, and Europe, handles the brand in eighteen countries, while DDB handles forty-five, which results in fragmented and uneven work across the world. McDonald's approach is thus *different* on a market-by-market basis and perhaps, from the corporate management perspective at this time, has to be this way. The objective for those taking IGMC seriously is to move from left to right along both continuums. However, for noninternational readers, the aim is to move along continuum A.

Forces shaping how global firms approach the competitive challenge at the organizational level have been conceptualized elsewhere. Radical reconceptualizations such as reengineering the corporation indicate the extent and need for organizational change. IGMC, likewise, is founded on the need for organizational change, to become more, not less, consumer oriented or, as we put it, *consumer driven*. The main problem is that virtually

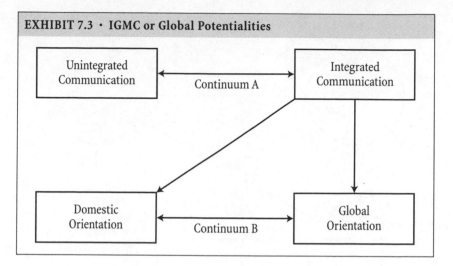

EXHIBIT 7.3 · IGMC or Global Potentialities

Unintegrated Communication ←— Continuum A —→ Integrated Communication

Domestic Orientation ←— Continuum B —→ Global Orientation

any change requiring restructuring encounters organizational resistance or inertia. IGMC requires radical new approaches in the organization and conceptualization of communication. It is worth remembering that how business was done yesterday is not as important as how business is done today and how it will be done tomorrow.

Given that firms face a competitive scenario in which restructuring may be demanded, how can firms proceed with creative and innovative marketing communication programs? Marketing communication may be tackled from a domestic perspective through the following stages:

1. Determine the target buying incentive.
2. Establish brand core values.
3. Identify brand perceptions.
4. Know the competition core values and brand perceptions.
5. Determine the competitive consumer benefit.
6. Focus on the confidence-building motive.
7. Determine tonality and personality.
8. Determine communication objectives.
9. Decide on perceptual change variables.
10. Seek to manage customer contact points.
11. Move from here to there.

This model is a useful overview of how to proceed in markets where market research or database evidence strongly indicates that a global brand-building approach would be unsuitable. IGMC strategy then indicates that an appropriate global approach would be developed as shown in Exhibit 7.4.

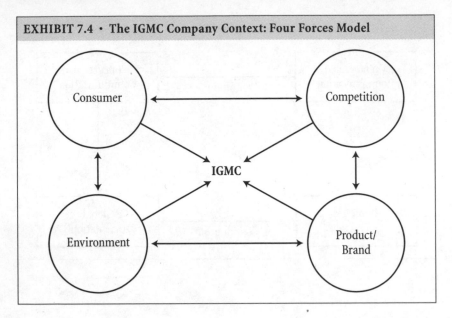

EXHIBIT 7.4 · The IGMC Company Context: Four Forces Model

Consumer

Competition

IGMC

Environment

Product/
Brand

Four variables will constantly impact IGMC strategies in the international context: (1) consumers, (2) competition, (3) environmental circumstances, and (4) levels of brand development. Thus the underpinning databases must be configured to gather material and information on these elements as they change over time. The next step will be to develop creative messages to targeted customers or potential customers to create satisfactory and sustainable exchanges.

CREATIVITY AND IGMC

Creativity or what is perceived to be creative may vary significantly from country to country or from consumer to consumer. From a brand-building perspective the use of integrated communication is derived from consumer needs and wants. By adopting this approach, perceived values (recognizable to consumers) are built into messages to differentiate and position brands from competing alternatives. If perceived value, either emotive or cognitive, is greater than that accorded to the competition, brand purchase behavior and loyalty generally will follow. However, loyalty can be sustained only when the use or consumption of products or services actually delivers what the marketing communication promises.

What do consumers seek from creative ideas? Let's assume that the creative drive for IGMC is spearheaded or led by advertising. Consumers seek information from advertisements much as they might seek information from a fairy tale or play—*they know it isn't real, but they believe its message to be useful in their real lives.* The question for the marketer is how this belief is created and sustained. Advertising and associated marketing communication techniques have to reach the sense organs of those who are to be communicated with (be seen or heard), have to gain attention (or the allocation of cognitive or emotive capacity), have to be seen as the path to a goal (must stipulate a meaningful and real benefit or value), and have to be retained in long-term memory to lead to a behavioral outcome. Effective creativity, at least from an advertising perspective, can be seen as incorporating at least six key elements, as shown in Exhibit 7.5.

Exhibit 7.5 suggests that marketing strategy and objectives *and consumer orientation* drive the integrated approach. We emphasize not just advertising but all the elements of the integrated campaign. Marketing communication speaks the language of the market, and it brings real benefits. Marketing communication is inherently competitive in nature. Consumers almost invariably discount "me too" campaigns.

Creativity is perceived as the essence of effective marketing communication, and there certainly is a need for creativity to help deal with IGMC issues. One could use any of a variety of techniques:

• considering how creative ideas are conceived and developed

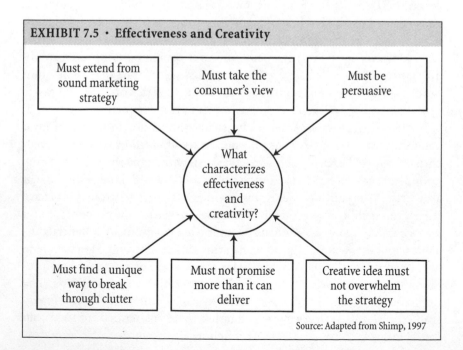

EXHIBIT 7.5 · Effectiveness and Creativity

- Must extend from sound marketing strategy
- Must take the consumer's view
- Must be persuasive
- What characterizes effectiveness and creativity?
- Must find a unique way to break through clutter
- Must not promise more than it can deliver
- Creative idea must not overwhelm the strategy

Source: Adapted from Shimp, 1997

- using structured approaches—brainstorming and other relevant creativity inducing techniques
- understanding the consumer decision-making process—issues of high- and low-involvement products/marketing communication campaigns
- potential use of stereotyping
- development of core benefits and focus on USP (unique selling proposition)
- creative use of endorsements
- types of message appeals and their appropriateness
- creative approaches in practice—space advertising, merchandising, events, and activities that create news (marketing, public relations, and sponsorships)

Each of these techniques and approaches may, however, soon be supplanted or replaced by the creativity template approach.

Creativity Templates

The four forces model depicted in Exhibit 7.4 drives creativity in advertising or in an IGMC approach. Generally the use of templates involves the generation of a large number of concepts. The assumption is that generating a large number of ideas outweighs the costs. However, such ideation (or idea generation) tends to be highly informal and unsystematic. Often these methods are based on the *divergent thinking* approach, whereby judgment is suspended and ideas emerge in a limitation-free environment.

However, even in such an environment certain patterns of creativity may emerge and be applied. Creative teams often seek ways to become more productive as they progress through an iterative series of creativity tasks. *Common patterns* relevant to different domains are sometimes identified. These may then be applied to marketing communication in a given cultural context or even transplanted or transported to other cultural contexts. Such patterns tend to be more stable and less transient than the abundance of random ideas that emerge in the process of associative thinking. Patterns will also assist in "organizing" the creative process by developing routes that have been proved to lead to productive creative ideas that are meaningful and memorable to customers and consumers and lead to mutually beneficial outcomes. Simultaneously, unproductive ideas can be sidestepped or avoided.

Recent studies (Goldenberg, Mazursky, and Sorin, 1999–2000) presented a new framework for creativity in marketing communication. The premise of the study is that certain patterns are identifiable, objectively verifiable, universal, and learnable and that these patterns, termed *templates,* can serve as a facilitative mechanism that channels the ideation process, enabling those responsible for creative development of marketing communication to be more productive and focused. This study indicated that a small number of templates can accurately predict more than 50 percent of creative outcomes.

From a marketing communication perspective, successful advertisements (crucial in spearheading many global campaigns) share and are characterized by certain abstract patterns, which the study terms *creativity templates*. Six major templates were derived from a sample of 200 ads in the first study. Expert judges found that six creativity templates explained 89 percent of these ads. Following a formalized description of the templates, a second study comparing 200 award-winning and 200 nonwinning ads indicated that the two groups differ systematically in the number and distribution of creativity templates. The templates could explain 50 percent of the award-winning ads as opposed to only 2.5 percent of the nonwinning ads. In a further study designed to examine the robustness of the template approach, individuals were trained in the template approach, in an association technique, or not trained at all, prior to an ad ideation task. A group of experts subsequently rated the ideas. Findings showed that template knowledge was associated with creating high-quality ads in terms of creativity, brand attitude judgments, and recall, although templates were found to vary in triggering emotive responses such as humor.

The template approach implies a means to achieve greater expertise in creativity. Moreover, unlike the divergent thinking approaches in which the required expertise (such as group moderating) is not related to the creativity process itself, the creativity template approach is trainable and has the capacity to improve creativity outcomes. In fact, training in creativity templates may result in higher levels of creativity. The template approach serves to focus cognitive efforts involved in ideation, enhances the capacity to access relevant information, and increases the memorability of the reduced sets of information for task performance.

The Template in Action

Given the recent nature of the template approach, finished ads resulting from the use of creativity templates are not yet available. However, let's take recent examples from the pages of one of the world's leading newspapers—the *Financial Times* (March 18, 1999). Among the many advertisements in the newspaper appeared the two ads for computer-related technologies reproduced here. The primary message of the Siemens ad, shown in Exhibit 7.6, promoting the Scenic Mobile 750 is "Hundreds of Brains in a Well Designed Box." Accompanying pictures show the Siemens model with various in-built

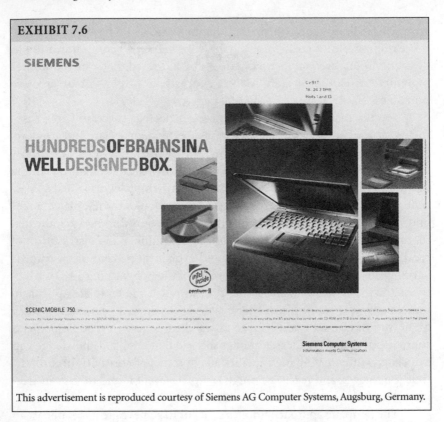

This advertisement is reproduced courtesy of Siemens AG Computer Systems, Augsburg, Germany.

technologies—screen, CD-ROM, floppy port, removable display, etc. The accompanying text emphasizes the unique functional features of this model. The ad describes product benefits and features in a creative yet functionally oriented, highly visual way.

By comparison, the headline of the ad for Unisys, shown in Exhibit 7.7, is "Sure we go on vacation. But we never quite get away from it all." The accompanying visual display shows two pictures. In each, the head of the relaxed individual (shown on skis or in casual clothing) has been replaced by a computer screen. The accompanying text does not concern functional benefits as such but rather focuses on client needs, in this case for Amadeus, a global travel reservations system. The first ad focused on functional product benefits in a traditional format with a highly innovative headline. The second focused on creative display, with an emphasis on consumer orientation. One could argue that in the second example a major cultural driver or symbol (the head or face of a consumer) has been *replaced* by another visual symbol (computer screen), which, rather than suggesting cultural drivers, suggests *global needs*.

EXHIBIT 7.7

The creativity template approach, at the simplest level, could work by replacing a cultural driver—in this case a symbol—with another symbol. If one adopts the creativity template approach, the communicator needs to find out what has served successfully as a consumer-oriented driver for a specific campaign, say in the United States. Such an approach can then be developed in other cultural contexts, without necessarily searching for new creative ideas. For example, a new location could be Japan or Germany rather than the United Kingdom. In each case product space remains the same, but the symbols set would vary. Creatives can then work inside the symbols set and have a constrained ideation approach governed by the cultural circumstance in which the approach is to be deployed. However, replacing symbols via a *replacement template* can be extended to other products. The authors of the studies described earlier are also working on developing a taxonomy of templates for application in new product development. These templates have significant resonance for IGMC processes, particularly when adapting, altering, or using successful marketing campaigns in new or different cultural circumstances.

THE THREE-STEP TYPOLOGY FOR APPLICATION OF IGMC PROCESSES

We have already differentiated between those activities that build returns in the short term (business building) and those that build returns in the longer term (brand building). In this chapter we translate these two types of activities into marketing communication concepts. However, there is a third type of building activity for those corporations with a multiplicity of brands. In these situations the corporation may act as a brand in its own right. We call this *corporate branding*, or *raising the corporate umbrella*. Admittedly, for some firms, there may be little or no differentiation between brands that are purchased and consumed and the corporate brand. These building mechanisms reflect the dual effects of interaction and synergy and are conceptualized in Exhibit 7.8.

Business Building

All those activities that stimulate sales for a given product or brand within an annual marketing planning period are business building. The annual marketing plan for a brand usually contains the following elements:

- situational analysis
- clear description of the target market
- marketing objectives and goals

EXHIBIT 7.8 · The IGMC Triangle

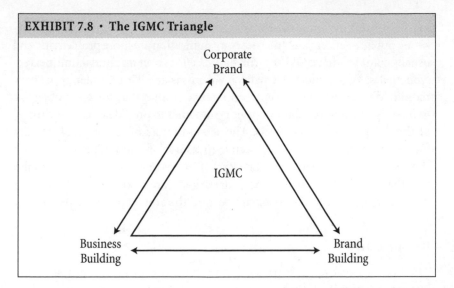

- overview of marketing strategy
- delineation of marketing tactics
- control and implementation criteria
- summary and appendix information

Under the heading of marketing tactics appear the promotional planning processes, and usually there are separate plans for each promotional element. However, from our perspective, the following annual elements can be identified:

- target markets (customers, prospective customers, swing customers)
- objective setting for each group
- budget allocation for each group
- mixture and interaction of promotional elements (marketing, public relations, advertising, personal selling, sales promotion, direct mail, Internet, point-of-sale, etc.)
- selection of appropriate messages
- selection of appropriate media
- evaluation and measurement criteria (see Chapter 9)

What we are attempting to do with this mixture of promotional elements is to manage as many of the contact points for consumer or customer messages as possible. We wish to measure behavioral outcomes. For personal selling, sales promotion, and direct mail, this is straightforward. Advertising, marketing public relations, and Internet communication are more problematic and usually contain what could be termed *weak effects* over an annual time period. Nonetheless two authors (Demetrios VaKratsas and Tim Ambler, 1999) have recently distinguished between econometric studies that focus on objective marketing mix and purchase behavior outcomes to provide reliable estimates of the size of behavioral effects. The second range of "conceptual" studies focuses on prepurchase and subjective measures of knowledge or cognition (beliefs, recall, and awareness) and affect (feelings or emotions). It is our view that these second groups of conceptual criteria are associated with business *and* brand building and thus extend beyond the annual planning period.

Brand Building

The building of brands is partly tied up with the annual planning period but extends significantly beyond this period. Brand purchase, and indeed brand loyalty, is not just an expression of current promotional or IGMC campaigns. Such behaviors are a function of past brand usage and current intent. What this means from an IGMC perspective is that brand building should be part of a continuous process of development. Thus advertising, which is regarded as the ultimate mechanism for creating warm, nonrational feelings for a product or brand, needs to be part of consistent and ongoing development that delivers core values in new and creative ways. Marketing communication for a brand, combined with the ongoing search for associated marketing public relations (MPR) techniques cannot be seen as an annual cost on sales. Instead it should be seen as an ongoing investment, producing year-on-year measurable returns. However, such communication programs may or may not be replicated in every country; whether they are replicated depends on product category, stage of product life cycle, the competitive environment, other marketing mix components, and so forth. Inevitably long-term investment in IGMC, and indeed shorter-term execution, relies on the quality of information contained with the database concerning different customer typologies.

Corporate Communication

As we discussed in Chapter 4, in some cases the identity of the company is readily apparent—Shell and IBM are examples. In others subsidiary companies have their own identity, but the parent company is also visible in the background—General Motors, L'Oreal. A further range of companies can be described as "branded"—Unilever, Procter & Gamble—where subsidiary companies have their own style and brands and the corporate entity may not be known to the uninitiated. Differences between the different corporate typologies have been ably tackled in the literature. In the 21st century, firms will be unable to maintain the third option. Consumers want to know about the companies behind the brands. While expenditure on corporate communication is dwarfed by expenditures on product or brand marketing communication programs, such expenditures are nonetheless necessary in today's world. To complete this task properly, corporations are starting to appoint corporate communication executives who in turn engage specialists in the field of marketing or corporate communication to develop programs for internal and external publics in a manner consistent with the corporate identity. The gap between identity (corporation) and image (publics) that needs to be bridged constitutes the planning framework using such mechanisms as public relations, public affairs, investor relations, government relations, labor market communication, social responsibility, corporate advertising, and media relations.

There are at least three other senses in which corporate communication is necessary and desirable. The first stems from the need to build not just the individual brands in a corporate portfolio but the corporate brand as well. Corporate entities play an increasingly important role in the global economy. They exert significant economic and political influence and form a significant aspect of news in their own right. If BMW seeks millions of dollars in resources from the British government to bolster a flagging Rover brand, it is an important media, social, political, and economic issue. If genetically modified food products are proven or suspected to cause health problems, this will lead to the need for proven long-term testing and subsequent retail action and legislative influence throughout the world. Brands are being globalized, corporations are becoming globalized, but news has been global for some time. Corporations need to protect, nurture, and strengthen themselves by building interactive and synergistic relationships with all publics that can impact corporate performance.

The second reason corporate communication is necessary is to protect and nurture strategic business units and brands to enable them to grow. Inevitably brands are powerful corporate assets in their own right, often reflected in balance sheet accounting and reporting. But brands need a powerful business backing them. Increasingly, these businesses are global in scope and scale.

The third sense in which corporate communication is necessary lies in the sense that primarily marketing and corporate executives are spearheading the drive for IMC and IGMC. It is our contention that IGMC has to be driven by senior management. Note from Exhibits 7.1, 7.2, and 7.3 that IGMC is driven by both sectors of management. At yet another level all resources are allocated to SBUs and their brands *by corporate management*. Thus, for customer-driven IGMC programs to work, and for the organization to learn continually, requires strong top-down corporate commitment.

CONCLUSIONS

- There are ten factors at the nexus of marketing strategy: objective, initiative, concentration, economy of resources, maneuver, unity of command, coordination, surprise, simplicity, and flexibility.
- The corporate reengineering you will need to effect must be a top-down effort.
- Make creativity be *effective*, not merely unique.
- Apply IGMC processes to building your business, brand, and corporate identity.

8

IGMC Drivers and Agency Interaction

As illustrated throughout this book, the need for organizations to move toward adoption and utilization of new models and processes is inescapable. In this chapter we illustrate the primary drivers of IGMC and then show how these drivers operate from an agency perspective. Agencies servicing client needs are commonly an integral part of developing meaningful communication that leads to success. While we use the term *advertising agency*, we prefer the term *communication agency*, for major corporations in today's world do not seek just advertising solutions to marketing communication or business problems. Instead they seek effective marketing communication solutions that increase market share and expand brand, business, and ultimately corporate performance in terms of sales, profits, enhanced relationships and behaviors, and more positive mind-sets from all publics.

TECHNOLOGY DRIVERS

The marketing scene, at least over the last five years, has been rocked by the impact of new media, including the development of interactive television, the rise of the Internet, E-commerce, interactive telephone, and faxing. As we have indicated elsewhere, the amalgamation of these technologies resulted in the passing of control from marketers into the hands of consumers and customers. Market segmentation heralded the introduction of narrowcasting that has been doubly pushed forward by the new media explosion. Both segmentation and narrowcasting signify the growth of one-to-one communication opportunities; hence the reference to marketspace as opposed to marketplace in earlier chapters. The brand, as discussed in Chapters 3 and

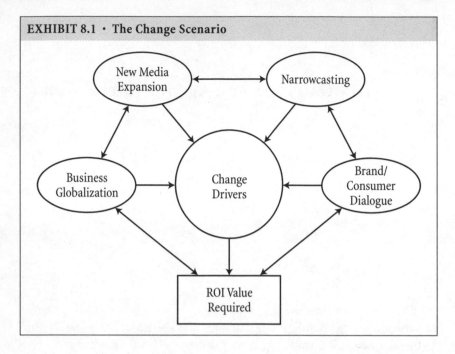

EXHIBIT 8.1 • The Change Scenario

4, has become central, most importantly in the ways consumers interact with brands. The image of brands, in the mind-sets of customers and consumers, is central to IGMC. Because the mind-sets may well vary from country to country and between corporate and individual brands, corporations that wish to grow brands globally still need to know where brands "exist" in terms of individual country performance. The real driving force, however, is the ever greater accelerating pressure for marketers to show or prove return on investment for marketing activities. And since marketing communication forms by far the greatest bulk of brand investment (not expenditure), Chapter 10 addresses this crucial issue of ROI or, as we describe it, ROCI. All of these change drivers are illustrated in Exhibit 8.1.

CULTURAL DRIVERS

We have shown that the age of mass marketing is rapidly closing in most developed markets. In an age where IGMC mechanisms proliferate, corporations need to access and use multiple tools to reach and influence consumers. Micro- and niche markets and one-to-one markets do not necessarily exhibit different behavioral characteristics. But appealing to their

EXHIBIT 8.2 • **Cultural Characteristics**

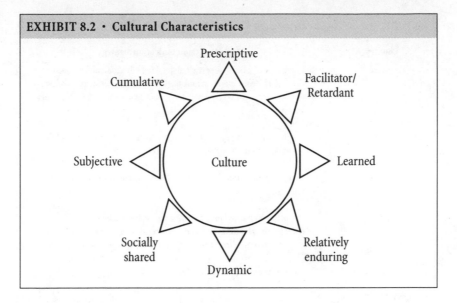

needs, wants, and desires may need to be approached differentially because of cultural criteria.

Marketing strategy for different consumers may need to be differentiated on the basis of culture. And, taking this to the corporate brand level, publics, including internal staff, require different types of communication. Yet culture represents nothing new to marketers. The major characteristics of culture from an IGMC perspective are illustrated in Exhibit 8.2.

Taking these characteristics as givens means that marketers constantly have to revisit and adjust marketing communication strategies to ensure they meet the needs of target audiences or target publics. An old but still relevant example of how strategy can be similar but differ in terms of a potential IGMC format was found when Renault launched the Renault 5 throughout Europe—one of the world's major small-car markets. The basic elements of cultural factors, admittedly drawn from a rather arbitrary selection of European countries, are shown in Exhibit 8.3.

What is telling about the Renault example is that only once (in the case of Holland) did the company decide to alter product line policy. In every other case the same car was being marketed, but *differentially*, apparently determined by company awareness of market cultural factors. And again, customization for IGMC is not impossible. But it is improbable in our view that such customization will work everywhere, in all cultures. Exhibit 8.4 indicates why adaptation may be required.

EXHIBIT 8.3 • The Renault 5: A Culturally Adjusted IGMC Approach

Country	Marketing Communication Strategy
France	Fun image of a little "supercar" adapted to both urban and highway driving. The copy platform took the form of a cartoon strip, showing a bouncy chatty car with eyes and mouth drawn in on the headlights and bumper.
Germany	Emphasis on technical superiority; key features were the safety of the car and its modern engineering and interior comfort.
Finland	Emphasis on technical superiority; focus on solid construction and reliability.
Italy	Importance attached to road performance, focus on mechanical features, road handling capacity, and acceleration. Importance of creating an individual personality for the car was relegated to second place, and the name Little Supercar transformed into La Cittadina del Mondo, "the citizen of the world."
Holland	Revised product line policy. Car positioned as small, high quality, and expensive. Management decided to go into the market with the Renault 5TL, its top luxury model.

Source: Adapted from Douglas and Dubois, 1977

EXHIBIT 8.4 • Communication Influencers

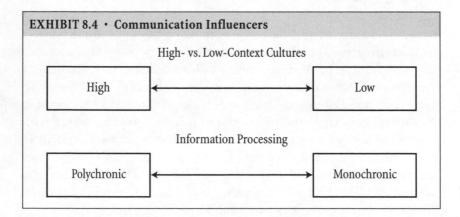

The terms *high-* and *low-context cultures* connote receptivity of a culture to in-depth background information. Thus, for example in Japan, Spain, and Italy, communication may be indirect rather than direct. The words used do not necessarily convey messages accurately. Instead the sender's position, social status, and values convey the major part of the message. Personal relationship-building approaches, therefore, are likely to work well in these cultural contexts. On the other hand, in low-context cultures such as Germany and the United States, words are used to convey the majority of information. What is said, not the way it is said or who is saying it, conveys most of the information.

The second information-processing continuum also indicates a potential need for adaptation. Polychronic information-processing cultures work on several fronts simultaneously. Direct eye contact, superficial friendships, and moving with immediacy to "close the sale" are seen as confrontational and potentially aggressive. Monochronic cultures, on the other hand, are permeated by a sense of time, and these characteristics are seen as standard business practice. In these cultures wasting time would be perceived as annoying and irritating by certain types of businesspeople. On the other hand, pushing for schedule completion or contract closure may be seen by Japanese or Hispanic cultures as "pushy" or impatient. These influences, well known to international marketers, may be sidestepped or deemed unimportant in the drive for globalization. Unfortunately, in these days to ignore them is a potentially fatal mistake.

THE MARKETING COMMUNICATION PARADOX: DIVERGENCE AND INTEGRATION

Marketers are faced with a paradox. At the very same time of divergence of consumer and public behavior and accelerating multidimensionality in media alternatives, the organization is under pressure to integrate. But the impetus to integrate is a reflection of many factors, as conceptualized throughout this text and depicted in Exhibit 8.5.

The forces affecting the corporation are many and varied. For example, Exhibit 8.5 can be considered from either the individual or corporate brand perspective. The brand structure may be multiplied by many hundreds in the case of, say, Procter & Gamble or Unilever. The stakeholder set will vary brand by brand but would probably be unitary at the corporate level. Channels would vary based on consumer custom and practice and the messages to be deployed. Thus the question of what to integrate must be addressed from a consumer audience or public perspective and may include messages, tonality, media, teams, planning processes, database requirements, and ROCI analyses (see Chapter 10) to deliver the benefits of coherency and efficiency leading to behavioral outcomes. So the answer to the questions of how and what to integrate is driven by marketers' proactivity with respect to consumer needs.

With these factors in mind, how is IMC developing in advertising agencies around the world? First we will look at agencies in five countries; then we'll examine how one global agency is responding to its client's desire

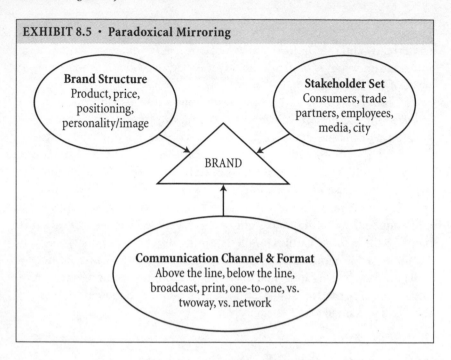

EXHIBIT 8.5 • Paradoxical Mirroring

for integrated approaches. Finally, we will discuss issues that impact media systems and distribution of messages and incentives needed by agencies to service client needs with new integrated approaches.

THE IMC STUDY FINDINGS

During 1997 and 1998, a series of studies was carried out to ascertain the level of development of IMC from an agency perspective in the United States, United Kingdom, Australia, New Zealand, and India. This study was reported in the *Journal of Advertising Research* in 1999.

The study found a remarkable degree of unanimity concerning what IMC was and how it had developed over time. The study suggested that IMC was developing as a response to, and in conjunction with, changes affecting the field of marketing communication worldwide. We have already indicated developmental paths along which firms could go in developing IMC and IGMC. However, the extent to which IGMC or IMC can be implemented depends on what firms decide to do given potential differing contextual circumstances and perhaps cultural constraints.

From the international perspective, however, there was little to suggest that firms had progressed beyond the first stage of IGMC, namely the inte-

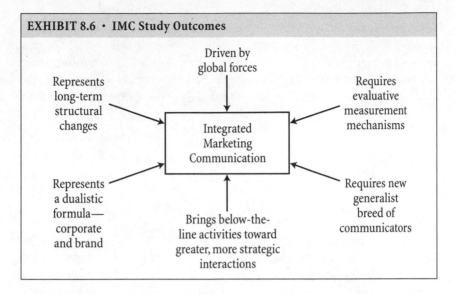

EXHIBIT 8.6 • IMC Study Outcomes

Driven by global forces

Represents long-term structural changes

Requires evaluative measurement mechanisms

Integrated Marketing Communication

Represents a dualistic formula— corporate and brand

Brings below-the-line activities toward greater, more strategic interactions

Requires new generalist breed of communicators

gration of tactics. The definition of IGMC used in the study found acceptance of, but not wholehearted agreement with, our executive respondents. Based on responses, executives expressed the need for a revised definition, together with a series of methods to evaluate or measure the effects of IGMC programs. Both of these have been provided in this book. However, as we have argued throughout, in a world of multiplied product and message options and unique cultural circumstances, corporations have to choose whether and how to reorganize communication from an IGMC perspective.

Despite the fact that the study showed widespread agreement concerning the benefits of using IGMC approaches in the five countries in terms of *standardization of meaning*, it was virtually impossible to assess *standardization of practice*. Exhibit 8.6 summarizes the other major findings of the five-country IMC study.

Let's now see how agencies may need to restructure to respond to these new initiatives on behalf of client-based organizations in Europe.

THE INTEGRATED AGENCY PERSPECTIVE

Corporations wishing to compete globally require the assistance of agencies. Put another way, they need access to the creative, planning, and media skills major agencies provide to develop integrated campaigns. They can use one large international agency whose approach generally mirrors corporate requirements. This allows for communication centralization and control. Such an approach can be used for larger divisions, strategic business units, and global brands (both existent and wannabes). Or it can be used for managing and directing the corporate image on a worldwide basis. Quite a number of global companies have consolidated marketing communication with one global communication group. The following are the major global marketing communication groups that have in effect *mirrored* global firm requirements and sought to service all client communication needs:

Organizational/HQ Location	Gross Income U.S.$ Millions
WPP Group (London)	2,768
Interpublic Group (New York)	2,211
Omnicom (New York)	2,052
Dentsu Inc. (Tokyo)	1,642
Cordiant (London)	1,432
Young & Rubicam (New York)	1,059
Euro RSCG (Levallois-Perret)	813
Grey Advertising (New York)	809
Hakuhodo (Tokyo)	774
Leo Burnett (Chicago)	677

Advertising Age, 1995

An alternative is to have the lead agency or client hire local agencies, which tend to be better informed about the national consumer culture and would also know about national media constraints. Often local agencies are subsidiaries of international groups. They also possess a significant depth of national knowledge. Hiring a leading public relations or public affairs firm to tackle corporate brand issues could also access this local knowledge. Global agencies that produced gross income in excess of $600 million in 1995 are these:

Agency	Gross Income U.S.$ Millions
Dentsu Inc.	1,569
McCann Erickson Worldwide	1,063
J. Walter Thompson Co.	881
Hakuhodo	774
BBDO Worldwide	737
Grey Advertising	701
Leo Burnett	678
Lintas Worldwide	666
Euro RSCG	640
DDB Needham Worldwide	629
Ogilvy & Mather Worldwide	611
Saatchi & Saatchi Advertising	602

Advertising Age, 1995

Intermediate solutions attempt to effectively balance worldwide coordination and localization of marketing and corporate communication efforts. These strategies are sometimes referred to as *glocalization*. Considering the two preceding tables again, these are not mutually exclusive alternatives but rather service arrangements that firms can choose to use as strategic partners in developing standardized or differentiated IGMC campaigns.

Each or any of these approaches needs then to be translated, first into a creative brief and planning process and then into a media brief and planning process. The following elements have been developed in conjunction with Keith Crosier, who has worked as an advertising manager for a major multinational and who became a university teacher at Strathclyde University in the United Kingdom.

The creative brief involves these steps:

1. Background: Previous work for client? What worked?
2. Target audience/public: Behavioral aggregation, attitudinal, socioeconomic, and psychographic segmentation.
3. Proposition: What is the proposed behavioral/attitudinal outcome?
4. Support: Main media, message, interactive marcom roles?
5. Tone: Tone of voice required?
6. Desired response
7. Current behavior/attitudes: Derived from the database.
8. Mandatory and other requirements
9. Other data, brand level, media, dates, budget

This list assumes the client has delegated the creative planning process to a communication agency. The sequence depicted is not rigid, nor are the steps necessarily sequential. The aim of the creative team, which includes account planners and managers, creatives, and a media representative, is to produce marketing communication that will achieve client objectives and simultaneously outmaneuver the competition. (See Chapter 7 for more detail on the creative process.) The creative planning process may then proceed as follows:

1. Identify creative objectives.
2. Generate ideas.
3. Formulate communication concepts.
4. Cross-check with media plans.
5. Develop executive concepts.
6. Pretest.
7. Formulate postevaluative creative strategy.

The creative process has to be matched with the media brief and media planning process. Note that at these levels there is significant opportunity for every element of marketing communication to be focused on behavioral outcomes.

The media planning process as depicted by Keith Crosier includes the following steps:

Media Requirements
- Client?
- Product/service/brand/corporation?
- Objectives?
- End users?
- Decision influencers of promotional message? (needs adaptation?)
- IGMC period?
- Budget?
- National/international/global?
- Season/timing/sequence?
- Space/size/IGMC approach integrality?
- Constraints?
- Other agencies/interactions?

Background Data
- Consumer database scenario
- Competitive scenario
- Current/past marcom approaches
- Sales/market share
- Creative brief
- Marketing or corpcom strategy/strategies
- Any mandatory requirements

The media planning process includes these steps:

1. Identify media objectives and promotional appropriations.
2. Monitor competitors.
3. Match targets to media.
4. Draft strategic plan.
5. Cross-check with creative plan.
6. Select media options and set media schedule.
7. Implement operational plan.
8. Review and revise (following postevaluation of media strategy).

The media brief and media planning process represent procedural principles that can apply in any culture from an IMC or IGMC perspective. Let's now consider what happens when this process is translated into an international context.

The Corporate Communication/Marketing Communication Plan

1. **Raw Materials**
   What are we offering/communicating to whom?

1.1 Product/Service/Organizational Profile
Specification: What can it/we do?
Benefits: What can we/it offer?

1.2 Company/Organizational Profile
Specification: What do we do?
Identity: How do we present ourselves?
Image: How are we viewed/seen?

1.3 Audience/Market/Public Profile
Behavioristics: How have they behaved in the past?
Sociodemographics: Who are they, and where located?
Psychographics: What do they want to be/want us to be?

1.4 Market Profile
Structure: What does it look like?
Competition: Who is there with us, and how do they compete?
Culture: Is this important; if so,why; and how to evaluate?
Dynamics: What's coming?

2. **Constraints**
What is beyond our control?

2.1 Marketing Mix
Product policy: What effect on IGMC approach?
Pricing policy: What effect on IGMC approach?
Place/distribution policy: What effect on IGMC approach?

2.2 Givens
Precedents: What is traditional/expected?
Mandatories: What is compulsory?

2.3 Budget
Appropriations: What funds are available?
Allocations: How and where are they to be expended?
Control: How will cost effectiveness be monitored?

3. **Objectives**
What do we need to accomplish?

3.1 Goals: What are the overall annual and long-term aims?

3.2 Targets: What are the intermediate aims of the plan?

3.3 Criteria: How will effectiveness be measured? (short/long term)

4. **Strategy**
How will we achieve our objectives?

4.1 Communication: What do we want to say?

4.2 Creative: How do we want to say it?

4.3 Media: How will the message(s) reach consumers/publics?
(contact points and contact preferences)

5. **Timetable**
How will our strategy become an integrated campaign?
5.1 Time scale: How soon must objectives be met?
5.2 Schedule: What needs to happen when?
5.3 Interaction: Which partners are we working with?
5.4 Control: Who is in overall charge (lead agency/client)?

6. **Implementation**
How will the campaign be measured?
6.1 Authority: Who can say yes or no?
6.2 Responsibility: Who will coordinate it? (See timetable.)
6.3 Delegation: Who are the subcontractors?
6.4 Procedures: How will we monitor progress?
6.5 Evaluation/Measurement: How are results to be measured?

This marketing communication planning framework can be adapted in conjunction with the creative and media briefs and planning process for use in any culture. However, whether the actual campaign or promotional element is adapted depends on the given contextual circumstances of a product, service, or brand.

Let's consider how one agency in London, Saatchi and Saatchi, tackled the twin issues of IGMC (international) and IMC (national focus). The older amalgamated company had dropped *advertising* from its title as early as 1993, when it became known as a "through-the-line" communication company. By 1997 Saatchi and Saatchi had become a hothouse for worldwide change in creative ideas. Back in 1997, all of its major clients were ranked in the top five in terms of market share in the countries in which they competed. Studying a selective sample of these client companies revealed a wide disparity of use in terms of marketing communication elements deployed:

Industry	*Marketing Communication*
National Lottery (UK)	Television, posters, radio, trade point-of-sale, game design
Electrical Retailer (UK)	Direct marketing, sales promotion
Computer Related Hardware (Europe)	Television, press, retail promotion, point-of-sale materials, trade communication, loyalty schemes, CD-ROMs, Internet, screen savers
Health and Beauty (Europe)	Television, press, mail inserts, door drops, point-of-sale
Motor Vehicle (Europe)	Television, press, posters, test drive phone-ins, promotions, radio
Business Stationery (United Kingdom)	Press, direct mail, Internet

What is interesting about these examples is the large span of marketing communication activities created and managed by the agency. Both the span and mechanisms deployed are all different. Thus, while Saatchi and Saatchi still has some specialists—database marketing, marketing public relations, sales promotion, etc., as well as advertising—the specializations are deployed according to client need for an integrated solution. This supports our oft-repeated statement that if IGMC is to work effectively, it depends on the will and influence of senior executives in global organizations. Agencies, in other words, are not the driving force behind IMC or IGMC; clients are.

Increasingly clients see their role as that of integrator. Sylvia Meli, formerly with Saatchi and Saatchi and now with Grey Advertising, has said, "For many clients integration is not just a philosophical issue, but has become an economic necessity." Demonstrably, from an agency perspective, clients have moved and are moving toward IMC and IGMC. Some of the underlying reasons are illustrated in Exhibit 8.7.

Communication agencies are always concerned with revenue generation. The worldwide move toward below-the-line activities, as compared to above-the-line advertising, means that every agency has to widen its ability to provide nonadvertising services. Moreover, a strategy emphasizing consumer loyalty and curriculum marketing has overtaken conquest marketing as the number-one priority. The old adage that five times as much money is spent on attracting each new customer as on retaining existing ones has finally come home to businesses of all kinds and in all industries. Exhibit 8.8 indicates how marketers believe communication works.

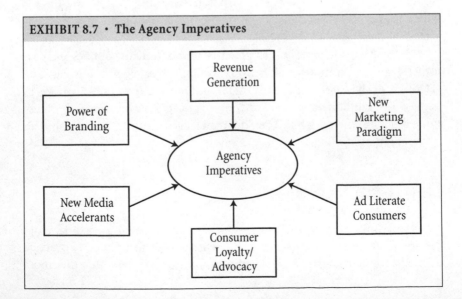

EXHIBIT 8.7 · The Agency Imperatives

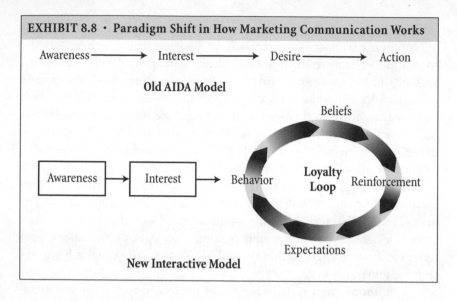

EXHIBIT 8.8 · Paradigm Shift in How Marketing Communication Works

Awareness ──────▶ Interest ──────▶ Desire ──────▶ Action

Old AIDA Model

Awareness ──▶ Interest ──▶ Behavior · Beliefs · Loyalty Loop · Reinforcement · Expectations

New Interactive Model

Our measurement models and processes in Chapter 10 work alongside the new interactive model in terms of dealing with existing customers from an individual and corporate brand perspective.

New media are not only here but also are now far more than hype. They amount to a new type of interactive, consumer-controlled communication in its own right. Clients expect agency planners not only to know about new media developments but also to be able to recommend them as part of integrated campaign development. But integration, as we have seen, is also about branding, and one key question is how to extend the brand franchise. Another question is: What about corporate branding and *all* the brands within the corporate portfolio? Exhibit 8.9 indicates the broad-ranging parameters of these issues.

Exhibit 8.9 does not show all potential brand franchise publics and customers, nor does it indicate all delivery mechanisms. What it does indicate is that IGMC has more targets to aim for and more delivery mechanisms to use—which could be perceived as contact points for consumers and customers. In the emerging IGMC world, managerial attitudes, even within an agency scenario, will have to change.

MEDIA SCENARIO

Although some international markets may be homogenizing or globalizing, the ability of firms to standardize approaches may be forestalled in practice by media infrastructures in given cultural contexts. We have seen that most

---

EXHIBIT 8.9 · Expanding Brand Integration: Broadening Influences

← ———————— Brand Franchise ———————— →

Internal	Channel	Retail	Customers	Influencers	Analysts	More Targets

Sponsorship		
Advertising		
MPR	More
Sales Promotion	Delivery
Direct Marketing	Mechanisms
Point of Sales	
CD-ROM	
Internet	

---

media expenditure is concentrated in the triad areas (North America, Europe, and the Pacific Rim dominated by Japan). Availability of press, radio, television, and electronic and other forms of mailing systems varies from country to country. Even where television is available, the times available for advertising may vary considerably, as is the case across Europe (eighty minutes a day in Italy versus twelve minutes a day in Finland). As the following comparison of the United States and the Pacific Rim shows, the potential volume of media messages—a reflection of media availability—varies widely both between the United States and these countries and between the countries themselves.

Media Availability	USA	China	Hong Kong	Taiwan	Singapore	Indonesia	Malaysia
TV Stations	2,070	700	2	3	6	6	4
Newspapers	1,532	900	60	275	17	42	38
Magazines	11,500	7,000	600	4,442	134	120	220
Radio Stations	12,142	n/a	3	33	15	750	17

Issues of fragmentation and consumer choice are prefigured in the tables and exhibits presented earlier. There are relatively few global media save those available by cable systems (e.g., MTV, BBC, and CNN) and regionalized newspapers such as the *Financial Times* or the *Wall Street Journal.* The Internet forms a potential global medium on its own. Currently the Internet can be positioned as an intermediate medium that is neither personal nor mass. Certainly the Internet has to be integrated with other forms of communication, yet it has the potential to reach most, if not all, consumer sets worldwide. Predictions of wide Internet usage, though relevant, do not mean that old modes of communication will disappear. As Alan Rosenshine said in an *Advertising Age* article about five years ago, "Traditional advertising and new media will co-exist and, increasingly, complement one another. . . . In any event, it will be quite some time, if ever, before the new media replace the old. Films didn't doom books. TV didn't doom radio, magazines or newspapers. Cable didn't doom the networks."

Development of the Internet does, however, provide impetus for the methods by which a company builds relations with its publics and customers and for the company's organizational structure. The Web does change customer participation in the marketing communication process. As interactive media evolve further, other media, and the creative processes involved, will have to change to adapt to Web-oriented customers and publics.

As we have argued repeatedly, however, the availability of media is not an overriding issue from an IGMC perspective. The approach for a given set of customers has to be driven by an understanding in a given cultural context. We have also indicated (see Case Studies 2 and 4) that the only significantly globalized form of media is advertising, closely followed in some cases by sponsorship or public relations. This means that, when successful, campaigns that use television in one country (for example, the United States) would potentially have to be adapted in other cultures (for example, China or Hong Kong).

MESSAGE INCENTIVES

Sales promotion activities in the form of incentives are usually indigenous. Nonetheless, such incentives are significant in building strategically integrated marketing communication. The following issues are relevant here:

- Repeated price promotions weaken the added value produced by advertising.
- Price promotions lower consumer reference price levels.
- Consumers attribute low quality to frequently promoted brands.
- Consumers may become accustomed to and plan purchases based on discount availability.
- Trade promotions, which receive the lion's share of budgetary appropriations, produce the weakest long-term sales effects.
- Non-price-related sales promotions have much more potential to further strengthen and enhance brand image.

• Sales promotions generally do not change the attitudes or behavior of consumers who are already strongly loyal or strongly negative.

Andreas Laspadakis, 1999

Price promotions are a complicated aspect of the current marketplace. Retailers in many parts of the world form such a significant proportion of distribution capacity that they can demand price reductions. However, repeated price promotion tends to result in the demotion of brands to commodities. There may always be a need for some price promotion, but we prefer to see such promotions being driven by strategic brand-building issues rather than just masking current weakness associated with other marketing or promotional mix elements. Nonetheless, sales promotion can provide an important mechanism for attainment of a brand's long-term objectives. Both price- and non-price-related promotions have to be deployed in such a way as to be consistent with the overall IGMC strategy. Too much emphasis on price-related promotions can, and often does, produce negative returns to the brand image. Non-price-related promotions might not produce equal short-term effects but reinforce and enhance brand image in the longer term.

As with the media scenario, deployment of price- and non-price-related sales promotion depends on the contextual circumstances of consumers in a given cultural setting. Very few sales promotions (save perhaps for credit cards or financial services) have crossed international boundaries. Yet incentives may need to be given to achieve annual national or local sales objectives. In the longer term, however, we suggest promotions be considered from a brand-building perspective and the use of nonprice promotions clearly linked to core brand values that enhance the planned brand image.

IMPLICATIONS FOR INTERNATIONAL MEDIA RESEARCH

Few can doubt that many global communicators are keen to integrate their marketing communication activities. Media research provides ongoing and salient research data gathered from syndicated and audited research services to aid in the media planning and buying processes. The difficulty is that about 95 percent of all media is still negotiated and placed locally. There are few genuinely international media, and this complicates the global media buyer's task. Moreover, several problems are facing international media research and researchers that have resonance for the continued development of integrated approaches to communication:

• Sustained technological innovation and economic development appear to underpin the trend of marketing and marketing communication moving from a national focus to a global perspective. Despite emergence of an increasingly geographically borderless world, the boundaries of consumers' minds are not crossed as easily, resulting in the glocalization of marketing communication strategy, spearheaded in many instances by advertising, while message incentives vary country by country.

• Despite the numbers and depth of a range of media research vehicles in developed economies, few media purchases are underpinned by sound understanding of the dynamics of to-be-served markets. Far too many multinational media buys are driven by statistics, and statistics do not necessarily equate to understanding. These surveys, and many others, while currently underpinning many marketing communication strategies and very useful at identifying broad macroeconomic trends, don't really serve to adequately identify consumer attitudes toward companies, products, services, brands, or marketing communication activities, and certainly don't reflect consumer behaviors. This in turn may suggest implementation of integrated approaches (led by advertising) without really understanding how and in what way(s) markets may respond. For example, a global advertising strategy deployed by American Express used the theme "places you want to go, people you want to meet," with the proviso that the ads developed would give cardholders the same campaign they see at home but look like a domestic effort to locals. Meanwhile, Colgate Palmolive, having attempted a global approach across Europe during the 1980s, switched to local country autonomy in the 1990s, even though it uses a global marketing communication company to operationalize the strategy.

• Building an international brand image is often painfully slow because of different product life cycle stages and different levels of understanding about what a brand conceptually and emotionally represents among different cultures. Another barrier may be company organizational structures that lend themselves to neither internationalization nor integrated approaches. Developments in either direction have to be driven by a strong center, and yet in a series of interviews carried out with ten major packaged goods multinationals, eight of the ten corporations adopted a devolved international managerial structure. Thus integration, from an international perspective, is unlikely to develop without preceding organizational change. For these companies, international media research will continue as currently offered, but again with a need for more qualitative research.

• It is still possible to *plan* global campaigns centrally. Information about many markets is available, and media operations are becoming more standardized worldwide. Budget allocation, relative media efficiency, and media weight can all be taken into consideration. The difficulty is that at the very same time increasing amounts of data are being generated internationally, other issues are coming to the fore.

• In the global market media vehicles are proliferating. Cable TV, satellite TV, pay-per-view TV, and other forms of television delivery mechanisms are rapidly taking away share from broadcast channels. Yet lack of standardized quantitative media research is retarding the growth of global campaigns. In the United States, multiplication of media alternatives has resulted in audience shrinkage while simultaneously costs of advertising to smaller audiences have expanded significantly from year to year. The best option for media planners is to plan internationally using data extrapolated from national television research (e.g., Barb in the UK, GFK in Germany, Intomart in the Netherlands). Print media do not fare much better. In Europe international planners access data from nonstandardized and often incompatible national readership surveys and extrapolate accordingly. Purely numerical evaluations, it has been claimed, will never be enough to ensure development of truly integrated international/global campaigns.

• There is evidence to suggest that media fragmentation will further accelerate by the convergence of computer, communication, and information technologies. Direct selling, underpinned by database technology, may further subvert micromarkets to units of one.

• The idea of the world being bound together by mass media, speaking one language, sporting similar brands, is already defunct. Consumers and would-be customers throughout the world are fragmenting, diversifying, and splintering in their media consumption. We have moved irreconcilably from mass to micromarkets, from marketplace to marketspace. Tomorrow's consumers may be individualized in their consumption of television, a further phase of development from marketspace to mindspace.

The dilemma for global communicators is simple: how to reach across the globe while at the same time coping with its immense diversity. An answer to this question may be difficult, but is worth attempting:

• Communicators must speak the language of the listeners. Marketing communication must be integrated, not from an outbound, outmoded sender mentality but from an inbound, interactive, consumer-driven perspective. The control of information technology is passing from senders via channels to receivers.

• Advertising, and the whole range of other communication variants, must in an integrated fashion convey the same values country by country but be far more personalized. In other words, quantitative data must be a starting point for research but be underpinned by qualitative data gathered by international media research organizations or by companies themselves.

For example, in two recent studies research findings by means of focus groups suggested that for the *same subject areas* (brands, product categories, social activities in Europe and the United States) attitudes of consumers varied significantly. The implication was that marketing communication copy needed to be recrafted to take advantage of conceptual relevance amid cultural diversity.

As media continue to fragment and consumers exercise choice diversity, implications for international media research seem to crystallize. To produce IGMC that effectively crosses geographical and psychological boundaries, homogenization must be supplanted and replaced by approaches that take into account cultural and linguistic diversity. Such diversity can be understood, in our view, only through a sound understanding of the dynamics of markets. In other words, international media providers and international media research face tremendous growth opportunities.

CONCLUSIONS

- You must understand the cultures into which you wish to send your communication—is it high context or low context?—and adapt where necessary.
- In general, you will require the assistance of a communication agency to compete globally. Try to choose one whose competencies mirror your requirements.
- If one approach won't cross all borders, consider glocalizing.
- Non-price-related promotions are preferable to price promotions—cutting the price too often commodifies the brand.

9

An Integrated View of IGMC Management and Vendor Compensation

Traditionally management of the marketing communication area has fallen to a functional specialist, either a marketing communication manager or perhaps an advertising director. In some cases it might be the sales manager or director who adds communication responsibilities to his or her portfolio. Thus communication has been managed as an organizational activity or element based on functional objectives. The goals of the communication unit are typically set by senior managers who are often responsible for broad areas of the organization. Likewise, senior management has determined communication budgets either based on requests by the functional manager or simply as allocations made during the annual budgeting cycle. Commonly funds dedicated to marketing and communication have come from the general resources available within the organization or, increasingly, have been allocated into a common pool by the various strategic business units (SBUs) as part of their budgeting process.

In marketing communication program development and support, the marketing communication manager relied on either an internal department, commonly staffed by media, creative, or visual specialists, or an external organization such as an advertising agency or communication development and placement organization. Compensation of the external groups was often based on some type of media commission for space or time purchased, markups on purchased supplies or materials, and perhaps fees for time invested in the development of plans and programs. Increasingly today, compensation for external organizations appears to be based on a combination of commissions and fees. Thus, from the view of the marketing communication manager, many of the agency services or other resources were "free of cost" since payment was covered in commissions from the expenditures made in support of other external communication programs.

In both managing and financing various marketing communication programs, the amount spent by the marketing organization was taken as a fixed expense by the firm. That is, it was budgeted at the beginning of the accounting period, and withdrawals were made from a reserve set up for the purpose as the programs were executed. Thus the senior management assumed marketing and communication expenditures were a sunk cost or an accrual account that could be "raided" near the end of the accounting period if expenses needed to be reduced or funds moved to shore up the bottom line. Therefore, marketing communication in most organizations has deserved little or no top management attention since (a) it was difficult to measure results, (b) it expensed costs, and (c) little or no immediate business impact was felt as a result of adjusting the level of investment. Thus, while marketing communication has been important to the persons involved in the function, unfortunately, the same cannot be said for senior management in many firms. (Recall from our discussion of the three types of organizations that product- or distribution-driven organizations believe the product superiority or availability of product is the critical element in marketplace success.) Thus the systems used to manage the marketing communication function and to determine how and in what amount communication program development should be funded or measured have received little attention outside the immediate areas of the functional activity.

Much of the lack of management involvement in the budgeting and evaluation of communication investments is due to the difficulty of measuring or at least determining the returns on the marketing and communication investments. If you don't know what you're getting back for what you spend, then the best approach is to spend the least possible and hope for the best. This seems to have been the approach used by many organizations over the last four decades. This is not to say that many organizations don't believe marketing and communication are critical to their success. Indeed the very basis for organizations such as Procter & Gamble, Unilever, Nike, Coca-Cola, and others has been the result of highly successful marketing and, particularly, communication programs. But, for the vast majority of organizations, marketing communication, whether integrated or not, is not a major issue. As a result it has often been shorted on the development of fundamental issues such as management structures, funding for program development, and the like. We will deal with the issue of measurement in Chapter 10. Our discussion there will provide the basis for determining how much the organization should invest in marketing and marketing communication and how to measure the results of those investments.

In this chapter we deal first with the management of the marketing communication function or activity in the organization and second with how much and under what circumstances the organization should pay for the development and ongoing activities falling under the marketing communication banner.

A TRADITIONAL APPROACH TO MARKETING COMMUNICATION MANAGEMENT

For the most part marketing communication has been designated as a function or a department or an area of activity in most organizations. Thus it has come under the traditional approaches of command and control management. Exhibit 9.1 illustrates a typical corporate organizational structure.

There are generally three or more basic activities of the organization—operations, finance, and sales/marketing. Under each activity a number of groups deal with the specific area related to that function. Operations controls manufacturing or development and distribution. Finance deals with accounting, billing, and payroll. Marketing deals with customer contact, market planning, product management, and so on. Each is a separate department, and each is a functional activity reporting upward to the senior management of the firm. Interestingly, in most organizational structures few functional groups interact with each other or their sibling groups in the organization. For the marketing communication manager to interact with the

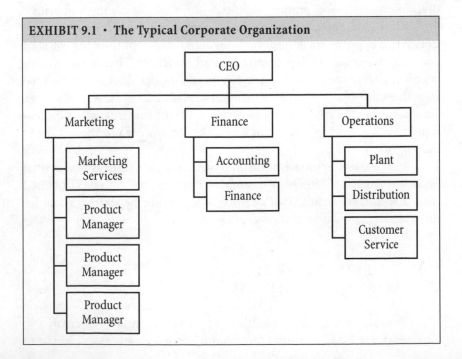

EXHIBIT 9.1 • The Typical Corporate Organization

production department, he or she generally has to go up the line or chain of command and then down the same chain in the other department or group. Thus the primary coordination occurs at the top of the organization, with senior managers making decisions that impact the actual daily activities of the organization in the field.

It is clear from this organizational structure that there can be little or no integration within the total organization. Each functional element is separate and has its own areas and activities for which it is responsible, and each is managed and rewarded on what it *does*, not what it *accomplishes*. From the view of the functional manager, he or she is a separate and unique activity unrelated to the whole of the organization. "If I do my job right and others do their jobs right, everything will be OK" is generally the management rule of thumb for these organizations.

Yet, as we have demonstrated throughout this book, the customer and the consumer do not consider the organization to be separate and individual sets of activities and/or functions. They see the organization holistically: "You all have the same name. You all work for the same organization. Why can't you tell me what's going on with my account or my product or my service?" The basic dichotomy in many organizations, in fact, is that the customer views the organization holistically while the organization views itself as pieces and parts. Therein lie many of the problems in global marketing and communication. The lack of connection or knowledge or understanding not only among countries and regions but also among departments and divisions makes global programs difficult if not impossible in these firms.

The IGMC approach to marketing communication management takes exactly the opposite track from traditional management thinking: we start with a customer view of the organization and work back. That develops management approaches that fit customer needs, rather than organizational structures and flowcharts that fit managerial goals. Along the way, of course, we must bring the customer needs and organizational structure and capability together, but the concept of a *customer-centric* organization is key to our approach.

In brief, our approach to management and structure is to ask what needs to be managed to satisfy customers, not what needs to be structured for management control. That question will provide the starting point for our approach, structure, and process.

WHAT NEEDS TO BE MANAGED
TO SATISFY CUSTOMERS?

If the organization takes an inside-out approach (recall our discussion in Chapter 1), the management of the communication function will equate to managing the communication output of the firm. Management will be focused on managing the advertising program or the sales promotion activities or direct marketing mail drops or public relations events. Thus the communication people and managers will be focused on what gets done, not on the impact of the programs the group is implementing. Focusing on the outcomes rather than the output, again is a major difference in how the marketing communication group views itself and its responsibilities. It's the IGMC approach.

Managing the communication activities with and for a group of customers and prospects transforms the structures, focus, and activities of the marketing communication group, as shown in Exhibit 9.2.

The real task for the marketing communication group and the marketing communication manager is not the management of the communication delivery vehicles but (a) how to attract and acquire new customers for the organization, or (b) how to retain desirable present customers, and/or (c) how to manage acquired and retained customers through the product portfolio of the organization. Each of these tasks is unique, and each requires a different set of marketing and communication skills, tools, and tactics.

From a marketing communication management standpoint, the first issue for the IGMC manager is "How can I best invest the finite resources of the organization in marketing communication to attract new customers?" Then, once a prospect has been attracted and retained, the next question is logically "How can I manage the new customer through our product portfolio so it will provide benefit to the customer and to the firm?" That, of

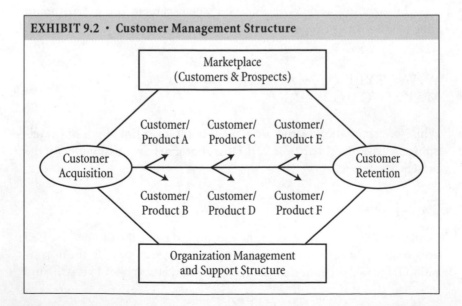

EXHIBIT 9.2 • Customer Management Structure

Marketplace
(Customers & Prospects)

Customer/
Product A

Customer/
Product C

Customer/
Product E

Customer
Acquisition

Customer
Retention

Customer/
Product B

Customer/
Product D

Customer/
Product F

Organization Management
and Support Structure

course, demands a totally different form and type of communication program from the one used initially to attract customers to the brand. Finally, the management issue of the marketing communication manager and group becomes "How can we assist in retaining the customers we have attracted and are migrating through our product or service assortment so that they remain with us over time?" Again, retention demands a different type of communication program from acquisition or migration, and it demands a different type of approach and communication mix. In some cases advertising may be very important; in others, it may not be used at all. The approach of managing customers and customer communication requirements is vastly superior to the management of traditional communication delivery vehicles.

If the organization views the management of customers as its primary activity, the managerial issues become totally different, as do the activities in which the organization invests its resources or budgets. In this approach different types of managers may be needed. Different skills are generally required of the people involved in the management of the process. Different capabilities are needed among the external resources or suppliers. It is this type of managerial change that is driving the new forms of integrated global marketing communication. Obviously the requirements of a global marketing and communication manager who is responsible for the acquisition of customers from all over the globe are radically different from those of an advertising manager responsible for the purchase of time, space, and other exposure vehicles even in multiple marketplaces. Indeed, it is this change in the view of the responsibilities and goals of the marketing communication manager that differentiates him or her from the traditional international or regional marketing communication director or manager.

Inherent in this new view of IGMC management is the structure in which these managers operate.

WHAT TYPE OF MANAGEMENT STRUCTURE MAKES IGMC WORK?

While the organizational structure of many IGMC organizations is still developing, we have identified three forms that appear to have possibilities for the present and future.

A Revised Brand Management Structure

Exhibit 9.3 illustrates one way of moving toward being a customer-focused organization. Rather than being focused on products or brands, the organization is focused on customers and market segments. (Note: This structure

EXHIBIT 9.3 • Market-Focused Organization

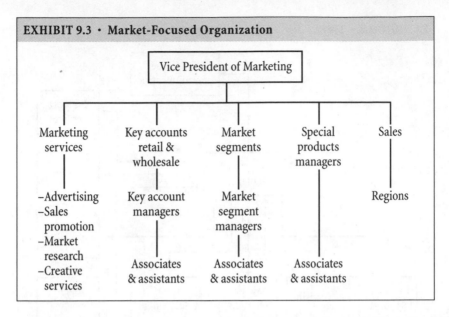

assumes an organization selling through channels where key accounts are important.) Further, another group is responsible for the various market segments that have been identified; for example, heavy or light users or present customers and prospects and the like. Yet another group focuses on new or special products—managers who identify new market segments or who identify new products that can be developed for existing customers.

There are also two support groups in this design: (1) marketing services—the support group that provides expertise in the marketing communication areas—and (2) sales—the face-to-face contacts that occur with customers and prospects.

Centralized Marketing Communication Activities

Another way to become customer focused is to control all marketing or brand communication through a central office or marketing communication manager, as illustrated in Exhibit 9.4. This approach is being used increasingly by organizations that are attempting to move from a sales-oriented to a marketing- or brand-oriented approach to marketing and communication.

Often called the *communication czar* or *corporate communication director*, this manager is designated to consolidate control and responsibility for all forms and types of corporate and product brand communication in one place, increasingly in the office of the CEO or chairman of the organization. For many groups attempting to build their brand value or simply to gain

EXHIBIT 9.4 · Marketing Communication Management Structure

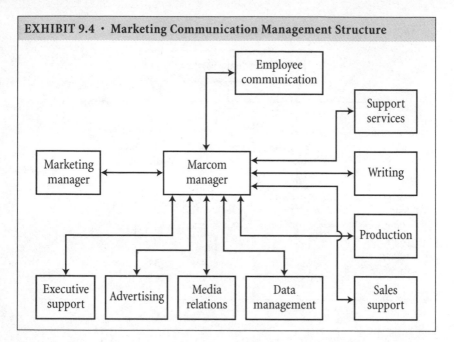

control over the communication being distributed about the brand or the organization, this approach makes good sense.

In this structure all activities related to the brand or brand communication and therefore market or marketing communication are brought together in one office or one central location. This group sets brand and communication standards for the organization that are then implemented in the field. In many cases a watchdog approach is used initially (that unfortunately sometimes ends up with "logo police" as the equivalent) to set standards and enforce conformity. As the organization gains capability in managing the communication activities, often the restrictions are reduced and responsibility for implementation is pushed out to the various operating divisions.

A recent development in this area is that the communication director, or czar, centralizes the actual content of the communication programs, either electronically or in hard copy form, and then makes that material available to the field personnel, from which they can construct their own communication programs. In other words, the local marketing communication manager can select from preapproved and consistent communication elements and assemble them in any manner that seems appropriate on the local level. We have observed this type of approach in organizations varying from insurance to heavy machinery to computers.

Increasingly the centralization of brand activities is occurring at the most senior levels of the organization. CEOs and CFOs are beginning to recognize the value of the brand as a method of building shareholder value. In addition, increased interest in driving the organization into the global marketplace gives impetus to the need for carefully planned and well-executed marketing and communication programs around the globe.

The Market Segment Design

The market segment design is illustrated in Exhibit 9.5. It is based on the concept of being totally customer oriented and developing and delivering services to satisfy customer needs through a focused approach.

The primary value of the market team design is that it is in line with the increasing focus on teams and work groups within many organizations—the famous "flat organization." In the team approach the traditional hierarchy is abandoned in favor of a group of specialists who come together for long or short periods of time to attack specific problems and opportunities.

In the structure illustrated in Exhibit 9.5, a unique team of functional specialists comes together to manage a group of customers. Almost all activities required to provide products and services to a group of identified customers or prospects are represented within the team. Granted, the team may need to draw on production and distribution activities from the central organization, yet it contains the resources needed to acquire, manage through

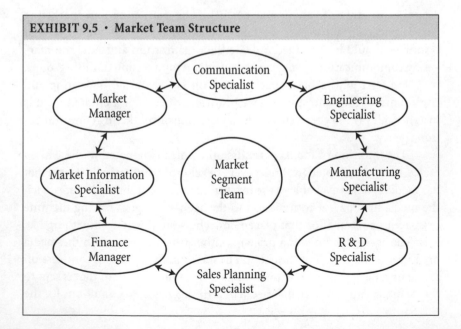

EXHIBIT 9.5 • Market Team Structure

the product or service portfolio, and retain a group of customers either locally or around the world.

In our view this market team design is the most appropriate for a global marketing organization. The market team is focused on the customer wherever that customer or prospect might be located. The goal is to manage the customer, not the geography or the products or services.

Doubtless there are and will be other organizational designs that can be used by organizations marketing and communicating on a global basis. For example, some organizations have chosen to abdicate marketing communication decisions and outsource it to their advertising or public relations agencies. We believe that is a mistake. The customers belong to the firm, not to an agent. Customer success comes from ongoing relationships that only the organization is capable of developing and maintaining. To believe these ongoing relationships can be managed by an external resource, no matter how dedicated or enthusiastic, simply ignores the reality of the value of ongoing associations and involvement of the organization with its customers.

Still, external suppliers, vendors, and agencies certainly can and will be used. How should the organization select those resources, and what type of compensation system should be used is the next question.

A TASK-BASED VIEW OF EXTERNAL RESOURCE SELECTION AND COMPENSATION

Again, as we did with the management of the marketing and marketing communication activities, we take a customer-focused view of what resources should be obtained outside the organization and how the marketing communication manager can consider remuneration of those groups.

We start with a bit of background on how external marketing and communication organizations have historically been compensated. In this instance our primary reference is the advertising or marketing communication agency.

The tradition of media commissions, which originated in the United States, has been adopted in almost every developed country in the world that has media systems available to the marketing organization. By that approach the media firm pays a commission to the agency or agent buying the time or space as a reward for that placement. The system works something like this: The agency negotiates a price for either time or space with the media organization on behalf of the client. The medium then grants a commission to the negotiating agency that is deducted from the statement that is sent to the client. In other words, the media bills the agency a gross amount for the time or space. That billing is then passed on to the client company for reimbursement. The agency collects the full amount but remits only a net amount—the total statement less the agency commission. These commissions are generally in the range of 15 to 25 or perhaps even 30 percent in some countries. Thus we have the rather unique situation where the agency is working for the marketing organization but being paid by the media firm. As one might imagine, this has created concerns and questions about the impartiality of the agency over the years.

The other compensation method is generally some type of fee for hire. In this system the agency sets some type of hourly fee or rate for the various services it provides the client. These fees are commonly based on some type of hourly rate for employees plus an overhead charge. Based on these fees, the agency estimates the time and other costs to develop specific marketing and communication activities on behalf of the client. The client is then billed by the agency for the time and costs involved in the development and preparation of the various marketing communication activities. In some cases the commissions earned by the agency from the media are credited back against the fees being paid by the client.

There are numerous variations on these two themes, but they provide the bulk of the compensation arrangements between clients and agencies or external suppliers around the globe. In short, compensation is based either on how much the client invests in various forms of media or on the amount of time required to develop and administer a communication program by the agency.

Again, these strategies emphasize the output of the marketing communication program, not the outcomes. Because external resources such as agencies are not compensated on the basis of marketplace results, views of what is practical and useful compensation to them have long been a major point of discussion and sometimes even disagreement between client and agencies.

In the IGMC approach to developing and implementing global programs, we take a different view of how external groups should be compensated. We recommend viewing the purchase of these resources on the basis of expected returns, not on the basis of developmental or spending levels.

Understanding the Marketing Communication Process

Eight steps are involved in developing and delivering a marketing communication program, illustrated in Exhibit 9.6. While some of the activities may blend across the various boxes we have illustrated, these are generally the activities involved.

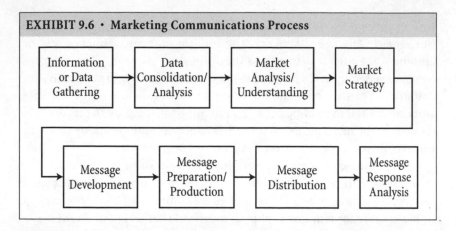

EXHIBIT 9.6 · **Marketing Communications Process**

Information or Data Gathering. This is the process of gathering information, knowledge, and records about customers and prospects, markets, and marketing systems in the marketplace to be served. Commonly this is done by research organizations or perhaps database organizations. In some cases it falls to an internal information technology group. Compensation for these groups has generally been made on a project-by-project basis, although there are also subscription approaches whereby the researcher provides the services for a set monthly or annual fee to client and agency organizations.

Data Consolidators and/or Data Analysts. These are firms or people who take the raw data gathered in the first step and consolidate or bring the data together to examine what customers are doing in the marketplace. Commonly these are organizations that compile data and provide it to organizations for analysis such as A. C. Nielsen, Information Resources, National Family Opinion, SMRB, and TGI. While these organizations gather the information and consolidate it, they do not attempt to provide detailed analysis or understanding. That occurs in the next step. Compensation for these groups generally comes through project fees or subscription fees that are charged monthly or annually. Commonly, there is some base fee arranged and then additional activities are billed in addition.

Market Analysis to Develop Market Understanding. These firms take the gathered and consolidated information on markets and customers and analyze and attempt to understand how the market operates, how customers buy, how products are used, and so on. Organizations that provide this service might include Spectra, Claritas, Market Metrics, EDS, Epsilon, and Targetbase Marketing. Increasingly management consulting organizations such as Ernst & Young, Andersen Consulting, and Booze, Allen and Bain

& Company provide this service. A few advertising agencies still operate in this area, but increasingly those activities are being outsourced to external groups. Again, payment for these services is generally made on the basis of some type of project or ongoing service fee that may or may not be tied to the amount of time invested in the project by the supplier.

Market Strategy Development. Traditionally this has been the province of the marketing organization and the brand and/or product manager. Increasingly, however, consulting organizations and market research and database firms are entering this field. For those using inside resources, this is typically an organizational cost with perhaps some transfer pricing being involved. For those hired from the outside, the common approach is a fee for the services that may or may not be tied to amount of time involved in the task.

Message or Incentive Development. Historically the advertising agencies have provided this service. Agencies took the strategy the organization developed and turned it into messages and or incentives ready to be distributed. As was discussed in Chapter 8, increasingly the advertising agencies are turning into holding companies with operating units in all the specific marketing and communication activities ranging from advertising to public relations to sales promotion. Advertising agencies have offset the costs for message or incentive development through the commissions gained based on the placement of time or space that has been allowed by the media organizations. In those cases, where media commissions have not been great enough to cover the costs of development and implementation, the agency has charged an additional fee to the client organization.

Message or Incentive Preparation or Production. Again, this has historically been the province of the advertising, promotion, or communication agency. While those agencies have often employed specific production organizations such as television producers, type and film houses, and the like, the agency has operated as the consolidator of those services and presented a unified package to the client organization. For the most part compensation for these services has been made on a project basis that may or may not be tied to the amount of time and effort involved in the task.

Message or Incentive Distribution. Distribution of marketing messages and incentives usually occurs through various forms of media organizations ranging from newspapers to television to cinema to direct mail. The media generally base their time or space costs on the number of persons reached by the medium, their delivery cycle, and their production costs. As discussed earlier, agencies often receive their compensation from the media in the form of a commission or discount on the amount of time or space they purchase. While there are some fixed charges by medium, often prices and programs are negotiated. Thus it is often difficult to determine what the actual costs of a marketing communication program might be until the agency or client actually enters the media-purchasing marketplace.

Message or Incentive Response Analysis. As has been stated throughout this book, measurement of the effect and results of marketing communication programs has not been well developed in any specific market and certainly not in global terms. For the most part measurement has focused on the marketing communication output—measures to assure clients and agencies that the media delivered what they agreed to deliver or that the audience exposed to the medium was of the size and geographic location promised or expected. Increasingly the area of marketing communication measurement is being developed by specialized consulting organizations that are focused on developing this area. For the most part they operate on some type of fee or project basis. Examples of these organizations might include Interbrand, Financial Analysts, and Agora, Inc.

With this overview of the various functions needed and necessary to plan, develop, and implement an IGMC program, we can now move to our task-based approach to marketing communication selection and remuneration.

Getting Out of or Staying in the Box

While the marketing communication process just described includes all the activities and steps needed to develop a marketing communication program and sounds like an orderly process, that is not the case. Many of the organizations that occupy each of the boxes have become specialists in their particular area. Yet they are now attempting to escape from the box they occupy, for this simple reason: there are simply too many competitors occupying the same box. As a result competition is severe and margins are eroding. For example, in the media arena almost all sales are negotiated. While media organizations attempt to hold to some type of rate card or established rate structure for time or space, there always seems to be some competitor who is willing to reduce prices or negotiate better arrangements or rates.

Because of the intense competition in each of the separate boxes, the most logical opportunity for any organization is to attempt to move up or down the process. Thus we see the research organizations, the data consolidators, and the database organizations attempting to move into the market analysis and strategy development areas. When they do, they come into direct competition with management consulting firms and internal strategy development groups. Alternatively, media, through various means, are attempting to move back up the process chain. They are now offering to develop the messages and incentives that organizations use and to produce those in various forms of media. This puts them in head-to-head competition with their supposed customers, the advertising agencies. Management consultants are moving down the process line from strategy development into message areas by suggesting and overseeing the activities of agencies and other external communication suppliers. In other words, every organization wants to get out of its box and into allied fields either upstream or downstream in the marketing communication process. While this is causing some confusion on the part of who does what in the field, we believe it can work to the advantage of the marketing communication manager who understands the pressures and new strategies that are rapidly being developed.

With this view of the marketing communication process, we are now prepared to rethink how compensation of external organizations should be developed.

Buying What Is Needed, Paying for Value Received

Our premise in external supplier and agency compensation is simple: we should be willing to pay for what is needed and base that rate on the value that service, information, or activity will likely return to the organization. We believe the acquisition of marketing communication services and activities should be approached in the same way as investing in customers and prospects based on their current and potential value to the organization (see Chapter 5).

This approach to compensation is based on a clear understanding of how marketing communication works for the organization, its value, and its return. If the marketing firm has solid, detailed knowledge of its customers and prospects—can identify and value them in some way over time, can estimate or calculate their share of purchases, and knows how much to invest and can estimate some type of return—additional knowledge in this area would not be terribly valuable. Therefore the organization would pay only small amounts to enhance or improve its information gathering, data consolidation, and market analysis. Having all this information and knowledge, it might, however, be willing to pay large sums for the development of effective marketing and communication strategies and even more to determine if those strategies were effective in the marketplace. Likewise, other organizations might be willing to invest heavily in the first three boxes simply to know and understand their customers, for that would allow the firm to move on to the next stage in the process.

Inherent in this approach is the idea that the organization will buy what it needs and pay for that value if it will enhance or improve its returns from customers. Purchases then should be made on the basis of what is valuable and useful and helps improve the overall process and return to the organization, not on how much the organization invests in various types or forms of marketing communication, and certainly not in how much it invests in various forms of media.

The second concept in the approach is as controversial. That is, the organization should pay for marketplace success, not marketplace development or activity. Simply put, the organization must find some way to reward supplier groups in the marketing communication process chain based on what outcome they help create, not on what output they develop. The most simplistic approach under this concept would be to have the supplier's return tied in some way to the success of the program in the marketplace. If the advertising works, the agency that created it is rewarded for marketplace success. If the advertising doesn't work, the agency isn't paid or at least is paid only a nominal amount. The same approach could be taken with almost any of the suppliers in the marketing communication chain except for those that are simply supplying resources or filling preset requirements. For the most part, however, there simply must be some movement from the traditional reward for spending, that is, from creating communication outputs to generating marketplace returns. Measurement of the results of marketing communication programs can provide a great impetus to the approach, and we describe in some detail the approaches we have developed in Chapter 10.

We are sure the traditional media commission and fee for hourly work cannot be overturned in any short period of time. We do, however, believe that negotiating the external resources on the basis of the value they might return to the organization can do much to provide a new and more relevant method of compensation for suppliers, vendors, and agencies in the future.

CONCLUSIONS

- The key to relevant compensation for external vendors and agencies is being able to measure the return on marketing communication investments.
- Marketing and communication managers today pay little attention to data gathering, consolidation, and analysis and all too much attention to message development, production, and delivery.
- The acquisition, retention, and management of customers require different strategies. Know which goal you are trying to reach.
- Consider paying your suppliers based on outcomes, not on outputs.

10

Developing IGMC Investments and Measurements

Traditionally funds for a global marketing communication program have been budgeted at the very beginning of the process. Management either approved a specific amount of money or simply allocated a sum for the process. Using the amount available, the communication manager, along with the ad agency, planning group, or others, allocated the available resources among the various communication tactics or activities that either had been planned or were developed based on the available funds.

This allocation approach to budgeting for marketing communication programs is known as *inside-out*. The organization starts with a projected level of sales or volume it expects during the coming year. From that, costs of operation are deducted, leaving a contribution margin. From that contribution margin the marketing budget is derived, from which marketing communication is then allocated. Marketing communication decisions are then made, and activities and tactics are devised based on available funds. The basic premise of the inside-out approach is illustrated in Exhibit 10.1.

The chart in Exhibit 10.1 shows that marketing communication investment is derived from the level of sales achieved or expected, which means that if sales don't reach expected levels the marketing communication investment must be reduced, being a function of sales volume. The clear message in this approach is "Marketing and marketing communication do not contribute to sales. In fact, they are a drag on profits from sales." Little or no regard is given to the communication needs of customers and prospects or of the organization. It's a simple, mechanistic approach that ignores any contribution marketing communication might make to the enhancement of sales and profits.

EXHIBIT 10.1 • **Inside-Out Budgeting**

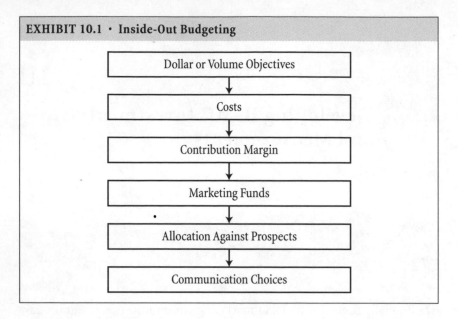

FROM INSIDE-OUT TO OUTSIDE-IN

The approach we take in IGMC is outside-in, starting with customers and their value and working back toward strategy and allocation, as illustrated in Exhibit 10.2.

Outside-in budgeting recognizes that each customer group creates some flow of income for the organization. That income flow is used as the basis for developing marketing communication plans. Recall from Chapter 6 the discussion of valuing customers and prospects and the income flows they generated for the organization.

Each customer, no matter what his or her status, has either current or potential value for the firm. Those income flows directly determine the amount the organization should invest to maintain, increase, or enhance those income flows. Assume Sally has been purchasing products from our company for three years, providing us approximately $1,000 in contribution margin each year. The question for the marketing communication manager is "How much should we invest in marketing communication directed toward Sally to maintain that $1,000 income flow at the contribution margin line?" When posed this way, the answer is fairly simple. We could invest up to $1,000 in marketing communication programs toward Sally to maintain her income flow, and the firm would still break even. If we spent less, we would develop more profit. In other words, the less we spend or invest in marketing communication, the more profit we make. This is not a welcome thought for most marketing communication managers. Generally the goal

EXHIBIT 10.2 · Outside-In Budgeting

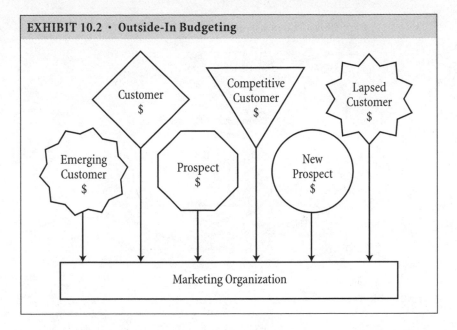

of the marketing communication manager has been to obtain larger and larger budgets and expand the marketing communication program every year. Yet, when viewed as outlined here, the truly successful communication manager always tries to drive spending down and profits up.

The preceding example is not a very common way of looking at how an organization should develop a marketing communication investment plan. Very seldom do we think of customers or prospects and their income flows as being the basis for investments. Instead marketing communication managers tend to think about advertising campaigns or direct mail drops or public relations events as investments in marketing communication programs, not in customers or prospects. So, when we start to think about customers and prospects and income flows and returns to the organization, it becomes clear that we need a new way to think about marketing communication investments and returns.

THE CLOSED-LOOP SYSTEM

With this example of income flows from customers as the driving force in the development of marketing communication investment plans, we can now summarize the approach we propose with the closed-loop system described in Chapter 6 and illustrated in Exhibit 10.3.

In our closed-loop approach we identify the value of customers and prospects now and into the future. By knowing the customer value, we are

EXHIBIT 10.3 • Closed-Loop Systems

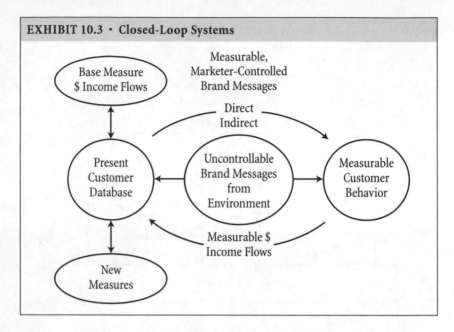

able to make managerial decisions about how much we would be willing to invest to retain Sally's $1,000 income flow at the contribution margin (CM) line. If we know the CM of Sally is $1,000 per year, we can make a managerial decision that we might be willing to invest 10 percent of that income flow, or $100, to attempt to grow Sally's purchases in the coming six months. By making this decision, we have determined the marketing communication budget, we have set a target return on our investment, and we have set up a process whereby we can measure the impact and effect of our marketing communication spend.

What we have also done is set in motion a process that defines what type of return we must get on our marketing communication investment in Sally to determine whether or not it was a success. Recall that Sally presently generates a $1,000 CM return to the company each year, which, for the purposes of this discussion, we can break down to about $500 every six months. If we invest $100 in Sally over the next six months, we must generate income flows of $600 from Sally at the CM line to break even (the $500 we would have expected based on past experience, plus the $100 invested in marketing communication). Anything over the $600 return from Sally is a positive return on our investment. If we got back $700 in contribution margin, we would have generated an ROCI of 100 percent ($100 invested, $100 in increased response over and above our communication investment, or a 100 percent return on our investment in Sally as a customer).

Inherent in this approach is the idea of incremental return. That is, we had an ongoing income flow from Sally that we could estimate in advance.

Thus, to demonstrate that our marketing communication investment was valuable for the organization, we had to maintain Sally's income flow ($1,000 total or assumed $500 for six months), and we had to recover our marketing communication investment of $100 simply to get back to where we started. The fact that we got back an additional $100 ($700 total) means we got back $100 over our expected return and our communication investment. In other words, we achieved incremental revenue as a result of our marketing communication investment. This concept of incremental revenue is critical to our measurement process.

THE CONCEPT AND PRACTICAL APPLICATION OF INCREMENTAL REVENUE TO THE FIRM

Incremental revenue is based on the simple concept that the return must be greater than the cost and greater than what would have been expected without the expenditure, as illustrated in Exhibit 10.4.

Line A in Exhibit 10.4 represents the current income of the firm. That income is assumed to continue whether or not the organization invests any additional resources. While we show the income flow as a flat line, most organizations have some sort of peaks and valleys in sales and income. We use the flat line for illustration only.

Line B is the maximum output of the firm—the total amount of revenue the organization could generate if all its resources were put to use: the total production of a manufacturing plant, the total number of hotel rooms available in a building, or the total number of seats on an airplane, for instance. Incremental revenue occurs when the organization invests *some* of its resources to drive current sales higher than would be expected in the period

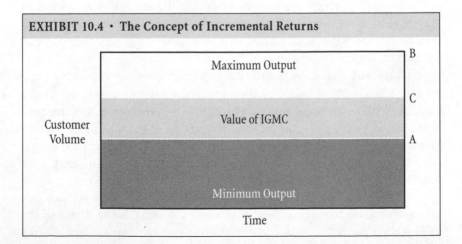

EXHIBIT 10.4 · The Concept of Incremental Returns

Maximum Output — B

Value of IGMC — C

Customer Volume

Minimum Output — A

Time

but to less than full capacity. That is what marketing communication fundamentally is all about. The firm assumes it is able to achieve *a certain level* of business with no marketing communication investment, due to the nature of the product, the location, or inherent demand that exists in the marketplace and so on. For a marketing communication investment to be profitable, returns must exceed the amount invested. This is a key element in the IGMC approach, for it suggests that marketing communication must not only recover the investment made in the activity but provide additional returns as well.

This concept of *incremental returns* is notably absent in many traditional marketing communication measurement systems. Often total sales or unit volume are taken as evidence of the impact of the marketing communication program, with no view of incremental returns. However, by using such measures there's no assurance that the marketing communication investment was even recovered, much less any incremental return achieved. More troublesome, when communication effects are used as the measurement yardstick, incremental financial returns cannot be measured at all since there is no way to relate product or communication awareness or attitude changes to the amount invested or returned.

Calculating Return on Customer Investment

Exhibit 10.5 provides a basic spreadsheet to illustrate how investments are related to returns in the IGMC approach.

As shown in the spreadsheet, we are estimating the ROCI on three groups of customers or prospects: present customers, competitive customers, and emerging customers. We estimate the current value to the firm for each customer group and then estimate the value of a marketing communication program. The spreadsheet is broken into four parts to differentiate the various steps in the process.

In the first section (lines 1–5) we estimate the value of each of the customer groups. This comes from the analysis and valuation of customer groups discussed in Chapter 6. In other words, we determine the total CM for each of the groups.

Once we know the expected CM for the customer group, we estimate what the income flow would be if no investment were made in marketing communication. In other words, relating this to our incremental revenue concept chart, what would be the expected income to the organization at line A if we invested nothing? That provides the baseline. Again, note that we start with total income flow and then convert that to a contribution margin for each of the groups. (See lines 6–7.)

The third section requests that we estimate the income flow from each group if a brand communication investment is made (line 8). That income flow is then converted into a contribution margin in line 9. From that we

EXHIBIT 10.5 • Basic ROCI Process			
	Present Customers	*Competitive Customers*	*Emerging Customers*
1. Present Income Flow in Category	$	$	$
2. Share of Requirements	%	%	%
3. Customer Income Flow to Brand	$	$	$
4. Contribution Margin %	%	%	%
5. Contribution Margin $	$	$	$
6. Income Flow Without a Brand Communication Program	$	$	$
7. Contribution Margin Without a Brand Communication Program	$	$	$
8. Income Flow with a Brand Communication Program	$	$	$
9. Gross Contribution Margin with a Brand Communication Program	$	$	$
10. Brand Communication Investment	$	$	$
11. Net Contribution Margin	$	$	$
12. Difference in Contribution Margins with and Without Brand Communication	$	$	$
13. Incremental Gain or Loss	$	$	$
14. Return on Investment	%	%	%

deduct the investment in the marketing communication program to convert this to incremental revenue and incremental contribution margin at line 10. Line 11 is the net contribution margin, that is, the CM expected from the customer once the marketing communication investment has been made. That investment is then deducted from the overall return (line 11).

The fourth section compares the return from customers with and without the marketing communication investment for each of the three groups. That is, we calculate the difference between the contribution margins with and without a brand communication investment (line 12) with the result being an incremental gain or loss (line 13). If the return with a marketing communication investment is greater than without, our ROCI will show a positive return. If the return is less than the cost of the marketing communication investment, the number will be negative. As long as we get back more for investing in marketing communication, less the cost of that investment, than we would have gotten without the investment, marketing communication is producing a positive ROCI. Of course a key element is the percentage of return that is being obtained. Generally if the return is greater than the return that could be obtained on other forms of investment, the communication planner is on solid ground. Often organizations set "hurdle rates" for investments—minimum percentage returns that must be achieved for any investment—which must be considered in the final evaluation of the value of the marketing communication investment.

At the end of this chapter we provide a full example of how the ROCI investment and measurement process works along with a hypothetical example.

MEASURING SHORT-TERM AND LONG-TERM RETURNS ON MARKETING

The ROCI process just described provides a useful and managerially acceptable approach for measuring the returns on a marketing communication investment in the short term, that is, during the current fiscal year. Recall, however, from Chapter 6, that some marketing communication programs provide returns in the short term, that is the current fiscal year (those we termed *business building*), and some communication programs are designed to generate long-term returns, that is, returns over several fiscal years. Those we called *brand building*. The process with the spreadsheet provides an excellent way of estimating or calculating returns in the current time period, that is, the current fiscal year. The question then is "How can we measure the return on longer-term communication investments?" Our communication planning matrix from Chapter 6 provides a solution, illustrated in Exhibit 10.6.

While the decision as to whether we are delivering messages or incentives is important in the planning process, for measurement we are interested only in the financial returns achieved. Thus the planning chart provides an excellent reminder, but our emphasis will be on when the returns are obtained, not on what type of program or activity was delivered.

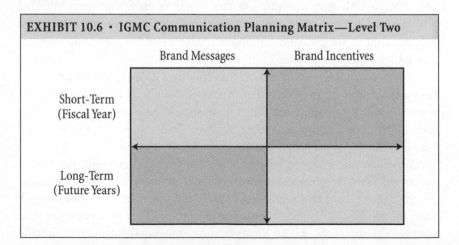

EXHIBIT 10.6 · IGMC Communication Planning Matrix—Level Two

	Brand Messages	Brand Incentives
Short-Term (Fiscal Year)		
Long-Term (Future Years)		

For short-term returns, when we measure the current income flows from customers and prospects and turn those into contribution margins, we are in essence converting those income flows not only into incremental returns but also into marginal returns to the organization. The concept of marginal investments and marginal returns is based on the economic concept that as long as the organization gains a greater return from the activity than the cost of the activity itself, it would theoretically continue to invest in the activity. That is, as long as marketing communication investments generate greater returns than the cost of the investment, no limit will be placed on the investment level. Thus, as long as we can generate a greater return than the cost of our investment, the organization should continue to invest in marketing communication programs. That, of course, demands that the marketing communication manager be able to demonstrate those financial returns in the short term, or in the current fiscal year.

But what about long-term, brand-building returns? At the end of every fiscal year the organization's books are closed and a new year starts. Since the organization has no way to recognize long-term returns, and returns on brand-building activities commonly occur over several fiscal years, the use of marginal returns and incremental revenue becomes less relevant. The answer to this conundrum is to look at customers and customer income flows in a different way.

In truth, customers are the true assets of the firm; they are the primary things that generate income for the company. While tangible assets (plants, equipment, land, inventory, or cash) are the primary measures of the value of an organization, we are beginning to understand that the cash flow the organization generates is often more critical to success than the tangible assets the organization controls. Tangible assets, unless they help generate income flows from customers, have little cash flow generating value to the organization.

If we start to consider customers and the income flows they create as the real assets of the organization, we can start to treat them as assets the same way tangible assets are valued and maintained. In other words, we would start to manage customers and customer income flows as assets that have value and generate returns.

For tangible assets the organization generally invests in some way to maintain the value of those assets. For example, in a hotel, if the property is not maintained, the value of the hotel to the customers will decline and the hotel will cease to provide returns to its owners. The same is true of customers. If we don't invest in customers on a regular basis, with marketing and marketing communication programs, they too will decline in value and stop providing the same level of income flow that the organization has enjoyed in the past. Thus, investing in customers through marketing communication programs is the same as investing in tangible assets to keep them producing income for the firm.

The only problem with this approach is that at the present time there are no accounting procedures that recognize future income flows. That is, the income flow from a customer can be measured only during the current fiscal year. At the end of the year every customer is wiped from the books when a new fiscal year or accounting period is started. Since we can't recognize future income flows, we must find other ways to determine the value of customers over multiple fiscal years. Thus, we need a measure of *brand building*.

In brand building we move from calculating income flows to measuring brand equity among customers and prospects that have been generated by our marketing communication programs. In other words, since we can't measure the financial returns, we must measure the surrogate for those values—how the customers and prospects value the brands or the relationships that exist between them and the company. (Remember that brand equity is the value of the brand as viewed by the customer, not by the organization. Thus we must find ways to measure this brand relationship and convert it into a financial measure to determine if our investments in marketing communication are actually paying off.)

While most measures of brand equity are still in the development stage, a number of approaches are available. For example, you can measure the value of a brand to a consumer on the basis of whether or not she is willing to pay a premium price for the brand compared to competitive alternatives over time. If so, that measure can be converted into a financial return now and into the future. You can also measure customer advocacy: is the brand strong enough that customers will tell other customers or prospects about it and become advocates of the brand? A third way to measure brand value is to track the increase in the share of requirements filled by the brand among consumers over time. If the share of requirements is increasing from year to year, then brand value to the consumer is obviously increasing as well. Again, this increase in share of requirements can be calculated and turned into a financial measure of the success of the marketing communication program. While these measures are somewhat different from traditional approaches, they can reveal the true value of a brand to customers.

Perhaps the easiest and most convenient way to measure long-term brand returns is to connect attitudinal data to behavioral data. That is, if we know the ongoing value of a customer to the brand or company (we can measure the financial value of the customer in the form of income flows), by connecting this data to attitudinal change we may be able to understand the relationship between attitudinal change and marketplace success. This use of attitudinal data is, in a sense, the opposite of traditional uses. Attitudinal data is most commonly used to *predict* marketplace actions by consumers. In the IGMC approach, we are using it to *explain* why certain marketplace actions occur. By using attitudinal variables to explain behavioral observations, we might well be able to determine the long-term returns from marketing communication investments.

UNDERSTANDING THE NEW ACRONYMS: ABC AND EVA

Two new concepts holding great promise for future financial management and evaluation of marketing communication programs are activity-based costing (ABC) and economic value assessment (EVA). Each is gaining favor in global organizations and can be related to marketing communication management.

Activity-Based Costing

Simply put, activity-based costing is a term for calculating the specific costs of each activity in the organization and then allocating those costs back to the specific activity. Historically most organizations have used very general rules to allocate costs. For example, if operating overhead for a plant was $1 million, that total cost was allocated proportionally to each of the products produced in the plant—if there were ten products, each was charged one-tenth of the total. Everyone knew that some products cost more to make than others did, but because data handling and cost allocation were so complex, a general rule of thumb was used rather than actual costs. ABC simply allocates specific tangible costs to each activity. As a result of such reallocations, many organizations have learned that not all products are profitable, that some customers are unprofitable, and that some services simply don't pay any returns. The ABC process has opened the eyes of many managers to what is *really* profitable and what is not, which products should be promoted and which shouldn't, and so on.

The importance of ABC to the communication manager is clear. If specific service or management costs can be attributed to individual customers, it will be easier to develop and determine actual contribution margins generated by each customer. That will only strengthen the IGMC approach.

Economic Value Assessment

Economic value assessment is a concept designed to calculate how the economic value created by the organization benefits stockholders. In other words, rather than simply using the value of tangible assets as the basis for the value of the organization, EVA is a process of determining the *economic worth* of the organization. The basic premise of EVA is that if organizational (and therefore shareholder) economic value can be built at a cost lower than the cost of capital, the organization should invest in those activities to build shareholder wealth. If we apply this approach to marketing communication, it means that if economic value to the organization can be shown to accrue from investments in marketing communication that create greater customer income flows or marketplace value, and the return would be greater than the cost of the capital employed, the organization would wisely invest in such marketing communication programs. The value of EVA is that it recognizes the current and long-term value that marketing communication might develop for the organization, unlike the reliance on continuous short-term sales returns on communication programs.

The key point here, of course, is that the marketing communication manager should be alert to these new financial and accounting concepts, for they could well have great value in terms of management of the IGMC programs of the future.

COMPLETE SPREADSHEET ON ROCI *

As discussed earlier, the key element required to effectively measure the return on brand communication investment, or the return on customer investment, is the ability to separate business-building brand communication from brand-building brand communication. While the line between the two will not be sharp and distinct all the time, the basic separation between short-term returns (within the organization's fiscal year) and long-term returns (over periods longer than the fiscal year) is critical because of current accounting standards.

The premise of the proposed ROI measurement system is that all business-building brand communication programs will contribute incremental returns to the organization. In other words, our goal is to account for additional revenue generated by the brand communication program, or estimated expected revenue. This distinction is important. Almost all organizations have some form of income flow from present customers, or they expect income flow from prospects. Therefore additional investments in brand communication programs should either enhance or protect that revenue stream or, in some cases, alter the income flow to create more profitability for the organization. This incremental revenue approach helps the organization truly understand the return it is receiving from brand communication investment.

---

*The following information is provided courtesy of the Association of National Advertisers, Inc. Copyright 1997, Association of National Advertisers, Inc. All rights reserved. Reprinted by permission. The ANA book *Measuring Brand Communication ROI*, from which the rest of this chapter is taken, may be purchased on-line at www.ana.net.

Our proposed incremental revenue approach is possible because technology enables us to have some measure of income flow from customers, or knowledge of the value of a customer group prior to executing the brand communication program. Thus the goal of the brand communication calculation or estimation is to determine the incremental financial returns rather than the determination of total sales volume generated or total profits, as commonly are measured by traditional approaches. This incremental value approach works just as well for a customer retention strategy because we can estimate what it costs or will cost to retain a customer's income flow, and from that the ROCI can be determined.

Similarly, we can estimate or calculate the cost to acquire a new customer since his or her initial income flow to the organization will be zero until he or she makes a brand purchase. Thus the proposed process works equally well with almost all types of customer or prospect marketing strategies. This is critically important in a very dynamic marketing environment.

A key element of the process, which will be explained in more detail in the following examples, is that it is designed to work primarily with customer or prospect groups. While it would be wonderful if we could estimate or calculate the return on brand communication for each and every individual customer, that capability is still some time off for most organizations. So while our approach can accommodate one-to-one brand communication calculations, we focus on customer groups in this chapter since that is what the majority of all marketing organizations will be using in the foreseeable future.

We illustrate our measurement process through a basic spreadsheet approach. An important part of this process is that it can be used either to calculate the actual return or to estimate in advance what the return might be using various "what if" scenarios. The approach is illustrated in Exhibits 10. 7 and 10.8.

The Basic Concept

Before leaping into an explanation of the spreadsheet, it is useful to review the basic concepts of the process. This is illustrated in the basic business-building ROI spreadsheet shown in Exhibit 10. 7. As we have stressed before, the spreadsheet can be changed or adapted by the organization. It simply provides a standardized framework for the process of calculating a return on customer investment that can be used across the organization.

As can be seen in the column across the top of Exhibit 10. 7, customers or groups have been aggregated by their behavior. For the brand or organization to be analyzed, these groups can be as broad or as narrow, and as many or as few as needed. Along with each customer group, we have specified the behavioral objective we hope to achieve or have achieved in the measurement period. Examples of behavioral objectives would be to acquire new customers,

EXHIBIT 10.7 · Business-Building Return on Brand Communication Investment or Return on Customer Investment

	Aggregated Customer Group: Behavioral Goal:	Group A	Group B	Group C
Category Requirement Assumptions				
1. Estimated Category Demand	*Historical Data/Estimate*	$	$	$
Base Income Flow Assumptions				
2. Base Share of Requirement	*Historical Data/Estimate*	%	%	%
3. Base Income Flow to Us	Line 1 × Line 2 =	$	$	$
4. Noncommunication Costs (Product, Fixed, G&A, etc.)	*Operating Estimate*	%	%	%
5. Contribution Margin %	100% − Line 4 =	%	%	%
6. Contribution Margin $	Line 3 × Line 5 =	$	$	$
Scenario A: No Communication Investment				
7. Change in Share of Requirement	*Estimate*	±%	±%	±%
8. Resulting Share of Requirement	Line 2 + (Line 7 × Line 2) =	%	%	%
9. Resulting Customer Income Flow to Us	Line 8 × Line 1 =	$	$	$
10. Less: Noncommunication Costs (Product, Fixed, G&A, etc.)	−(Line 9 × Line 4) =	−$	−$	−$
11. Less: Brand Communication Cost	$0	−	−	−
12. Net Contribution	Line 9 + (Line 10 + Line 11) =	$	$	$
Scenario B: Communication Investment				
13. Brand Communication Efforts (A−*m*)	*Estimate*			
14. Brand Contact Points (*n*)	*Estimate*			
15. Total Brand Communication Investment	*Estimate*	$	$	$
16. Change in Share of Requirement	*Estimate*	±%	±%	±%
17. Resulting Customer Income	Line 2 + (Line 16 × Line 2) =	%	%	%
18. Resulting Customer Income Flow to Us	Line 17 × Line 1 =	$	$	$
19. Less: Noncommunication Costs (Product, Fixed, G&A, etc.)	−(Line 18 × Line 4) =	−$	−$	−$
20. Less: Brand Communication Cost	−Line 15	−	−	−
21. Net Contribution	Line 18 + (Line 19 + Line 20) =	$	$	$
ROCI Calculation				
22. Incremental Gain/Loss vs. "No Investment" Scenario	Line 21 − Line 12 =	$	$	$
23. Incremental ROCI	Line 22 ÷ Line 15 =	$	$	$

retain the business of existing customers, or grow the share of business we are obtaining from our existing group. There are even times when we may want to divest ourselves of certain high-maintenance, low-profit customers, but that needs to be done in such a way that it does not damage our reputation among our broader base of customers and prospects or reduce our volume level, which might impact economies of scale in our operations.

Down the side, there are five major sections that provide the basis for the ROCI calculation. In the first two sections we calculate or estimate the

EXHIBIT 10.8 • Consumer Product ROCI Example

	Aggregated Customer Group:	*Loyals*	*Switchers*	*New or Emerging*	*Problem*
	Behavioral Goal:	*Retain*	*Grow Share*	*Acquire*	*Divest*
Category Requirement Assumptions					
1. Historical Category Demand		$1,000.00	$1,000.00	$1,000.00	$1,000.00
2. Environmental Changes in Demand		2%	5%	20%	−20%
3. Demand Adjusted for Environmental Changes		$1,020.00	$1,050.00	$1,200.00	$800.00
4. Impact of Competitive Activities		−1%	−5%	−5%	−5%
5. Demand Adjusted for Competitive Activities		$1,009.80	$997.50	$1,140.00	$760.00
Base Income Flow Assumptions					
6. Base Share of Requirement		60%	40%	10%	15%
7. Base Income Flow to Us		$605.88	$399.00	$114.00	$114.00
8. Noncommunication Costs (Product, Fixed, G&A, etc.)		75%	80%	80%	90%
9. Contribution Margin %		25%	20%	20%	10%
10. Contribution Margin $		$151.47	$79.80	$22.80	$11.40
Scenario A: No Communication Investment					
11. Change in Share of Requirement		−20%	−20%	−30%	−20%
12. Resulting Share of Requirement		48%	32%	7%	12%
13. Resulting Customer Income Flow to Us		$484.70	$319.20	$79.80	$91.20
14. Less: Noncommunication Costs (Product, Fixed, G&A, etc.)		$(363.53)	$(255.36)	$(63.84)	$(82.08)
15. Less: Marketing Communications Cost		$—	$—	$—	$—
16. Net Contribution		$121.18	$63.84	$15.96	$9.12
Scenario B: Communication Investment					
17. Brand Communication Effort A		$3.00	$4.00	$4.00	$5.00
18. Brand Contact Points N		2	1	1	0
19. Brand Communication Effort B		$2.50	$3.75	$3.50	$4.00
20. Brand Contact Points N		2	1	2	0
21. Brand Communication Effort C		$2.00	$2.50	$2.75	$1.00
22. Brand Contact Points N		2	2	1	0
23. Brand Communication Effort D		$1.50	$1.75	$2.00	$3.50
24. Brand Contact Points N		2	1	1	1
25. Brand Communication Effort E		$1.00	$1.00	$1.00	$1.00
26. Brand Contact Points N		0	1	1	1
27. Total Brand Communication Investment		$18.00	$15.50	$16.75	$4.50
28. Change in Share of Requirement		0%	10%	40%	1%
29. Resulting Share of Requirement		60%	44%	14%	15%
30. Customer Income Flow to Us		$605.88	$438.90	$159.60	$115.14
31. Less: Noncommunication Costs (Product, Fixed, G&A, etc.)		$(454.41)	$(351.12)	$(127.68)	$(103.63)
32. Less Marketing Communications Cost		$(18.00)	$(15.50)	$(16.75)	$(4.50)
33. Net Contribution		$133.47	$72.28	$15.17	$7.01
ROCI Calculation					
34. Incremental Gain/Loss vs. No Investment Scenario		$12.29	$8.44	$(0.79)	$(2.11)
35. Incremental ROCI		68%	54%	−5%	−47%

customer's total category requirement in dollars spent at the factory level. Next we determine our share of that requirement and then our baseline income flow and contribution margin. The next two sections adjust our share and contribution margin estimates under alternative levels of communication investment. From this comparison we isolate the incremental change in revenue attributed to the brand communication efforts. From that we calculate our ROCI, or return on customer investment. As mentioned before, this is based on the incremental gain or, in some cases, loss on our investments.

Category Requirement Assumptions. This section estimates the customer's entire demand, or requirement, within a given category, spread across all available vendors.

Line 1: Estimated Category Demand is based on historical or "what if" data about customer purchase behavior. In this exhibit we show it only as a single line entry, but this estimate can become quite sophisticated and complex. Later in this chapter we discuss how historical data can be adjusted up or down to take into account changes in demand due to environmental factors, competitive activity, and so on. For now the point is that potential total demand for the current period is the basis for our calculation, and it is expressed in dollars, not units, shipments, or other nonfinancial measures.

Base Income Flow Assumptions. This section combines basic assumptions about the brand's share of customer requirements and brand cost dynamics. These are factors that are then applied under alternative scenarios calling for differing levels of communication spending.

Line 2: Base Share of Requirement represents the proportion of the customer's total category requirements that our brand provided in the past, or we might estimate for a future time period. Again, the base is, in most cases, the firm's fiscal year. These base numbers are supported by historical or scenario data. As with all other measures in the process, this reflects dollars, not units. So, our share of requirements reflects the proportion of the customers' dollar spending that comes to our brand, not the proportion of units they acquire. In categories with wide variances in prices between competitors, this could be an important distinction.

Line 3: Base Income Flow to Us is the customer's total category demand multiplied by the percentage of that demand that comes to our brand. In other words, this is the income flow in dollars to our brand that the customer or group represents.

Line 4: Noncommunication Costs is a cost factor subtracted from the base income flow. This covers all fixed and variable costs of running the business excluding brand marketing communication costs or dollars taken as profit. For the sake of simplicity we have shown this as a simple percentage of the income flow. While this single percentage approach will be adequate for many organizations, it should be acknowledged that the dynamics of fixed and variable expenses in some companies may require a more complex, volume-sensitive calculation. However a company factors its expenses, we want to isolate all costs other than brand communication and profit to develop the contribution margin line.

Line 5: Contribution Margin Percentage is equal to 100 percent minus the percentage used in line 4 to account for nonbrand communication costs. Recall from Chapter 6 that we defined contribution margin as only profits and brand communication funds. Here we are estimating that margin as a percentage of the income flow from each customer or customer group.

Line 6: Contribution Margin is the brand contribution margin expressed in dollars. It is obtained by multiplying line 5, contribution margin percentage, by line 3, base income flow. In other words, it is what is left over after all fixed and variable costs (other than those for brand communication and profit) have been removed from the customer income flow. If there were no communication efforts against the customer, this figure would equal our net contribution to the organization's bottom line for the period. However, to the extent funds were or might be spent on brand communication programs during the period, this line reflects the combined total of those expenditures plus the organization's profit. At this point we do not need to specify just how much was spent on communication in the past. The key question is: will the brand be better off by making an investment in communicating with its customers? That question is addressed in the next two sections.

Scenario A: No Communication Investment. This section establishes a baseline of profitability if the brand made no further communication investment. If there were no communication efforts, how much business would the brand receive from each of its customers or customer groups? It is, of course, unlikely the brand would lose 100 percent of its customer base support without brand communication in the fiscal year. However, chances are that some change in demand or share would occur. In this section we calculate or estimate just what that impact might be—that is somewhere between 0 percent and 100 percent—and then reproject the brand's income flow, costs, and net contribution based on the factors established in the previous section.

Line 7: Change in Share of Requirement represents the estimated or actual results of what would or did happen to the brand's share of requirement in the measurement period (if there were no brand communication investment). How much would the brand decline from what it presently receives from each customer or customer group? For the sake of simplicity, we assume that even though we are not communicating actively, the customer will be likely to maintain the same overall category requirement. A mother with an infant will still need approximately the same number of disposable diapers each day whether or not the brand is actively communicating to her. What will likely change is the share of requirement the brand receives, expressed as a percentage decrease or increase in customer share of requirement. In most cases this will result in a negative number, such as a 15 percent decrease in the SOR.

The key question for many organizations will be how to develop an accurate estimate of its change in requirements. Companies with a great deal of historical data probably can extrapolate from past experiences. Others may have done split-market tests that could provide a starting point. And, in many cases, there may be nothing other than the manager's own best professional judgment and insight. In truth assumptions about what would happen if there were no communication are made every day, albeit indirectly. Managers often maintain levels of communication spending because they are afraid to change them. Or they underspend because they have never closely examined the impact of additional communication investment. Our process forces the manager to make viable and supportable decisions, not just maintain the status quo, or the traditional spending patterns.

Line 8: Resulting Share of Requirement is the result of adjusting the initial share of requirement in line 2 by the factor increase or decrease specified in line 7. For example, if the brand's initial share of requirement was 50 percent, but we felt that our share would decrease by 25 percent without communication support, our resulting share of requirement would be .50 + (.50 × -.25) = 37%.

Line 9: Resulting Customer Income Flow to Us multiplies the adjusted share of requirement from line 8 by the customer total category demand on line 1. Recall that we did not alter the customer's overall need for products in the category; we just estimated or calculated how much of that business we expected to get or got. This line, then, represents what would happen to our income flow for the period if we made no brand communication expenditures.

Line 10: Less: Noncommunication Costs (Product, Fixed, G&A, etc.) applies the percentage allocated to cover all noncommunication costs and profits from line 4 to the adjusted income estimate in line 9. Remember, this should include all costs with the exception of brand communication and expected/required profit.

Line 11: Less: Brand Communication Cost is $0 in this scenario since there are or will be no communication expenditures.

Line 12: Net Contribution is what remains after the costs associated with lines 10 and 11 are subtracted from the income flow estimate in line 9. This is our calculation or estimate of the brand contribution level under a scenario where no funds are invested in brand communication. It is this figure that is the basis for estimating the incremental gain—if any—that is to be achieved from an investment in brand communication programs, as follows in Scenario B.

Scenario B: Communication Investment. The next step is to estimate how the value of each customer group would change if we conducted a brand communication program directed toward it.

Line 13: Brand Communication Efforts (A-*m*) are identifiable and generally controllable programs that the organization can direct to specific groups of customers or prospects. There can be as many or as few efforts directed to each group as needed or required.

Line 14: Brand Contact Points (*n*) are simply the number of times each of the brand communication efforts we use are expected to result in brand contacts with the target segment.

As was discussed in Chapter 4, the real value of brand communication is in creating brand contacts with customers or prospects. These can come in any number of ways. Brand contacts need not be just media delivered, which is how we have traditionally tried to measure advertising results. They can be delivered via direct mail, via telemarketing, or even through the organization's sales force. We want to be able to accommodate any and all forms of brand communication activities. These can be either brand messages or brand incentives for the customer or prospect.

It is important to know that business-building brand contacts can occur multiple times within the context of a customer relationship or time period. Thus we talk about brand contact points, not just a brand contact point. This allows us to accommodate communication activities that may create multiple impressions or that may occur multiple times with no additional cost or investment by the organization. For example, a point-of-purchase display may deliver multiple brand contacts to the same customer once it is erected in a retail store. There is an initial cost of development and installation, but from then on the cost has been absorbed although the brand contacts continue.

Line 15: Total Brand Communication Investment represents the total investment in brand communication through all brand contacts with this group of customers. As was discussed earlier, this process is not an attempt to determine the ROI of the individual communication effort, such as one advertising insertion versus another, or a direct mail campaign against a public relations program. In a robust communication environment there is too much synergy between efforts and activities to measure accurately the impact of each with any accuracy. However, using the process described here, we can measure our total investment against a specific group of customers and compare that to the resulting change in the income flow to the brand.

Line 16: Change in Share of Requirement estimates what percentage increase (or decrease) we can expect in our share of requirement as a result of the brand communication program.

Lines 17, 18, and 19 recalculate our revised share of requirement, income flow, and noncommunication costs based on the factor used in line 16.

Line 20: Less: Brand Communication Cost is equal to the total brand communication investment figure in line 15. It is repeated here as a negative so that it can be subtracted from income flow along with the noncommunication costs.

Line 21: Net Contribution is the net income after all communication and noncommunication expenses have been deducted.

Calculation. The next two steps complete the calculation.

Line 22: Incremental Gain/Loss vs. "No Investment" Scenario compares the two net contribution estimates developed in lines 12 and 21. Note that these are incremental gains (or losses) to the brand as a result of the brand communication program. In addition, we can use this process to estimate or calculate the return to the organization from a customer income flow retention program.

Line 23: Incremental ROCI is the total incremental gain/loss (line 22) divided by the investment made in line 15.

Working Through the Return on Customer Investment Spreadsheet: Consumer Product Goods Example

Figure 10.8 illustrates the actual process of developing a return on customer investment on a brand communication program, using a consumer product example. We also expand upon the basic ROI model used earlier to incorporate more real-world situations.

The product illustrated in the example is sold through retailers. It is generally purchased three to four times per year by a household and has a high rate of penetration. There is limited brand loyalty in the category and substantial price promotion and discounting by competing organizations occurs.

We have divided customers into four groups based on their relationship with the brand. The specific behavioral objectives we have to achieve with our brand communication are shown.

The first group consists of loyals, long-term customers who give the brand 60 percent of their category business. We know that demand from this group is not growing significantly, but we obviously need to maintain what we have. Our goal is to retain their income flow at the same level as in the past.

The second group is switchers, a set of customers who switch between our brand and our competitor quite often. While the 40 percent SOR they currently purchase from us is significant, we feel we can strengthen our brand relationship and capture a greater proportion of their share of requirement.

Group three is an emerging group of customers just now coming into the market. This group is expected to expand rapidly, and even though our brand currently receives only 10 percent of their business, the goal is to acquire more of their income flow.

The last group of customers is our problem group. In some cases they give our brand only a small percentage of their business. In others their requirements are very low, and still others they continuously shop on price only. In addition, this group requires a great deal of support, and customer service costs to maintain them are quite high. Demand from this group is expected to decline in the coming period. We would like to reduce our brand communication investment in this group and actually divest some of these customers. But we can't afford to alienate them, because it could damage our reputation with other, more valuable customers, and in some instances we need their purchase volume to maintain our economies of scale in manufacturing.

On line 1, we have arbitrarily set dollar volume income flows at the factory level for each group at the same rate during the measurement period, i.e., $1,000. Most likely this would never be the case in the marketplace, but it is done to illustrate the dynamics of the process so that comparisons can be made.

Since this is a retail-driven consumer product, we ignore retail pricing. We are not interested in how much the customer actually spent to buy the product; we want to know the potential income that each group of customers can, or did, generate for our brand at the factory level.

Lines 2 through 5 are used to explain and adjust the value of each of the groups as a result of observations of activities in the marketplace during the measurement period (the fiscal year of the organization). Line 2 reflects changes in demand driven by environmental factors. Within some groups customers are purchasing increasing amounts of the product or service simply because they are interested or have increasing needs. An example might be computer software. Category revenue is growing at a rate of approximately 5 percent per year while unit sales are growing at approximately 12 percent per year. But even as consumer or customer consumption or usage increases, product prices are generally falling. Thus customers are buying more but paying less.

In our example our group of loyal customers is expected to grow by only 2 percent, while the projected growth rates for the other groups are 5 percent and 20 percent. Our problem group is declining by 20 percent. Thus, after growth factors are taken into account, our initial demand or available income flow of $1,000 becomes $1,020 for the loyals, $1,050 for our switchers, $1,200 for our emerging group, and $800 for our problem segment.

Having provided a way to deal with broad category or environmental changes during the measurement period, we also must provide some way to deal with competitive activities. Commonly competitors will attack certain segments or customer groups in the category. Normally they do this through price cuts or other forms of sales promotion or discounting, often offered at the retail level. Alternatively they simply may focus their efforts against various segments and drive the value of those groups down (or, in very limited cases, up) in terms of returns through various forms of promotion. This is what commonly happens in a price war: the price is driven down, promotional costs soar, margins are reduced, yet volume goes up. The recent customer acquisition programs of telecommunication organizations in the United States are prime examples of this phenomenon.

In our example, line 4 shows that competitive activities have only a slight negative impact on the income flow of the loyals group. It might be that those customers are very brand loyal or have some other reason not to react to competitive pricing tactics. However, competitive activities do have an impact on each of the other groups. As shown, each of the other groups' income flow is driven down by 5 percent as a result of competitive price discounting or other income-flow-reducing activity.

Line 5, therefore, is simply an adjusted income flow for each of the groups after taking into account environmental factors and competitive activities that will either increase or decrease each group's income flow. In effect it is the actual amount spent by each of the groups in our product category once the adjustments have been made (i.e., the available income flow from each group at the factory income level). Thus our adjusted estimated requirement for loyal customers becomes $1,009.80, $997.50 for the switchers, $1,140.00 for the emerging group, and $760.00 for the problem segment.

With overall category demand established, we can move on to determining the base value each customer group represents to our brand.

Line 6 details our share of requirement. In this case we have been receiving 60 percent of the income flow our loyals group spent or will spend in the category. This results in an income flow of $605.88. The switchers give our brand 40 percent of their business, so we receive $399.00 from them. The group of emerging customers' income flow of 10 percent SOR is $114.00. And the problem segment is using our brand for 15 percent of their requirement, which results in $114.00 income flow.

Next we must estimate our costs other than those for brand communication and profit. This is our allocation for all fixed and variable costs such as those related to product manufacturing and distribution, staff salaries, general and administrative costs, etc. Typically there will be some justifiable variation in costs attributed to different groups. For example, new customers generally incur greater administrative costs as accounts are established, promotional offers extended, etc. Established customers, on the other hand, are often the easiest and most efficient to serve. They understand the product, require less hand-holding, are acquainted with our products and services and can explain easily and quickly what they want or need, and are commonly receptive to our communication efforts.

In our example, we determined that 75 percent of the total income flow will be needed to cover all these noncommunication costs for our loyals group. As shown on line 8, they cost somewhat less to service than the switchers and the emerging group, both of which have more churn and therefore greater ongoing administration expenses. Finally, as explained earlier, the problem group requires an even higher level of customer service.

These cost factors give us the contribution margin available for each customer group in line 9. This is obtained by subtracting the percentage factor in line 8 from 100 percent. Line 10 expresses the contribution margin in terms of dollars. (Recall that contribution margin in this approach includes funds available for brand communication and profit only.) It ranges from $151.47 for the loyals group to $79.80 for the switchers to $22.80 for the emerging group and $11.40 for the problem customers.

At this point it is time to regroup. What we have just done is determine the value of the four groups of customers at the contribution margin line based on their income flows to the organization. If we could generate these income flows without investing any funds in brand communication, we might be able to justify serving each of them. However, even if we were able to drive our share of their requirements up substantially—getting, say, 70 to 80 percent of the switchers or emerging category—we still would have limited funds available for brand communication programs. This is the challenge that every brand communication manager faces when using this type of return on customer investment analysis. There are some customers against which finite resources simply can't be invested, or if the investment is made, it must be through some type of very efficient, low-cost communication activity, which commonly limits its power and impact. This is not to say that these types of brand communication programs are not possible or useful, but it does suggest that targeting and focusing on best customers or at least on those that provide the greatest opportunity for returned income flows is the first requirement of any brand communication program.

With this analysis of customer value, we can move to the next step in the process: identifying the incremental value created by brand communication programs. We do this by first estimating the impact on income flows if no brand communication investment was made. This is then compared with the results achieved when we develop and implement various brand communication programs. The results are often surprising.

First we create the "No Investment" scenario. This is done by estimating or calculating how much the customer group would decline or how much our share of its requirements would fall if we suspended communication activity during the measurement period. In our example we stated earlier that this is a competitive category with low loyalty and much competitive brand communication activity. On line 11 we estimate or calculate that we would lose 20 percent of the share we receive from our loyals, switchers, and problem groups if no brand communication programs were conducted. Even though loyals are familiar with our products, they have many alternatives and need to hear our brand messages to remind them of their value and to distinguish us from the crowd. Switchers and problems, without messages or incentives to encourage them, have little reason to consider our brand. The market tests that gave us that data indicated the emerging group is even more vulnerable. We could expect our SOR there to decrease by 30 percent during the measurement period.

You may recall from the earlier discussion that the customer's total demand or income flow in the category does not change as a result of our diminished communication activity. Just the proportion that we receive is impacted.

Lines 12 through 16 are a recalculation of all the components that lead to the net contribution:

- Since the share of requirement among loyals falls by 20 percent, the resulting SOR goes from 60 percent to 48 percent. Multiplying this by the group's category demand of $1,009.80 produces an income flow of $484.70. From this we subtract $363.53 to cover the 75 percent provision for product, administrative, and other noncommunication costs. This generates a net contribution from the group of $121.18.
- The share of requirement among switchers falls 20 percent as well, to an adjusted share of 32 percent. Given their category demand of $997.50 and the expected decline without brand communication, we now have an income flow of $319.20, 80 percent, of which ($255.36) is for allocated non-communication expenses. This generates a net contribution of $63.84.
- As was noted earlier, the emerging group was impacted more by the lack of communication. They are newer to the category, have little previous experience with our products, and in some cases are still experimenting with products and brands. Without brand communication, their share of requirement drops by 30 percent. We can expect to receive only 7 percent of their income flow dollars, or $79.80. Subtracting allocated costs of $63.84 provides a net contribution of $15.96 to our brand.
- Finally, we expect a 20 percent decrease in share from the problem group. Thus our adjusted share of requirement is 12 percent. This produces an income flow of $91.20. When allocated noncommunication costs of $82.08 are deducted, we find a net contribution of $9.12.

The net contribution income flow shown for each group becomes the basis against which we will measure the incremental gain or loss resulting from brand communication.

The next step in our analysis is to estimate or calculate the alternative scenario using one or more brand communication efforts against each group. Again, this example is for illustrative purposes only but will provide a view of the process. Those conducting an analysis within their own organization will have to adjust and adapt this particular chart to accommodate either more or fewer brand communication elements and activities than shown here.

In this illustration, we have five brand communication efforts, lines 17 through 26. Some of these efforts have been targeted to each group, although messages and delivery systems may be different. Others we sent to only one or two groups. As part of our analysis we must determine the cost of each of these brand communication efforts.

As can be seen, we have two lines for each brand communication effort. One is the identification of the program and the cost, and the second is the number of times the activity was used. For example, as shown on line 17, brand communication effort A costs $3.00 to implement against the loyals group. However, it costs $4.00 to implement against the switchers and emerging customers and, had it been used to reach the problem segment, it would have cost $5.00. The costs of delivery are based on message delivery systems that differ based on the ease or difficulty of reaching each group.

Line 18 shows the number of times brand communication effort A was used against each group. It was used twice against the loyals, once against the switchers and emerging groups, and not used with the problem group.

Lines 19 through 26 repeat this process for brand communication efforts B through E. As can be seen, there is a mix of communication efforts going against all of the four groups, with varying levels of intensity, based on the planned brand communication program.

Line 27 is a summary of investment against each customer group during the measurement period. This is simply an addition of the cost of each brand communication effort A multiplied by the number of times it was used. For example, for the loyals group we used brand communication effort A twice at a cost of $3.00 each or a total of $6.00. We used the same communication effort once with switchers at a cost of $4.00.

If we total all the brand communication efforts and the number of times they were used, we arrive at line 27. For example, we invested $18.00 against loyals, $15.50 against switchers, $16.75 against emerging customers, and $4.50 against the problem group.

In the previous section we dealt with the question "What if we made no communication investment whatsoever; what would happen to our share of requirement? And what would happen to our brand?" In this section we turn the question around to ask "What happens to our share of requirement and our brand if we invest all this money in these customers and prospects? How much—if any—will our business increase? And will our profits increase as a result?"

Just as in the "No Communication Investment" scenario, the key is to estimate or calculate the change in share of requirement that results from a planned brand communication effort. This estimate uses historical behavioral data, such as the responsiveness of customers and prospects to messages, incentives, and delivery programs. As was discussed in an earlier section, we are not trying to evaluate each individual, functionally specific communication effort. Instead we are attempting to determine the synergistic effort produced by all elements of a brand communication program.

Once we determine how much, if any, our share of requirement will change as a direct result of our brand communication program, we can recalculate all of the income, costs, and net contribution for each group.

• Even though we invested $18.00 in communicating with the loyals, there was no impact on share of requirement. However, since our original intention had been to maintain our current SOR level, our objective has been achieved. Our income flow remains at $605.88, with 75 percent ($454.41) of this allocated to noncommunication costs. However, we must now deduct our $18.00 communication expenditure to arrive at our net contribution of $133.47.

• We estimate that our share of requirement among switchers will increase by 10 percent, using our brand communication program, giving us a total share of their income flow of 44 percent. This would produce an income flow of $438.90. While income has increased, so have our costs; 80 percent ($351.12) of the income is allocated to noncommunication costs. After we subtract our brand communication investment of $15.50 we have a net contribution of $72.28.

• Emerging customers are very receptive to our messages, and we are able to increase our share of requirement by 40 percent, giving us a new share of 14 percent of their income flow. This produces an adjusted income flow of $159.60, 80 percent, of which ($127.68) is required for noncommunication expenses. When we subtract the $16.75 brand communication investment, we are left with a net contribution of $15.17.

• The problem segment unfortunately had a very slight change in share of requirement as a result of the brand communication program. The $4.50 we invested in this group produced a 1 percent increase in our share of requirement. Our income flow becomes $115.14, with $103.63 in noncommunication costs. After deducting our $4.50 communication investment, we are left with a net contribution of $7.01.

We now can develop the actual calculation of the return on brand communication investment or, better said, the return on customer investment. Only three lines are used in that calculation:

• Line 16, our net contribution under the "No Communication Investment" scenario.
• Line 33, our net contribution under a communication investment scenario.

- Line 27, the total amount of communication spending occurring under the communication investment scenario.

For each group we look at the incremental gain or loss in net contribution under the two scenarios. This is simply line 33 minus line 16. Because we are comparing net contribution values after all communication spending has been deducted, we are looking at the change in profitability that each group of customers or prospects can contribute. The return on investment is calculated by taking the incremental gain/loss (the "return") in line 34 and dividing it by line 27, total brand communication investment.

- Our loyals group received the largest portion of our communication spending, $18.00. That investment created no impact on our share of requirement versus our historical level. However, the alternative was to suspend communication, and in that event we likely would have lost 20 percent of our share among this key group. By spending the $18.00, we maintained our share and added to our profitability in the amount of $12.29 ($133.47 versus $121.18). Our return on investment is 68 percent ($133.47−$121.18)÷$18.00.
- Switchers increased their net contribution from $63.84 under the "No Communication Investment" scenario to $72.28. This is an incremental gain of $8.44, which, when divided by the communication investment of $15.50, produces an ROCI of 54 percent.
- Communication dollars against the emerging customer groups did not have as much impact. The net contribution actually fell from $15.96 to $15.17. While we were able to increase our share of requirement, the additional income was not sufficient to offset the communication costs. There is a loss of $0.79 and an ROCI of minus 5 percent. This illustrates why it is often true that new customers are expensive to acquire and their value often occurs over time and not immediately. In many cases organizations are better off trying to nurture the business they have established from existing customer relationships before investing significant amounts to acquire new customers. The true value of customer acquisition usually cannot be reflected in a business-building model such as this since the time frame is limited. There is, however, long-term value in acquiring new customers.
- Communication to the problem group also produced a negative impact on the bottom line. While share of requirement has a modest increase, net contribution went from $9.12 to $7.01, an incremental loss of $2.11 and an ROCI of minus 47 percent.

While this illustration is based on a real-world example, it has been adapted to illustrate the process. In other industries where this process has been used, similar results have been found.

What Is a Good ROI or ROCI and What Is a Bad ROI or ROCI?

The question often raised in this type of brand communication return on customer investment calculation is "What is a good ROI or ROCI? What is a bad ROI or ROCI?" Obviously brand communication managers want some sort of comparison with like organizations or with competitors. Unfortunately such yardsticks or rules of thumb do not exist or are of little value. All organizations are different. All have different strategies. All have different sets of expectations from management and stockholders. So, the only "good" or "bad" ROI or ROCI number is one that fits the financial requirements of the organization.

We have worked with clients who have set hurdle rates for brand communication programs in the 200 percent to 300 percent range, for this is the return they believe they can get with other uses of the organization's finite resources. Other organizations are pleased with returns in the 20 percent to 40 percent range, and still others have much more modest goals. The true determination of whether the ROI or ROCI is good or bad is what return could be expected from investing those funds in other corporate activities. If R&D is expected to return 40 percent, then that is a relevant comparison number. If new plant investments will return 18 percent, that is the relevant ROI to use in comparing communication ROI or ROCI. It is within this framework that brand communication must function now and in the future.

CONCLUSIONS

- Outside-in budgeting and the closed-loop system sensibly tie marketing communication expenditures to the revenue generated by customers.
- The incremental income approach reveals how investments in marketing communication programs yield bottom-line results that can be missed in traditional measurement systems.
- Long-term results can be captured only by systems that treat customers as tangible assets.
- Activity-based costing and economic value assessment may prove to be powerful tools in the struggle to capture the long-term (brand-building) returns of marketing communication investments.

The Way Forward: Overcoming Barriers with IGMC Solutions

In this chapter we describe and identify the barriers that could prevent the development of the IGMC approach we have been describing. These barriers cannot be sidestepped, minimized, or dismissed as inconsequential for they are real. They can, however, be overcome by new ways of thinking, acting, and managing organizations and communication groups in the 21st century. Thus, in the following sections, we have sought to accentuate the positive.

BARRIER 1: THE TRANSITIONING METAPHOR

As we pointed out in Chapters 1 and 2 the world of business is transitioning from domestically focused economies to a world that is global in scope and activities. Whether this can be described as a "brave new world" is debatable, but it is a world that requires new developmental paths for marketers *at all organizational levels.* So many of the firms we have interviewed, consulted for, or questioned are still positioned in the very first stage of IMC development—the one-sight, one-sound tactical approach. Admittedly, this is a good starting point. But it is an indictment of the marketing profession, which has trumpeted customer orientation for at least forty years, that so many communication programs are still developed from an inside-out rather than an outside-in viewpoint.

Managers and executives also have to transition in the ways they plan and operationalize marketing and corporate communication activities to achieve sustainable exchanges and relationships at a profit. Can managers make these transitional changes? The answer is, of course, a resounding yes. But that positive reply is dependent on absorbing lessons from the new paradigm.

The question may arise that if IGMC is such a powerful and provocative process, why doesn't every corporation, marketing communication agency, corporate communication department and public relations agency, and business school simply bow to the new received wisdom? It is difficult for cultures to transition to accepting a new paradigm, process, or system as *legitimate*, particularly when the old models and processes are still in operation and in many cases still producing successful results. Organizational heritages cannot be overtaken easily, and new ideas may percolate slowly. Cultural responsiveness does not necessarily have to act as a barrier to integrative processes. Perhaps a key starting point in overcoming managerial and organizational inertia vis-à-vis globalization and IGMC is to evaluate where the organization or brand is today and where it needs to be in the future. Notably, if the organization is fixed on products, processes, systems, and procedures, executives will need to ask the question "How can the products, processes, systems, and procedures be reconfigured so they are focused on exchanges with customers or publics?" Or, put another way, "How can we reconfigure the way we communicate with customers and publics to move this corporation as brand, and individual brands, *forward*?"

BARRIER 2: FROM MARKETPLACE TO MARKETSPACE

Worldwide demand for and acceptance of products or brands are underpinned by consonance with cultural norms and values. Today cultural factors are still as important, if not more so, and the drive for an IGMC strategy implies tactical adaptation as necessary. IGMC is as much about branding as it is about consumers. And consumers, their needs and wants, stand at the heart of brand loyalty. This suggests that all marketing communication tools have to be focused on the customer or consumer as the central hub, around which exchanges take place—not just advertising, but also sales promotion, direct marketing, point-of-sale, personal selling, package design, poster sites, the Internet. *All* fit into the new marketspace where consumers control what marketing communication messages they access and respond to.

One recent example of how control has passed into the hands of the consumer is the British automobile market. Prices in the United Kingdom average several thousands of pounds higher than those in the rest of Europe. Via television car programs, the Internet, and personal visits, British consumers are gradually realizing they can literally save thousands of pounds by buying their cars on mainland Europe, especially in the Netherlands or

Italy. And change in the marketspace has happened despite the deployment of the opposing arsenal of marketing communication tools by United Kingdom car manufacturers and their associated distributors.

BARRIER 3: ORGANIZATIONAL CONSTRAINTS

Firms will not rush lemminglike over the cliff of look-alike, sound-alike communication programs. Nor will they crowd to stumble upward through the staired stages toward financial and strategic integration. Instead some corporations may already be well advanced in all four stages; others may be at stage 1 (tactical integration); still others may be considering adopting an outside-in as opposed to an inside-out perspective.

Adaptation Versus Standardization

The old issue of adaptation versus standardization keeps cropping up. While commentators on either side of this debate keep up their respective ends, the only lucid approach is for communication to standardize where possible in relation to clearly defined markets and adapt where necessary. In fact focus on different customer groups *necessitates* differentiation in communication. Loyals do not need or require the same types of communication as switchers, and both do not need the same type of communication as potentials.

Internal Organizational Structure

At a recent global marketing conference someone asked, "What is the greatest challenge to creating a global marketing and communication program?" The answer: "Organizational structure." The reason for this is that many "global firms" are in fact not global at all but simply multidomestic. That is, they have simply replicated the domestic structure from the home country and created in effect semiautonomous strategic business units. These functionally oriented, vertically integrated, geographically focused organizational structures are simply too inflexible to deal with IGMC or marketing communication programs that work across many cultures with customers in mind. The solution is to redesign organizational structures around customers and customer groups, not products, services, or strategic business units. Just as much as organizations need to refocus and integrate marketing and corporate communication activities on key customer groups, the organization needs to think along the following lines:

- Stage 1: Start with customers and aggregate them into groups that are similar in behavior, attitude, needs, and wants.

- Stage 2: Make someone responsible for the welfare of that group of customers.
- Stage 3: The managerial task becomes to manage income flows for that group, not products, services, units, or geographies.

Managing such customer groups requires four capabilities, each of which needs support from manufacturing, logistics, systems, finance, and accounting:

- Capability 1: someone or some group responsible for new customer acquisition (switchers or nonpurchasers)
- Capability 2: someone or some group responsible for the care, nurture, and retention of existing customers (curriculum marketing)
- Capability 3: a third group responsible for managing the customers the acquisition group brings in. In other words, managing the customers through the organization's product or service portfolio, bringing new products on-line, ensuring that these new customers become loyal, and perhaps even eventually organizational advocates.
- Capability 4: a fourth group concerned with building relationships with key publics that could impact organizational performance anywhere in the world. For the sake of argument, we have termed this activity *corporate communication* and the output *integrated communication* to differentiate it from those communication programs focused on quid-pro-quo exchanges and relationships. However, where the corporation is a service or business-to-business organization or one with a unitary product line, then IGMC can be applied in both a corporate and marketing communication sense without the distinguishing application.

Undoubtedly, changing to such a customer-focused organization creates significant challenges for marketing management, at both the corporate and brand level. However, following from Chapter 9, we are concerned not just with promotional elements but with developing, maintaining, and increasing income flows from customer groups as well. Throughout, we have emphasized the strategic role of IGMC, not just tactical juxtaposition, even though we recognize and applaud organizations that are moving through the stages.

BARRIER 4: A RESEARCH-POOR CONSUMER ENVIRONMENT

Throughout the book we have noted that many corporations are starting to pay attention to cultural differences that correspond to what we have termed *glocalization* that ties into the IGMC process. Even here, however, the process of IGMC is not driven entirely by customer needs but more by organizational edict. We believe that firms need to access more and better information concerning the different customer groups they seek to serve. Businesses of all types need to build and derive information from the databases that capture behavioral and attitudinal information. To develop IGMC, firms need strategies that *work*. Such strategies can indeed be driven by organizational criteria, but there is also the necessity for firms to recognize and appeal to homogeneous segments among heterogeneous global markets. Likewise, recognizing homogeneity (along some variables) does not equate to similarity of decoding by consumers to similar global messages.

The recent past has shown that many multidomestic or global firms are keen to capitalize on new marketing communication developments. The difficulty continues to be that about 95 percent of all media is still negotiated and placed locally, and the majority of media available to marketing communicators in the international sphere is national or at best regional. With exceptions there are still relatively few genuinely international media.

Despite the numbers and depth of range of media research vehicles across Europe and Asia, for example, very few media purchases are underpinned by sound understanding of the market or customer dynamics. Far too many multinational media buys are driven by statistics, and statistics do not necessarily equate to understanding. These statistical reports and surveys do, however, currently underpin many marketing communication strategies and are indeed useful at identifying broad macroeconomic trends. But the broad trends are not really a substitute for behavioral and attitudinal evidence gathered from real exchanges and qualitative research data. However, purely numerical evaluations will never be enough to ensure development of truly international/global campaigns. What is needed, as we suggested before, is to focus on customers and the ways in which they come into contact with brands or the corporation and then to *manage these contact points*. At best, quantitative overviews of market factors are useful but no more than a supplementary resource to the database material that is required for IGMC.

BARRIER 5: CORPORATE/MARKETING BRAND INTERFACE

While we agree that communication is marketing and marketing is communication, we are convinced that two types of communication are required in a world where corporate business is *news*. Just as consumers buy, consume, and derive satisfaction from brands, they also subscribe to information networks that report on organizational developments. Who or what a corporation is, how it behaves, its image, and its persona are crucial to the various publics with which it interfaces and that allow it to continue to operate in today's world. Corporations must take very seriously the need to build relationships with publics—internal staff, business analysts, capital markets, the press and other forms of media, the communities in which they operate, and the markets they serve. Areas such as social responsibility, community involvement, issues management, lobbying, and corporate advertising are very real support mechanisms for every business and have to be managed just as rigorously, and as proactively, as the management of IGMC with customers. The corporation should be marketed as a brand in its own right. The identity programs developed by management should bear correspondence to the images before publics involved with and interested in corporate activities. The corporate brand has to be seen as the central core or hub that gives an overall sense of identity, meaning, strategic overview, and dynamic thrust to individual brands within the corporate portfolio.

Moreover, each individual brand needs to be protected and nurtured by the corporations in which it is located and managed. These brands are powerful irreplaceable corporate assets. However, as we have shown elsewhere, such brands may encounter different meanings and different competitive positions in each market. This means that IGMC cannot yet be a singular process in terms of tactics throughout the world but may for now be pluralistic in nature. Communication deployed will have to be altered in accord with customer needs, wants, and desires. But, as understanding of needs and behavior is transmitted continuously via the global database, IGMC messages and modes of delivery will become more uniform.

We have discovered in many corporations that the corporate and marketing communication functions are separate. Both communication functions, however, can and do learn from each other and should ally with each other so the values and identity associated with brands and corporation (and vice versa) become interrelated and synergistic.

BARRIER 6: THE TRAINING INVESTMENT

Corporations need invest not only in developing the relevant infrastructure but also in developing the communication staff who are to move forward with the IGMC approach. However, we suspect that businesses will not change unless made to do so by market forces—falling sales, declining customer retention, reduced profits, loss of market share. These factors may be the hard evidence that the models, tools, techniques, and processes that worked before do not work so well in the new information-intensive, globally oriented, choice-proliferating markets of the 21st century.

New competencies will not be developed overnight or even rapidly. Instead knowledge will be gained in the usual school of hard knocks, by developing brands, battling against competitors, communicating with publics and customers throughout the world. But training can also be developed by studying and applying the latest information. The greatest informational interface lies between world-class business schools, leading-edge corporations, leading business executives, and top-notch research journals. Every leader in tomorrow's business needs access to these materials. But training costs money. It is not just a matter of allocating resources; it is a matter of investment in the people who will build and maintain brands and business in the future.

BARRIER 7: MIND MAPS: STRATEGY AND CREATIVITY

We use the term *mind maps* as a metaphor for the ways in which managers and executives view the world. A simple analogy will suffice. Let's suppose we are visiting a new locality in some part of the world. Let's also suppose that the map we have is out of date and does not provide up-to-date information that enables us to progress easily to our destination. Sometimes people unwittingly operate from out-of-date maps. The problem with such maps is that they influence perception. Perception is not necessarily about reality but what we perceive reality to be. This can act as a significant barrier to the many new ideas, concepts, and processes of what IGMC is and why it is necessary in today's world.

The first part of the mind map we wish to redraw is to create for all managers and executives a customer-driven mode of thinking. Strategic imperatives cannot be driven by what worked in the past, for what worked yesterday may not work today. See, for example, Case Studies 1 and 2. In the former, British Telecom needed to build relationships with key existing and potential business customers. In the latter, De Beers sought to develop new ways of communicating using admittedly traditional media but involving substantively greater investment than before. For both corporations, and indeed for the other two cases, moving forward meant taking or adopting *the customer perspective.* As we have said before, products and services are simply means of delivering satisfaction. Satisfied customers come back. Dissatisfied ones do not.

The second part of perception that needs changing is creativity. Much IGMC strategy, once applied, is highly creative. We have also suggested using the new template method that is just starting to bring forth some very pertinent findings associated with creativity. Rather than using one of the unsystematic and informal creativity approaches, we have suggested following a more rigorous and structured process using patterns of thought and action that have proven successful elsewhere. We have suggested that these ideas and ways of successfully communicating be considered—not for wholesale adoption, but for potential adaptation in cultures that require differentiation beyond simple transliteration.

Corporate and brand marketing people need to work together to communicate what the business stands for and its concomitant brand positions. Most companies tend to be paranoid about releasing information, and the concept of empowering employees at different levels has been observed more in the breach than in the observance. Bill Gates, founder and CEO of Microsoft Corporation, recently advocated in his new book *Business @ the Speed of Thought* that all employees be given access to all company information. We agree with Gates. All employees, in every company, are involved with marketing, whatever their job title may be. Marketing is simply too important to be left to the marketing department.

BARRIER 8: THE AGENCY INTERACTIVE PERSPECTIVE

Strictly speaking change, in and of iself, is not a barrier to adoption of IGMC processes. The 21st century is about nonstop change. The world we live in now would be scarcely recognizable to someone from 1900. The 1990s alone saw changes in technology and marketing communication that have simply revolutionized the marketing world. The age of the mass market, on which so many marketing models were based, is rapidly declining in most developed markets. The age of the micro, niche, and even unitary market is now upon us. In these new markets communication control is in the hands of customers and consumers. Change, meanwhile, continues at an accelerated pace. Even as we write, the marketing communication experience curve is moving on.

There are those organizations that can assist in the process of managerial learning that needs to take place to implement IGMC. We know this process has to be client led, client driven. Nonetheless we believe that significant strides have been made by marketing communication agencies. Some have restructured to *mirror* client corporate requirements. These agencies are now in a position to move beyond the role of tactical marketing communication implementers or media buyers to being full strategic partners. Most successful IGMC implementation comes about when clients and agencies work hand in hand to develop, implement, and evaluate integrated campaigns. Moreover, such agencies are an important disseminator of workable practice. For the near or immediate future there may be no way around working with these "strategic partners." But agency practitioners should not be too tied to one marketing communication mechanism or discipline. Rather they should consider client needs from a customer perspective. Just as we suggested earlier that all staff need access to organizational information, so agency personnel will need answers to the many issues or questions raised in Chapter 8.

BARRIER 9: INVESTMENTS AND MEASUREMENT

The main problem encountered in terms of the continued development of IMC (rather than IGMC) was the failure to provide a set of methods and procedures to determine how much to invest in which customer groups, plus the added inability to measure outcomes from each set of investments in a robust manner. Managers and executives in our study groups and empirical investigations of IMC recounted this barrier to the continued and accelerated diffusion of IMC. In this book we have provided a straightforward spreadsheet-based approach to measuring return on customer investments. We admit that there are some anomalies overlapping between brand- and business-building investment and measurement and will continue to work on these for the future. However, the planning and evaluation processes, once implemented by organizations, should rapidly lead to case materials; that is where the organizations that have *learned* via marketplace realities are willing to share the outcomes of IGMC or IMC in practice.

THE WAY FORWARD

The barriers we have discussed can be overcome by managers and executives in possession of the skills, tools, knowledge, processes, and systems we have discussed in this book. We believe those communication programs, whether at corporate brand or individual brand level, must be orchestrated in such a way as to appeal to clearly defined customer groups or relevant publics. We believe that such communication cannot be delegated to individual country level or even left to brand or marketing managers. Instead there has to be someone with clear authority and the necessary power to develop and implement integrated communication programs that result in mutually beneficial behaviors. We believe that agencies can form powerful strategic partners in the development of these programs. We believe that in the 21st century the essence of marketing as a means of creating exchanges that satisfy individual and corporate objectives will be *communication*.

CONCLUSIONS

- Out-of-date mind maps and inflexible organizational structures may be the greatest barriers you have to overcome in moving toward a fully realized IMC or IGMC strategy.
- In the long run managing your customer contact points may yield greater benefits than buying loads of number-heavy research.

Appendix 1
Case Study 1: British Telecom[1]

British Telecom (BT) is one of the world's leading suppliers of fixed and mobile communication services. In the United Kingdom it supports twenty-seven million customer lines and, through its 60 percent stake in Cellnet, more than three million mobile connections. Its main services are local, national, and international calls (with direct dialing to 230 countries worldwide) and supplying telephone lines, equipment, and private circuits for homes and businesses.

Outside the United Kingdom, its strategy is to expand in chosen markets by developing a series of alliances and joint venture partnerships, and it has put in place one of the most comprehensive global networks of any operator. In Concert Communication Services, it has the world's leading supplier of global network solutions for multinational and global customers.

BT is also at the forefront of the development and marketing of a comprehensive range of advanced data and interactive multimedia solutions and technologies of the future.

As businesses go through the processes of internationalization and globalization, and as more and more people travel abroad, so the demand for international communication grows. In the last decade international communication—phone, fax, video, and data transmission—has more than doubled from thirty-three billion minutes a year to sixty-eight billion minutes.

This growth in demand has been complemented by the liberalization of telecommunication markets around the world. At the beginning of the

---

[1] This case has been provided courtesy of the head of content and communications strategy, BT Global Marketing. Grateful acknowledgment is extended for permission to use this material.

1990s only about 20 percent of the world's total telecommunication market was open to competition; by the end of the decade only about 10 percent was not.

BT's current geographical strategy is to focus on triad areas—North America, Europe, and Asia-Pacific—and to work with local partners. It now has a number of key partnerships around the world and significant investment in international services.

BACKGROUND

As one of the United Kingdom's largest companies and one of the world's leading communication groups, BT is continually offered sponsorship opportunities such as golf tournaments, formula one racing, rugby, soccer, and so on. While most of these events are based in the United Kingdom, relatively few opportunities have been presented to BT's global group that would help capture client and customer imaginations and be relevant to BT's growth ambitions. In 1994 Chay Blyth approached BT's senior management with a proposal that seemed to fulfill both criteria. The race he proposed was billed as the world's toughest yacht race, around the world against prevailing winds and currents and manned by nonprofessional sailors. The proposed route would also take the yachts to the key strategic areas where BT was rapidly expanding its business. The race was to run over nearly twelve months, providing a longevity that other sponsorships could not. The proposal, when packaged together, presented a great opportunity for BT to raise brand awareness and image in the countries concerned and simultaneously allow its senior executives to spend time with major existing and potential customers in the ports of call. Notably, both would also enjoy the spectacle of a fleet of fourteen state-of-the-art, oceangoing yachts.

The race would begin in July 1996, starting from Southampton in England, and then visit Rio de Janeiro, Wellington, New Zealand, Sydney, Cape Town, and Boston, before returning to Southampton in September the following year.

BT's global marketing group, while having no expertise in sailing, was skilled in mounting global events and exhibitions. The core team of five people was asked to take on the mammoth task of working with Chay Blyth's company (the Challenge Business), which owned the race, and at the same time to continue business as usual. Those duties included:

- developing and rolling out a global relationship program
- providing tactical support to BT's marketing teams around the world

- creating sales support tools for local and regional functions
- delivering marketing messages to its global customer sets[2]

In terms of BT's investment in the race, there were two clear options:

1. provide the minimum support but ensure that BT could exploit the race as a PR vehicle or
2. turn the sponsorship into BT's most ambitious global event— *the world's biggest relationship program*

The first option was clearly the easier of the two but would still demand a great deal of effort and resources from an already stretched team. Besides, BT was committed to support and exploit its sponsorship of the race as a global sporting event that would attract significant publicity in its own right. The initial decision to be the title sponsor had been made early in 1994 on the sound logic that there was a clear geographical connection between the race ports of call and BT's growing global capabilities in managed network products and services (telecommunication interconnectivity between and within countries around the world). Exploiting the interest raised by the yachts as they visited the ports of call would also allow BT to raise its corporate profile in strategic parts of the business world. The race would be used as a metaphor between the challenges facing the yachts (tough environments, continually changing conditions, need for strong leadership and state-of-the-art technology) and the challenges facing BT as it continued to expand into a very competitive global market.

The second option not only involved achieving these goals but also, with the same limited human resources, still with business-as-usual targets to meet, meant mounting a two-year intensive communication program that would span the entire world.

Such a program had never been undertaken in the communication industry. However, more important, it was becoming clear that the plan would also create an opportunity to work with the other yacht sponsors— companies such as Commercial Union, Toshiba, and Motorola, as well as the club sponsors, companies that had opted for a lesser sponsorship package,

---

[2] The BT Relationship Programs are designed to build and enhance relationships with its key existing and potential customers. A technical program (the Global Information Exchange) is designed exclusively for technological specialist functions in organizations and includes a newsletter, seminars, and a website (www.gie.com). For senior-level managers, a nontechnical program—the Global Executive Program—is designed to share information on all strategic and managerial issues. Both programs are running in all countries visited by the race yachts as well as other strategically important countries around the world.

which were also major multinationals such as Digital, Tandem, Sharp, and 3Com. Association and partnership with such well-known companies—which were both suppliers of products and services as well as customers of BT—helped provide increased credibility for the race and for the business programs of which they would be part.

MARKETING OBJECTIVES

With a blank sheet of paper facing the team, they devised the following plan:

1. Ensure that BT's sponsorship of the race was used to raise brand awareness among the selected audiences.

2. Create understanding of the "BT Offer" in terms of both its portfolio of products and services and its offer inherent in the relationship programs—shared knowledge and expertise about telecommunication technology (GIE)—and BT's understanding of global and local (national) strategic business issues.

3. Turn the company's sponsorship of the race into "the world's biggest relationship program."

4. Use the key stopovers as opportunities to mount strategic sales support programs.

5. Deliver consistent and integrated marketing messages to customers and prospects around the world.

COMMUNICATION OBJECTIVES

1. Explain to customers why BT is sponsoring the race.

2. Demonstrate, through relationship programs, how BT has an insightful and innovative view of the strategic and technical issues facing its customers.

3. Share with customers the BT view of the future of telecommunication and provide some valuable insights into strategic business issues facing companies in both global and local markets.

4. Demonstrate how BT can work with other major players in the industry to meet the needs of its customers.

5. Generate sales leads for the current portfolio of products and services.

6. Use the most effective and appropriate media to deliver BT and partner messages to the agreed target audiences.

STRATEGY

1. Exploit the race media coverage to attract attention to the business messages—use the race as a metaphor for the challenges that business customers face around the world.

2. Select key issues for debate and discussion with customers and examine them in detail in each of the ports of call. Observe the cultural, political, economic, and social differences and feed back to customers as fulfillment to the programs.

3. Mount semiprivate exhibitions (showcases) where BT and other sponsors (particularly the technology companies) could demonstrate leading-edge business solutions.

4. Integrate the key message—"Let's Talk"[3]—throughout all programs and the media used to deliver them to the targeted audiences.

TARGET AUDIENCES

In terms of BT's global customers, the key audiences (the direct remit of the global marketing communication team) were:

- senior decision makers in multinational companies—both technical and nontechnical
- opinion formers from consultants, governmental, and regulatory bodies
- local, regional, and international media

Each of these audiences would have its own marketing programs—ranging from conferences and seminars to senior-level one-to-one meetings and interviews.

THE BRIEF

It was recognized early in the program that the brief for the business elements associated with the race would need to be flexible to accommodate both

---

[3] The line "Let's Talk" originated from an advertising campaign developed by Saatchi and Saatchi in late 1994. The advertising concept grew from the premise "Better communication leads to better relationships, which, in turn, lead to better business and a better world." The take-out, or invitation, contained within the ads was ". . . so let's talk."

changes in the very dynamic communication market and ongoing learning and evolution as the year-long race moved around the world.

There were fixed elements such as the audiences and the key messages, but delivery and execution of the programs needed room to grow and evolve. Adopting such an approach would ensure that the program retained a freshness and topicality that would help attract continued attention from regional and international media while at the same time sustaining relevance for local audiences. Integrated and consistent messages are important, but not at the expense of being inappropriate.

THE TEAM IN THE UNITED KINGDOM

In the London office a core team of five people worked on the program full-time with another seven people working part-time but increasingly more as the race began. A project office was established and remained intact for nearly two years. This team was made up of:

- a project leader/project manager
- a strategy and business program manager
- an events specialist
- a public relations and television specialist
- an advertising manager

Other support members included finance, project management, organizational development, technology, and telecommunication specialists. The larger team worked through a process that centered on a central steering group that spun off a number of smaller teams driving the key programs. Integration of messages and pull-through into all programs would be achieved only through vigilant (and sometimes painful) steering group control. The single most difficult issue to manage was resisting BT's local offices' wishes to drive their localized messages into the core program as the key message. The whole business program had to be seen as a global event, discussing global issues in a local environment. Of course local input was essential (to provide relevance), but it was not key. The steering group and its strength and unity were fundamental to the success of the program. The fact that the steering group held the budget was important, but calling that shot was not advisable and was never used. Without local commitment and buy-in, the program would not work. Being a budget bully is never clever.

THE TEAM AROUND THE WORLD

At the ports of call similar setups were established where local managers formed teams to help manage the *show* when it arrived in town. This is but a partial list:

- Advertising had to be delivered to the local media (press, radio, and posters).
- TV and press interviews were arranged with BT and the Challenge Business managers.
- Sites were booked for the technology showcase, and then exhibits and demonstrations were installed.
- A media center had to be built and installed.
- Berthing for the yachts and hospitality sailings were arranged.
- Crew accommodation (and entertainment after weeks at sea) had to be arranged.
- Repairs and maintenance to yachts would be required.
- Local dignitaries would be invited to attend civic functions.

THE SUPPLIERS AND AGENCIES

To maximize both consistency and integration of messages, centralization of support agencies and suppliers was essential. Toward this end certain areas of promotional activities were relatively simple since BT already had arrangements and contracts with both advertising and PR support. These agencies were based in London but had delivery capabilities in almost all of the ports of call. Where no local supplier was present, affiliates were found, and a working arrangement was made to ensure that the local suppliers were part of the virtual groups. The part-time affiliates received the same core briefing and it was supplied to all agents.

The only exception to this strategy was for suppliers to build and install the showcase. Here a Boston-based supplier was appointed to oversee all design, configuration, and construction needs for each of the showcase sites (Sydney, Cape Town, Boston, and Southampton on the return leg). This supplier was responsible for briefing and arranging local contractors and labor for the physical work involved in delivering this element of the business program.

THE PROCESS

The processes that were put in place to deliver the various aspects of the business program were there to ensure consistency and integration of messages with the other aspects of the race. These centered on BT's own product set, including audio and video conferencing, E-mail, fax, and, of course, regular telephone contact with the partners. Considering the geographic spread of both ports of call and the distributed network of agencies, this meant that for almost two years a new way of living had to be established. From the center in the United Kingdom, where the core team was based, a working day could start at 6:00 AM—for conversations and discussions with Australia and New Zealand—and end around 2:00 AM the next day for audio calls with the United States. Teleworking became a necessity.

OUTCOMES FROM THE ACTIVITIES

Public Relations

The public relations value was estimated at £60 million in discounted advertising equivalent. This is a calculation reflecting how much BT would have had to pay to achieve the equivalent effects of communicating the messages through paid advertising.

Advertising

The role for local advertising (press and radio) was to let people know what the race was and that the boats would be in specific areas at specific times. The thousands of visitors to the docking sites indicated the success of the ad campaigns. From an attitudinal perspective, as part of its ongoing global awareness tracking program, BT's global awareness *and* understanding of its international activities and sales offers rose significantly throughout the race programs. In addition an independent research agency (Michael Herbert Associates) was appointed to conduct postevent interviews with guests to determine their views and levels of success. The general opinion from around the world was that the programs not only were enjoyable but also provided some valuable insights into the role and value of telecommunication as a strategic business asset. For example, one major customer viewed BT's sponsorship of the race as a positive means of communicating BT's pioneering and enterprising spirit. The nature of the race was seen as synonymous with the attributes of BT as a company—sailing against conventional wisdom voluntarily. Customers felt that the philosophy shows that BT is a company with new ideas for reaching its customers.

Face to Face

BT ran seminars for more than 2,000 specifically targeted customers in five major cities around the world and held private meetings with more than 250 presidents and board members from the world's leading companies. Also, BT managed to meet and greet around 3,000 local dignitaries and influencers from governments and professional organizations around the world.

The Internet

Forty million hits were made on the BT Global Challenge website over a period of ten months.

Events

Close to 3,000 people visited the showcases at the selected ports of call. Each visitor spent an average of ninety minutes in the showcase. Each of the four events was budgeted to cost around £80,000, yielding a cost per customer averaging just over £100 for a full day with BT. In return for this investment, new orders to BT and its offices around the world were in excess of £30 million over the following two to three years.

Hospitality

The total number of visitors who were exposed to some form of corporate hospitality fell somewhere in the region of 5,500, and although not particularly high, the quality and profile of these visitors were considerable. For example, having Bishop Desmond Tutu "bless the waves" before the yachts departed from Cape Town was a high point for many of the people associated with the race.

CONCLUSION

Global customers, global markets, global teamwork. By any standards the BT Global Challenge around-the-world yacht race was a great sponsorship opportunity. The race was a powerful opportunity to address BT customers around the world, and the result, by conventional sponsorship standards, was a huge success. Global media exposure for BT has been valued at £60 million. But more than this, the race was not seen as a one-shot event. BT has renewed its sponsorship for the BT Global Challenge in the year 2000 because of the success of the activities built into the race route. It is the world's biggest relationship program. For 2000 the yachts are bigger and have been redesigned in light of the experience gained in the first race. Major sponsorships are already in place, as are agreements on charity supports. BT Global Challenge yachts are being taken on mini-tours through Hong Kong, Japan, Malaysia, South Korea, New Zealand, and later in Europe and North America to raise enthusiasm and excitement for the main race.

EXCERPTS FROM FINANCIAL DATA

	1998	*1997*	*1996*
Turnover	£15,640M	£14,935M	£14,446M
Operating Profit	£3,657M	£3,245M	£3,100M
Earnings per share			
(before exceptional items)	31.7 pence	32.8 pence	31.6 pence

AUTHORS' NOTE

For readers interested in the dynamically developing telecommunication industry, the following materials may be useful:

1. "Dynamic Growth Shapes Industry of Tomorrow," *Financial Times*, special report on the Telecommunication Industry Worldwide, March 18, 1999.
2. Leer, A. (1999) *Editors of the Wired World*, FT Pitman Publishing, London.
3. Hills, T., and Cleevely, D. (1999) *Global Turf Wars*, Analysis Publications, Suite 2, Quayside, Cambridge CB5 8AB, UK.

Related links for more BT corporate information: http://www.bt.com; http://www.telfort.nl; http://www.viaginterkom.de .

Case Study 2: De Beers[1]

BACKGROUND

- Diamonds are mined in Australia, Zaire, Botswana, South Africa, and Namibia. Two hundred fifty tons of ore typically produce one carat of polished gem diamond.
- Gem diamonds have no functional value, and demand can be erratic. During the Great Depression, the diamond market shrank markedly. Thousands of miners in southern Africa lost their jobs.
- To combat market volatility, De Beers then founded the Central Selling Organization (CSO), contracting with the major diamond-producing nations (which represented 80 percent of world production) to purchase and value all annual output of rough diamonds at controlled prices, thus providing greater financial stability to underpin the cost of mining.
- In 1938 De Beers created the pioneering advertising slogan "A Diamond Is Forever." The phrase has now passed into common usage throughout the world and still forms the basis of the company's widely acclaimed marketing communication, which promotes diamonds as the "ultimate gift of love."

---

[1] This material has been reproduced and adapted with kind permission of the IPA and De Beers (1999). The original material was part of the IPA's Advertising Effectiveness Databank, which contains over 650 papers. Anyone can access any paper for a small fee; the IPA can also run searches on defined criteria. For further information about the IPA please contact IPA, 44 Belgrave Square, London SW1X 8QS. Tel: 0171 235 7020; Fax: 0171 245 9904. De Beers website: http://www.edata.co.za/debeers/

• De Beers promotes diamond jewelry globally to generate consumer demand or "pull." But, as the boom of the 1980s came to an end, investors, producers, and consumers strove to reduce their liabilities. In 1993, as rough-stone sales fell, retail jewelers continued to sell while simultaneously destocking to reduce liability.

• De Beers had to take significant steps to prevent the potential erosion of diamond jewelry sales and avert the long-term damage of the pipeline filling up, an ensuing oversupply and price drop, which in turn would impact stock prices, the mining and cutting industries, retail jewelers around the world, and the image saliency of diamonds.

OVERVIEW

Power in marketing communications is derived not just from creativity, but from the magnification and multiplication of the message through all forms of media and exploitation at potential customer points. Here we describe one creative idea, which adopted an IGMC approach by using a multiplicity of media vehicles but concentrated mainly on worldwide advertising developed by J. Walter Thompson Company (JWT) in conjunction with De Beers. It is important to note, and we state this in the text (see Chapter 8), that delegation of IGMC to agencies is usually predicated on a long-standing relationship of trust between client and agency. JWT is regarded as De Beers's global partner from an IGMC perspective. This relationship began in the early 1970s in Japan and then grew throughout the world to include twenty-six major countries.

MARKETING OBJECTIVES

The 1992–93 business objective for De Beers Consumer Marketing Division was to protect sales related to "core occasions" business segments in the face of deepening worldwide recession. Advertising was perceived to be the major IGMC mechanism. The role for CSO advertising was to manage effectively the esteem (and value) with which diamonds are perceived around the world.

MARKETING COMMUNICATION OBJECTIVES

1. to strengthen diamond jewelry's position as the ultimate gift of love in the face of a continued recession and increased competition
2. to translate those positive attitudes into purchase behavior

Strategy

Advertising was used as the primary IGMC driver, coupled with other below-the-line media, to present the core values of diamonds (beauty, rarity, uniqueness, brilliance, purity, etc.) via their emotional resonance as a gift of love. The challenge was for diamonds to "own" special occasions to the extent that consumers believe the cash investment to be emotionally, rather than financially, rewarding. This could be achieved by one of two methods according to market development:

• By maximizing the return from the mature markets by customers' "trading up" to more expensive pieces of diamond jewelry. These markets include the United Kingdom, United States, and Italy, where diamond ownership is around 70 percent.

• By growing developing markets via increased penetration of diamond jewelry ownership resulting in growth of the numbers of pieces sold. This "acquisition" segment includes markets such as Thailand, Mexico, and Arab countries, where gold is strong but diamond traditions are less well established. In Thailand, for instance, penetration is a mere 5 percent and is concentrated in cities.

CONTEXTUAL CIRCUMSTANCES

Engagement

Within Europe practices differ widely; 70 percent of United Kingdom couples currently buy diamond engagement rings. In Germany there is no engagement ring tradition; couples simply get married.

Marriage

In Islamic circles bridal sets (necklace, earrings, bracelet, and ring) symbolize parental care and are given by both sets of parents as a nest egg for the bride.

Other Occasions

American traditions include the "Sweet Sixteen" diamond for fathers to give to their daughters in recognition of their transition to womanhood. The birth of a child is often commemorated with diamond jewelry.

Other Jewels

Japan has historically had a pearl-based jewel tradition. There was no Japanese word for *diamond* until the 1960s. Japan now forms the second-largest consumer diamond jewelry market in the world, after the United States.

Other Precious Metals

In Eastern cultures, from Turkey to the Far East, everything revolves around gold as a form of security or portable wealth.

Social Changes

Diamond sales have historical links to the social traditions of marriage and celebrations, which not only vary in their significance between countries and cultures but are themselves undergoing change. In the West family structures have loosened; marriage rates are falling, and divorce rates are increasing. Marriage at later ages delays childbirth. In 1970 there were seven to ten marriages per 1,000 population, and the mean age at first marriage was twenty-three. By 1993 the number of marriages per 1,000 population had dropped from four to seven, and the mean age at first marriage was twenty-five. Additionally, the divorce rate increased by 50 percent between 1970 and 1993.

SUMMARY OF MARKETING COMMUNICATION STRATEGIC CHALLENGES

- to unify all the important mature and developing countries under a single approach flexible enough to recognize local needs
- to identify a single powerful consumer motivation out of a turmoil of national differences among markets as culturally, religiously, historically, and economically diverse as Europe and Asia, the Gulf States and the United States, Australia, and South America
- to provide guidance to enhance the creative idea rather than change it as it traversed those boundaries

TACTICS

A Change in Media

Historically De Beers ran predominantly women's print campaigns displaying a variety of jewelry to suit different markets' needs and budgets. The recession demanded more aggressive consumer media to successfully ratchet the emotional response to the "ultimate gift of love" message. Television and cinema were chosen as the major advertising media, together with deployment of retail point-of-sales support for diamond retailers. The public relations function supported the advertising strategy by accessorizing "stars" and leading models in fashion shoots and holding events in each country that supported the ultimate image.

Television advertising allowed De Beers to reach a broader target audience, consumers watching as couples and evoking a strong emotional response between them simultaneously. The media target audience was primarily adults over age twenty-five, although engagement ring cinema audiences were slightly younger. Due to the length of the purchase cycle, a policy of quality programming was deployed, where joint viewing was anticipated. This would enable high saliency levels to be reached and maintained.

Added Production Value

Each market historically had produced its own print campaigns of between two and ten different executions. Photographing diamonds, especially against skin, is notoriously difficult. They're relatively small and technically difficult to light. Each diamond is individual and reacts to light in its own way. Print production quality was always an expensive challenge.

- The estimated annual worldwide print production budget for De Beers was in excess of $1.5 million.
- For the switch to television, the use of new techniques with lasers and fiber-optic lighting combined with stark contrast of shadows provided the ideal backdrop to display the scintillation of each individual stone. The production costs for the first three TV executions, which ran for over three years, were $700,000.
- Not only was the advertising more effective in communicating the appeal of diamond jewelry to a wide audience, it was also more cost effective to produce, enabling markets that wouldn't normally warrant TV advertising to share its benefits.
- Usage of point-of-sale and accompanying marketing public relations enhanced and supplemented the imagery.

The Brilliant Creative Idea—Intimate Anonymity

The power of the resultant "Shadows" campaign idea lies in the anonymity of the people and the setting and the prominent showcasing of the jewelry at the musically climactic moment of giving. This apparently simple device carries a complex raft of messages and associations. Consumer feedback about the worth, desirability, and suitability of diamond jewelry emanated from a breadth of elements within the campaign, building to a whole greater than the sum of the parts—in other words, synergy.

A powerful music track captured the attention, communicated drama, emotion, and romance. It had all the sophistication to which all diamond advertising must aspire. The visual intrigue of the shadows was involving, providing something to decipher and imagine. The sophistication of black and white images stood out amid color commercials.

The anonymity of the shadows, while evidently human in form, was also mysterious, romantic, and allowed consumers to see themselves in the images. Race, color, class, and age become irrelevant in the shadow play— key to the cross-cultural acceptance of the message.

The story encapsulated a relationship. It was simultaneously involving and inspirational. And the production technique was a dramatic showcase for the product: big, beautiful, and highly desirable.

ACTION

The "Shadows" campaign ran in Australia, Austria, Belgium, Brazil, Canada, France, Germany, Great Britain, Italy, Japan, Kuwait, Mexico, Netherlands, Oman, Philippines, Russia, Saudi Arabia, South Africa, Spain, Thailand, Turkey, United Arab Emirates, and the United States.

Advertising spending was roughly 0.4 percent of sales, with a worldwide marketing budget of US$558 million, significantly dwarfing the previous magazine budget.

CONTROL

For several years De Beers has commissioned regular brand tracking surveys to investigate advertising awareness and diamond jewelry imagery and desirability among adult consumers in key markets.

The timing of these studies varies by market, and the questionnaires are not precisely comparable. Image parameters measured in one market may differ from another. The perfect continuous tracking study worldwide is an unaffordable option.

Nevertheless, advertising awareness, advertising "likability," and attitudes toward diamond jewelry and its desirability were measured.

RESULTS

The advertising and the promotional elements proved to be successful on a global basis. Tracking studies in major markets showed that consumers saw, remembered, and liked the campaign. Their positive attitudes toward diamond jewelry held strong, as did their "intention to purchase in the next 12 months."

These attitudes were reflected in steady value growth. The campaign helped bolster confidence among the conservative jewelry trade, who were happy to recognize the business contribution made by the advertising in their markets. As a result they stopped destocking and continued to offer the customer a good choice of jewelry.

American retailers reported an 8 percent increase in retail sales ($2,715 million). Since the United States is the world's biggest diamond market and received about 31 percent of De Beers's US$558 million worldwide campaign budget, this result alone represents a significant return on investment.

In short, mass media advertising, coupled with below-the-line elements, using a single campaign around the world, worked to build shareholder and trade confidence and maintained a healthy balance between short-term volume sales and long-term image exclusivity among consumers, in spite of the deep recession.

Sales Performance

Sales of rough gem diamonds by the CSO in 1998 were $3.35 billion, 28 percent below the previous year's sales of $4.64 billion. Sales in the second half of 1998 were $1.65 billion, 7 percent lower than in the same period in 1997. Trading conditions were difficult throughout the year, and anticipation that second-half sales would be higher than first-half sales failed to materialize as a result of the global economic uncertainties. Good levels of retail sales of diamond jewelry in the United States and to a lesser extent in Europe failed to compensate for lower sales in Japan and East Asia. Sales performance in terms of rough diamond sales by the CSO is given in Table 1, followed by some income data in Table 2.

TABLE 1
CSO Sales of Rough Diamonds 1988–1998

Year	Total Sales US$billion (rounded)
1988	4.2
1989	4.1
1990	4.2
1991	3.9
1992	3.4
1993	4.4
1994	4.3
1995	4.5
1996	4.8
1997	4.6
1998	3.6

TABLE 2
Combined Income Statement for De Beers

	1997 US$M	1998 US$M
Turnover	6,418	4,492
Headline Earnings	1,044	639

Consideration of the share price over the period 1994 to 1999 shows significant growth from 1994 to 1997, followed by a precipitous decline from late 1997 through all of 1998 and some growth in early 1999.

Case Study 3: Dow Chemical[1]

BACKGROUND

The Dow Chemical Company is a global science- and technology-based company that develops and manufactures a portfolio of chemical, plastic, and agricultural products and services for customers in 168 countries around the world. With annual sales of more than $18 billion, Dow conducts its operations through fourteen global businesses employing 39,000 people. The company has 121 manufacturing sites in 32 countries and supplies more than 3,500 products.

In the 1980s Dow discovered that its customers, like itself, were becoming deeply involved in the quality movement—improving processes and outputs, raising product quality, reducing errors, responding more effectively to customers and the marketplace, and so on. All the lessons that had been learned from Deming, Juran, and the other leaders of the quality movement were creating massive changes in how Dow's customers and prospects were operating and managing their businesses.

Most of these quality-oriented organizations began to focus their efforts on improving customer value and satisfaction, becoming more responsive to growing competition, and focusing on the need to drive costs downward and customer satisfaction upward. One of the objectives of this increased emphasis on quality was to develop programs and systems that would enable them to become more effective competitors around the world. Many of them began to develop interdependent systems with their own customers and to rely more on relationships than on price and promotion.

[1] This case was developed with the assistance of the marketing communications group at Dow Chemical in Midland, Michigan. We are indebted to them for sharing these insights.

EXTERNAL PRESSURES ON DOW

One major outcome of this quality initiative for many Dow customers was the standardization of processes, systems, and logistics throughout their organizations, particularly in manufacturing. For Dow, which was primarily a raw material or intermediates supplier, this move to standardization of both processes and products had major implications for how it related to customers and prospects. Where once it had supplied a variety of products and services based on the end products its customers developed for individual markets in a variety of geographies, Dow soon discovered its customers were becoming increasingly global in their needs and operations. That is, the internal standardization developed by their customers began to migrate down and impact Dow in terms of what products and services customers wanted and needed and so on. Thus Dow began to feel the effect on its business as a result of its customers' steps toward globalization.

To respond to its customers' initiatives, both internal and external, Dow began to standardize its products and processes in line with the specific products and systems that were being standardized by its customers. That meant changes in production, logistics, sales, and even marketing communication. Dow management reasoned, "If our customers are standardizing products and systems around the world, we must do the same." Thus, in the late 1980s, Dow took the first steps toward moving from a multidomestic or international to a truly global organization. While the standardization of products, services, and activities took many forms, one of the most critical was the standardization of information processes and technology and, most of all, communication both inside and outside Dow.

INTERNAL BARRIERS AT DOW

Over the years Dow, like so many other companies, had become quite decentralized. Managers of individual plants and product lines had developed their own manufacturing systems and processes, their own sales and marketing teams and systems, and their own communication approaches. The result? A worldwide agglomeration of products, information technology, service support, and resource allocation. Each functional area in the Dow organization was developing and delivering what it perceived to be the needs of its individual customers in its specific areas of responsibility. As a result, when attempts were made to cross borders or geographical boundaries, sometimes the solutions Dow facilitated didn't fit customer needs and requirements. Sometimes the solutions were successful, and sometimes they weren't. The problem was, the emphasis of the Dow solution was on what each Dow business deemed relevant rather than leveraging what the customer needed or wanted.

So, one of the first steps in globalization for Dow was to standardize its own internal operating systems. In other words, Dow Chemical had to get every employee, every plant, and every division—in short, the whole organization—operating on the same internal processes and methodologies. Not a small task for an organization that operated in 168 countries, had 39,000 employees, and supplied in excess of 3,500 products to its customers, not to mention the support and services that went along with those products.

Dow began the global process internally, not externally. To standardize and consolidate, Dow contracted with IBM to provide a common information and communication system that would tie the entire Dow organization together. By having a common information technology platform that would include internal communication, production, process, and management systems, Dow began to think like and act like a more contemporary global organization. Out with all the personal favorites, the software systems, the hardware, the laptops, everything. In with a system that would work for everyone so that all could work together.

BECOMING GLOBAL (AND TRANSPARENT)

Having standardized its internal operating systems, the next step for Dow was to offer that standardization approach to its customers. In other words, Dow began to consider how connecting its customers to its systems and bringing its customers closer to the Dow organization would improve business operations for both parties. Dow employees had to confront the prospect of customers accessing the Dow systems to get product information, place orders, obtain technological support, access research reports, view manuals, compare alternatives, or sometimes just get a Dow opinion on problems they were having. The Dow goal? To become transparent to its customers.

At the same time, Dow began to think about how to improve and enhance its delivery of marketing and communication materials. Traditionally Dow had developed and delivered its marketing and communication programs primarily as support for the sales force, to support existing products and processes, and to promote new products. While over the years Dow had moved aggressively to make its marketing communication managers an active part of the various business groups, this new move to globalization meant even more changes. One very successful move was to connect marketing communication's role in developing strategy and executing programs to the activities of customer inquiry response. In this way the return on communications investment and the capability to measure effectiveness were connected. In addition, and maybe more important, the customer and market feedback loop was built into the business, and marketing planning activities were enhanced.

Historically Dow had considered marketing communication an important but not necessarily a critical element in the Dow customer package. Like many other business-to-business organizations, Dow had focused its efforts on its technical and product superiority. Those had been the key elements in helping customers and prospects use Dow's raw materials to build and deliver marketplace products. Thus marketing communication had been focused on supporting the efforts of the sales force and the technical team. But the new approach of becoming more customer and market focused caused marketing communication management to radically rethink its role and its approaches. Rather than Dow deciding what products and services it wanted to promote, what if Dow let customers decide what information they wanted to access, when and where and how they needed it, and in the form they wanted it? What a radical thought—letting customers decide what they wanted to hear from Dow, not what Dow wanted to say to them.

So the first real steps in interactive, customer-oriented global communication were taken. Dow began putting most of its marketing communication material into various digital and electronic forms. While it is not practical to make everything electronic, as much as possible Dow was going electronic. Archiving the digital information was the foundation of this effort so that both the customers and the marketing communication professionals would have access to any information and delivery format that they desired. While there were major cost savings for Dow in this process, the more important result was that these new electronic systems and processes allowed its customers to access information and material in the form they would like and could use. For example, if one customer wanted hard copy, she could simply print it out in her own office. It's an easy task when the customer decides and Dow doesn't have to guess.

ORGANIZING FOR GLOBAL COMMUNICATION

This approach to putting the customers in control of communication created major changes in the marketing and communication groups. Giving customers access to all forms of information and data in the form they wanted it, whether that be print or electronic, hard copy or print on demand, became the process by which Dow began to globalize its business. Down came the traditional boundaries of time, space, geography, and culture. Dow became a twenty-four-hour-per-day, seven-day-per-week information supplier.

As globalization progressed, Dow recognized the need for a new organizational structure and approach. Global customers need global suppliers. As a result, in 1997 Dow went through a radical restructuring and reorganization. Today Dow is organized into fifteen basic business groups: Adhesives, Sealants & Coatings, Chemicals, Dow Agro Sciences LLC, Emulsion Polymers, Engineering Plastics, Epoxy Products & Intermediates, Fabricated Products, Hydrocarbons & Energy, Insite® Technology, New Businesses, Polyethylene, Polystyrene, Polyurethanes, and Specialty Chemicals.

These SBUs are focused on customers and solutions and Dow capabilities, not on plants and products and geographies. Increasingly, Dow is finding that its customers, through the standardization processes of the 1980s, are global in their needs and ways they wish to be served. So the new Dow organization is designed to provide global answers for these global customers. One team is assigned to a customer, and that group is empowered to fill that customer's global needs, solve its global problems, and service all its requirements no matter the geography.

THE FUTURE

Dow Chemical is on a continuous journey of globalization from a product, logistics, marketing, and communication standpoint. It has flipped the usual planning process upside down and turned marketing communication inside out. It hasn't been an easy task, nor is it completed. But it is under way, and it is working. Globalization is making major changes at Dow, creating whole new types of marketing and marketing communication programs, revising the roles of managers, and revitalizing every process.

Case Study 4: Orange PLC[1]

BACKGROUND

Since Orange launched in April 1994, it has maintained its brand image in both advertising and below-the-line marketing communication. In the process the London-based company has positioned itself as the mobile phone brand that "owns" the future of telecommunication. As a late entrant into the market, Orange had to carve out a niche for itself. At the time the market was cluttered with many different and confusing messages about mobile phones. To cut through the clutter Orange communication had to be consistent and motivating. While everyone else was talking about mobile phones, Orange talked about "wire-free communication" in a clean world that was both optimistic and uncluttered. This clean sense of optimism is consistent with everything Orange does.

Orange required much expertise from outside agencies. In the early years Wolf Olins created and has continued to develop and supervise Orange's corporate identity. WCRS is responsible for all above-the-line advertising and helps coordinate activity with the other agencies as new

[1] Grateful thanks are extended to WCRS for its kind permission to use the case material reported here. This case material has been adapted from the WCRS paper "The FTSE's Bright: The FTSE's Orange" submitted for IPA Effectiveness Awards, published in June 1999. The adapted material is provided with the kind permission of Cameron Saunders and Dan Izbicki of WCRS and the IPA. The resource is the IPA's Data Bank, which contains over 650 papers. Anyone may access any paper for a small fee, and the IPA can also run searches on defined criteria. For further information please contact: IPA, 44 Belgrave Square, London SW1X 8QS. Tel: 0171 235 7020; Fax 0171 245 9904.

campaigns are launched. Dutton Merrifield ensures that all copy and glossaries of terms are consistent and provides customer communication leaflets and bill inserts. OptionOne (now 999 [Scotland]) provided point-of-sale, and WWAV worked on direct marketing. All is managed and coordinated between the agencies and the Orange campaigns and design team. All agencies are based in London or have London offices.

Since launch, Orange has used a multimedia mix to create synergy across all sectors. Creative consistency and media phasing create a sense of ubiquity for the brand. The Orange audience is given a taste of a new campaign through the use of posters that hint at the message but do not tell the whole story. Television and print ads then follow to fulfill the campaign explanation. This is joined by shop displays, information leaflets, bill inserts, and fulfillment information for inquirers.

The compound effect is far more powerful than a disparate campaign that uses each marketing discipline independently. The end result ensures that the message is absorbed on several levels and is more effective. This saves Orange money. Rather than potentially confusing consumers with independent creative work by sector, a powerful brand image is formed and maintained, and Orange gets more out of each pound spent as messages and images are shared and remembered.

INTRODUCTION

This case study covers the period from April 1996 to April 1998, which represents the first two years of Orange as a publicly listed company (PLC) on the UK stock exchange. As a PLC, the purpose of Orange changed to one of creating *shareholder value*. This imperative represented a significant sea change in corporate strategy in terms of pre- and post-share-launch. Prior to going public, the focus had been on *volume share* to gain critical mass. With the new focus the company could not sacrifice margin for the sake of volume. In light of the business plan Orange PLC was precluded from two hard-hitting strategies pursued by the competition—price cuts and distribution growth. While the former would compromise short- and long-term subscriber values, the latter would either involve high fixed costs (building or buying a national network of wholly owned shops) or endanger short- and long-term revenues (through increased dealer incentives). Instead, to achieve *value share*, Orange PLC had three core objectives:

1. Earnings growth: Evidence that the market is growing at an acceptable rate, given macroeconomic and market conditions.

2. Earnings security: Providing investors with the confidence that the PLC's revenue is secure. Usually for a period of ten years hence.
3. Risk diversification: Spreading the risk for investors. Analysts look for a PLC's capacity to spread its investments over a number of potential growth areas. For Orange this relates directly to its ability to create a strong and transferable *brand*.

To achieve these objectives, Orange committed itself to an unequivocally brand-led strategy. If Orange could exert enough *brand pull*, this would likely prove the most effective value-enhancing insulation against relative weakness in terms of price and distribution. Heightened brand desirability would prove to be Orange PLC's key competitive advantage.

In this context, as the brand public face, integrated marketing communication spearheaded by advertising had a central role to play. Thus, for this case, it is unnecessary to make distinctions between communication and media strategy and the brand-led business strategy. The strategies are indivisible, since from its inception as a company in an increasingly ferocious business environment Orange PLC's integrated approaches have made a unique contribution across every element of the business. Here we attempt to demonstrate how IMC has helped Orange PLC deliver against the core drivers of the business strategy, illustrated in Exhibit 1.

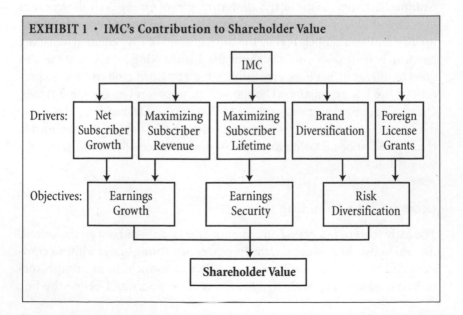

EXHIBIT 1 · IMC's Contribution to Shareholder Value

This case will demonstrate how IMC contributes to developing share price value, in this case from £2.45 at initial offer (April 1996) to £4.50 (April 1998). And this despite a period when Orange's volume share of the market has been under ever-increasing pressure, further confirming investor confidence in the brand-led, value-based strategy.

MARKET CONTEXT

Since 1996 there have been three significant trends in the UK mobile telecommunications market:

Competitive Price Cuts

The main competitors in the UK mobile telecom market are Cellnet, Vodafone, and One2One. As competitors have cut prices, the Orange core tariff proposition has remained unchanged. This means that Orange is now about 5 percent more expensive than Vodafone or Cellnet, and 20 to 35 percent more expensive than One2One. While this price premium has inevitably impacted volume share, it has not affected Orange PLC's value share of the market.

Tied Distribution

Significant changes in the distribution strategies of Orange's rivals were seen in 1998 and 1999. For example, Vodafone spent millions of pounds buying up distribution channels that by the third quarter of 1997 equated to having 250 wholly owned shops throughout the United Kingdom. One2One also grew to mirror its network expansion, which by April 1998 covered 98 percent of the UK population (Orange was at 96 percent at the same stage). One2One adopted a strategy similar to Vodafone's. Meanwhile, Cellnet also made significant acquisitions, expanding distribution beyond the nationwide chain of BT shops. During this time period, Orange opened thirteen self-branded shops.

Increased Ad Spending

The early years of integrated campaigning for Orange did not go unnoticed. All four networks now appreciate the power of a strong brand within a commodified market. The result has been heavy investment by all competitors in brand advertising, with significant media support and below-the-line

EXHIBIT 2 · Media Expenditure and Share of Voice, January 1994 to April 1998

Orange	Cellnet	Vodafone	One2One	Total	
£m	£m	£m	£m	£m	
72	58	39	67	236	Media Spend

Source: IPA. Figures rounded for sake of comparison.

activities. Orange has significantly outspent its rivals in the advertising stakes, as shown in Exhibit 2.

The effect of this continuous competitive activity is summarized in Exhibit 3, which shows the percentage of each operator's market share attributable to the key sales drivers within the marketplace.

Based on the data in Exhibit 3, it can be seen that Vodafone and One2One's market shares are most sensitive to distribution. One2One is most seasonal, especially in relation to fourth-quarter (Christmas) sales. Orange is the most susceptible to price sensitivity. Cellnet seems to be somewhat reliant on its familiarity and residual past effects. One2One is benefiting from renewed momentum since its relaunch in early 1996. One2One and Orange are the most advertising sensitive.

EXHIBIT 3 · Short-Term Market Share Sales Drivers

	Orange %	Cellnet %	Vodafone %	One2One %
Distribution	5.3	7.1	16.2	11.6
Pricing	12.3	0.1	9.3	0.1
Previous Sales	16.6	51.2	16.7	35.1
Seasonality	13.6	12.0	11.9	25.8
Other Features*	37.0	26.4	42.4	19.1
Short-Term Advertising	15.3	3.3	3.6	8.4

* This includes handset advertising, handset choice, cofunded advertising, coverage, macroeconomic factors, and long-term effects, as well as the multitude of sales promotional activities that are a constant feature of this market. The complexity of the mobile phone market makes it very difficult to disentangle these individual variables; hence here they are grouped together (see Chapter 10).

THE ORANGE BUSINESS STRATEGY

One very rapid way of increasing market share is by lowering prices. However, this would have fundamentally opposed Orange's long-term strategic development. Moreover, lower-cost tariffs would likely attract lower-value customers. In a business where high acquisition costs equate to low-contributing customers, this can result in overall network losses. Instead, Orange PLC pursued a brand-led, shareholder-value-enhancing strategy. We now assess marketing communication contribution against the following measures.

Earnings Growth

Earnings growth is enhanced by two factors: an increase in the net number of subscribers, essential in an expanding marketplace, and an increase in the revenue from those subscribers, a combination of quality and quantity.

Increasing the Net Subscriber Base. Orange has been the third-biggest network operator since it overtook One2One in January 1996, as Exhibit 4 shows.

Throughout the period April 1996 to April 1998, Orange was neither the cheapest nor the most readily available of the four network operators. The business strategy required the IMC process to exercise positive dispositions toward the brand by potential new subscribers. During this period the advertising-led process was ranked consistently above the three competitors. The best descriptor regarding the decision to connect to Orange was brand

EXHIBIT 4 · Network Subscriber Bases (as of April 1, 1998)	
Company	Subscriber Base '000
One2One	1,198
Cellnet	3,077
Vodafone	3,431
Orange	1,318

Source: FT Mobile Telecommunications

Note: Orange was last into the mobile telecommunications market, where it faced two established competitors (Cellnet and Vodafone) and a successful new entrant (One2One).

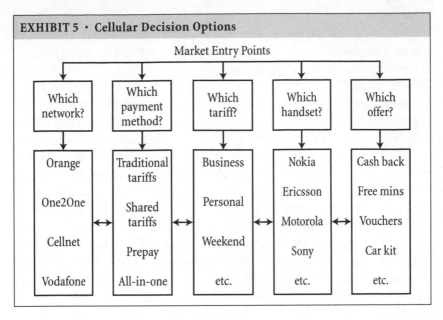

EXHIBIT 5 · Cellular Decision Options

Market Entry Points

Which network?	Which payment method?	Which tariff?	Which handset?	Which offer?
Orange	Traditional tariffs	Business	Nokia	Cash back
One2One	Shared tariffs	Personal	Ericsson	Free mins
Cellnet		Weekend	Motorola	Vouchers
	Prepay		Sony	Car kit
Vodafone	All-in-one	etc.	etc.	etc.

preference and promotional offers, accounting for 80 percent of stated decisions (58 percent and 22 percent, respectively). "Brand pull" was also exhibited by customers' consistently ranking Orange higher in terms of brand consideration (purchase intent).

The mobile phone market, in the United Kingdom as elsewhere, is inherently complex, and the decision-making process is equally complex. Potential customers must consider not only advertising per se but the whole range of marketing communication variables, illustrated in Exhibit 5.

The four key drivers of the decisions within the mobile network market were found to be pricing, distribution, the market trend, and seasonality. Using an advanced statistical model, analysis shows that communication, spearheaded by advertising, has contributed 15.25 percent of Orange sales since flotation. Given Orange has connected an additional 772,000 subscribers since flotation, this equates to 110,320 connections. Averaging this over lifetime network customer value is captured in the following equation:

$$(\text{annual revenue per subscriber} - \text{cost of acquisition})$$
$$\times$$
$$\text{customer lifetime}$$

IMC's contribution from April 1996 to April 1998 therefore represents £144.34 million [110,320 × (£497−£225) × 4.83 years], which equates to more than three times payback on this one measure alone.

However, the Orange business plan requires that earnings growth come not only from attracting a volume of subscribers but also from maximizing the revenue obtained from each customer.

Maximizing Subscriber Revenue. Marketing communication had the opportunity to maximize revenue in two ways: attracting high-revenue customers at the outset or encouraging all subscribers to increase their usage.

Taking the combination of these two factors, as well as company ability to retain its customers, has enabled Orange to increase its net share of market value (1996: 34 percent; 1997: 37 percent), despite a declining net market volume (1996: 29 percent; 1997: 25 percent). Orange has attracted the highest revenue per customer of the four networks.

The marketing communication role in this has been to attract appropriate customers through a very distinctive style and concomitant communication of specific messages. Orange PLC's response handling system is capable of linking all marketing-communication-driven (including advertising) inquiries. Simultaneously, Orange advertising continues to communicate many different services by various media (led by television), well ahead of the nearest ranked competitor. Notably, communicating Orange's value-added services not only helps attract new customers but also encourages greater awareness among existing customers. Communication also facilitates and underpins increasing usage.

Earnings Security

Mobile communication constitutes a growth market throughout the world, with the concomitant promise of long-term returns for shareholders. Maximizing shareholder value is a matter of not only attracting quality customers (which delivers earnings growth) but also maintaining them (delivering earnings security).

Maximizing Subscriber Lifetime. The marketplace's measure of loyalty is *churn*—the percentage of the base that leaves the network each year. Orange has the lowest levels of churn in the United Kingdom, as shown in Exhibit 6.

Orange's level of churn is influenced primarily by overall service and perceived quality of the Orange network. In addition, Orange PLC has capitalized on its customers' sensitivity to Orange marketing communication. Among numerous promoted products and services, there are two that research has identified as being particularly relevant to the subscriber base in minimizing churn—network coverage (58 percent) and price (21 percent).

EXHIBIT 6 • Network Churn Levels		
	Churn (%)	Customer Lifetime (years)
One2One	25.0	4.0
Cellnet	32.0	3.1
Vodafone	28.0	3.5
Orange	20.7	4.8

Communicating Improved Coverage. It is not enough simply to improve network rollout but to communicate this to customer groups. Campaigns were developed to achieve this objective and to encourage significant brand values. This allowed Orange customers to become brand evangelists (via positive word of mouth and legitimization), countering negative perceptions of Orange coverage among potential customers. It also increased Orange customer loyalty by countering the prime reason for churning off the network. During these campaigns, perceptions of enhanced coverage among customers increased.

Communicating Value for Money. In a highly price-sensitive market, it was imperative that Orange customers be dissuaded from switching to cheaper alternative networks, particularly given the price-led strategies of key competitors. Notably, in the months when marketing communication spending was low or nonexistent, satisfaction levels decayed rapidly. The effect of marketing communication overall, in this sense, was to maintain customer satisfaction levels. This was regarded as a long-term and growing contribution to marketing communication for the Orange brand.

Quantifying Marketing Communication's Contribution to Earnings Security. The combined effects of marketing communication were to reduce churn levels and enhance satisfaction, equivalent to an additional customer life span of 3.43 months. The average revenue per subscriber is £497.14 or £41.42 per month. Marketing communication can therefore claim £142.07 (3.43 months × £41.42) of the lifetime value of an average Orange customer connected during the period 1996 to 1998. The total number of new customers between April 1996 and April 1998 was 772,000. Marketing communication's contribution to earnings security can therefore be calculated as 772,000 × £142.07 = £102.6 million.

Risk Diversification

While Orange is a proven success in the United Kingdom mobile telecommunications marketplace, it has an obligation to create further shareholder value through diversification of its interests so that it is not reliant on one market.

Foreign License Bids. In the particular case of Orange, investors and analysts have remained concerned about the rate of growth of the UK mobile telecommunications market, which has lagged behind other European markets, as shown in Exhibit 7.

Opportunities for foreign license acquisition have formed a core element of Orange PLC's risk diversification. Many countries and governments are passing through an extended phase of deregulation in which fixed and mobile companies are now competing. The difficulty is in converting bids into awarded licenses.

Many of the bid situations are ongoing (e.g., Sri Lanka, Ireland, Austria). In some cases bids have already been successful (e.g., Northern Ireland, Israel, Switzerland). But where Orange has won bids as part of an international consortium, the Orange *brand* has been shown to play a pivotal role.

> Orange's experience in the UK mobile phone market, where it was a late entrant but now has one of the best recognized brand names, is understood to have counted heavily with the Swiss authorities.
>
> *Financial Times*, April 21, 1998

EXHIBIT 7 · Past and Predicted Cellular Penetration				
	1997 %	1998 %	1999 %	2000 %
Norway	34	37	40	45
Spain	10	14	17	22
Sweden	35	37	40	44
UK	15	16	18	22
Italy	17	22	26	31

Source: FT Mobile Markets

EXHIBIT 8 · Judgment Criteria for the PCN Swiss License	
Criteria	%
Capability	20
Network rollout	20
Coverage	20
Innovations	20
Marketing	20

This international success has been driven by the inherent transferability of the brand. In a global telecommunications market, plagued by the familiar problems of nationalized monopolies and consumer confusion, Orange marketing communication has been designed to offer international appeal. This has been researched successfully in countries as diverse as Belgium, Greece, Sri Lanka, the Netherlands, Israel, and Switzerland. Integrated marketing communication, spearheaded by advertising, has thus contributed significantly to the global potential or the Orange brand.

> Given that Orange has created one of the strongest world-wide cellular brands, we feel that it is an extremely attractive partner for those looking to bid for and run [personal communication network] licenses in Europe.
>
> SBC Warburg, Orange Analyst's Report, March 1998

In view of the fact that much of Orange PLC's international potential is latent, it is very difficult to put a full value on IMC's contribution in foreign license bids. A useful rule of thumb for contribution is quantified in relation to the successful Swiss bid for license, shown in Exhibit 8.

Marketing communication was perceived to play a significant role in gaining and maintaining the Swiss license (current value is estimated at £100 million; and the contribution of marketing communications to this amounts to £7.4 million).

This example indicates the enormous potential value of Orange marketing communication worldwide, with the implication being that this has contributed similarly to Orange's success. Indeed the Orange name is now considered to be so powerful that Hutchison Whampoa, the huge Hong Kong–based backer of Orange, is considering rebranding all its worldwide operations as Orange.

Appendix 2
The Oral-B Study Case[1]

GLOBALIZE OR LOCALIZE: CHALLENGES IN INDIA

This case illustrates the situation many marketing communication managers face: whether or not to use a global or a local approach in their communication program. It provides most of the data and information available to Oral-B managers when they were making the decision a few years ago. We have masked some of the data for proprietary reasons. We do not provide the solution developed and successfully executed, for we believe it is more important for global marketing communication managers to come to their own conclusions than to be presented with a single solution.

NEW DELHI, INDIA

Sanjay Kapoor was staring outside the window of his second-floor office onto the busy streets of New Delhi. He had just sent his fax to Redwood City, California, international headquarters of Oral-B Laboratories. That was where Steve Perry, the international marketing director for the firm, was located. Sanjay had recently joined Oral-B as the country manager. He had trained in the United Kingdom in various functions of the Gillette Company, of which Oral-B was an operating division, to prepare him for this new respon-

---

[1] This case is made available with the kind permission of Oral-B, Redwood City, California, and RK Swamy/BBDO, Bombay, India. It is not intended to evaluate management decisions and is to be used only as an educational tool in helping managers consider all aspects of the particular situation described.

sibility. Now back in India, his primary function was to orchestrate the launch of the Oral-B brand of toothbrushes and dental floss in the country. If the launch was successful, he foresaw a bright future in the organization.

After a great deal of thought and considerable deliberation with his small marketing team and his advertising agency, Sanjay had sent a detailed fax to Steve outlining the Indian marketing situation. He was seeking Steve's opinion on what type of introduction should be used. The fax was only an attempt to involve his headquarters in the decision. He knew the final decision was his to make.

Simply put, Sanjay believed he had three choices: (1) He could produce locally developed advertising and supporting materials for the launch of Oral-B toothbrushes in India. (2) He could run the available international advertising materials as they had been used in other markets. Or (3) he could adapt the international material for use in India. If he decided to adapt the materials, how could that best be done?

These questions had been bothering Sanjay for some time. He knew that he had to make up his mind soon and develop his final recommendation. His fifteen years of marketing experience told Sanjay that this was one of the most crucial decisions he would make in the launch of Oral-B toothbrushes in India.

If the communication package was done right, Sanjay knew half the battle in India would have been won. If they got the communication wrong, the product would not move, the company would experience stocking and return problems with the trade, and the substantial investment planned in advertising would be wasted. Indeed the launch itself would be a fiasco.

Thinking about the available international creative materials, Sanjay knew they had been used successfully in many parts of the world, including many parts of Asia. He knew the advertising focused clearly on the strong dentist heritage Oral-B had established over the years. The advertising was also quite simple and focused. He also knew that if he used the international advertising in India, headquarters would automatically endorse it. In addition, the cost to produce a new TV commercial and other materials would be saved and the entire available budget could all be spent in media.

But the question was: Would the international advertising that had worked so well in other countries work as well in India?

Sanjay knew he had a tough market to crack. He was up against the international giants that operated in the Indian market—Colgate and Unilever. In addition, the market was flooded with a host of local toothbrush competitors, all of whom were competing ferociously by offering lower-priced products that were of fairly good quality.

Although most international toothbrush marketers had lots of international communication materials to use, most companies tended to use locally produced advertising and marketing communication materials. Sanjay was not sure whether the international Oral-B commercials and approach would appeal to the Indian consumer. He especially had doubts about whether the commercials would cut through the clutter and give Oral-B the quick awareness and trial that the brand required for a smooth takeoff in the Indian market.

No matter which way he went, Sanjay knew that he would be responsible for the outcome. Well, I suppose that's why they are paying me all this money, he thought as he turned away from the window.

REDWOOD CITY, CALIFORNIA

Steve Perry liked to start his day early. At 7:30 A.M. when he walked in, the first thing he noticed was a fax from Oral-B's Indian operation. As he read the Indian market review, which was very well organized, he came upon the questions. These are tough decisions, Steve thought. I need to work through them just like the Indian team has done to provide them with any real help in their decision.

In the fax, Sanjay Kapoor, the country manager in India for whom he had great respect, had asked for Steve's opinion on what Oral-B should do with its advertising to introduce the Oral-B line of toothbrushes. Should it use its proven international materials, or should it be producing new materials in India, particularly a TV commercial?

Steve Perry had moved into his job as international marketing director of Oral-B three years ago. In that time he had overseen the expansion of the brand into many new countries in Eastern Europe, Asia-Pacific, and Latin America. Some of these markets were quite small; thus the question of localization had never come up before. Many of these new markets simply couldn't afford to produce new materials. Indeed these markets were grateful for any materials they could get from headquarters to reduce their costs.

Steve knew India could not be classified as a small market by any stretch of the imagination. Still, he had a simple philosophy. When you had something, particularly in advertising and communication, that seemed to work, you didn't really want to change it. Steve also preferred to invest all available funds in media rather than spend any part of it in producing additional commercials. He was also concerned that Oral-B's media investments always seemed to be significantly less than those of the competition. He was naturally concerned about diverting any media money into production.

Steve also had another concern. He was not sure of the quality of television production Oral-B could obtain in India if they developed a local commercial. He knew the top management of Oral-B would simply not have a shoddy commercial representing its brand to the consumers in any part of the world. Sanjay had covered this aspect in his memo, stating that Oral-B could produce a good commercial in India with local talent for around $40,000. He argued that was really affordable given the overall Indian advertising budget of more than $600,000. Still, Steve was not sure. What was Sanjay's view of quality? And was this really consistent with what Oral-B expected?

Steve also knew some other things about Oral-B that Sanjay could not know. In spite of being marketed in thirty-five countries, Oral-B had never produced a TV commercial outside the United States. Therefore, if it decided to produce one in India, this would raise many questions among top management about the necessity of the expense.

With all these issues flashing through his mind, Steve still knew the questions raised by Sanjay were valid and needed careful thought. Steve had visited India several times in the previous year, going through the markets and visiting shops in many parts of that big country. Every time he made the trip, Steve was struck by the size and complexity of the market. He attended media reviews conducted by the agency, where again he was struck by the scope of Indian media, the complexity of various languages and cultures, and the fact that all their international competitors with a long track record in India always seemed to produce local creative materials.

Steve knew from his long years in marketing that nothing was as simple as it seemed on the surface. He still had to ask himself the question: Would the international Oral-B television commercials work in the Indian marketplace? That was really what Sanjay was asking him to comment on in his return fax.

Steve knew he had only an advisory role to play in the marketing and advertising issues in India. The final responsibility for success or failure would rest with Sanjay Kapoor and his marketing team. Still, he knew the questions raised by Sanjay regarding advertising were critical to the success of the Indian project. The matter needed very careful thought. "Globalize or localize?" seemed to sum up the question for both Steve and Sanjay.

BACKGROUND

Oral-B is a successful marketer of toothbrushes headquartered in Redwood City, California, just outside San Francisco. After many decades of independent operation the Gillette Company acquired Oral-B in 1990. Oral-B had been highly successful in its base market, the United States, accounting for over 20 percent share in toothbrush sales.

Based on its U.S. success, Oral-B started its international expansion. The brand is now available in more than fifty countries around the world, with manufacturing operations in half a dozen countries. Oral-B viewed its international expansion as a fundamental business strategy for growth and was keen to establish a strong presence in the emerging markets of Asia.

Asia was particularly interesting to Oral-B because of its huge population base (Oral-B sold a basic product of everyday human use) and the relatively lower penetration of toothbrush use on that continent. Oral-B could foresee a future in which its sales in the Asian region could well exceed the sales in its home country. The Oral-B corporate strategic planners estimated this could happen by the year 2010, provided Oral-B was successful in breaking into the markets of China and India.

Oral-B was founded by a dentist who believed the concept of a brush that cleaned the teeth only was inadequate. Oral hygiene required that the gums, and indeed the whole mouth, be cleaned as well. Therefore, he came up with the concept of a brush that was a complete "oral brush," hence the name Oral-B.

Oral-B built its business primarily by building relationships with dentists, relying less on mass media and direct consumer contact. The company had a field-based sales force that called on dentists, explained the virtues of the product, and carried out extensive sampling. Ideally the dentists would then recommend Oral-B to their patients, which, over time, would result in more and more people converting to the brand and forming a very loyal base of users.

Oral-B was proud of this rich dental heritage and implemented this professional relationship strategy in new markets as it expanded. This strategy, over time, also gave the firm its international advertising proposition: "Oral-B is the brand used by more dentists themselves around the world."

Oral-B was now planning a market entry into India. A country manager (CM) and a core marketing team, all based in New Delhi, had been employed to carry out this task. The team had already made arrangements for contract manufacturing of toothbrushes to Oral-B specifications. The product would be ready for the market in four months.

The Indian team had also done its homework on the distribution front. Being a part of the Gillette Company was a major advantage. The CM had arranged for the Gillette sales force and distribution network to carry and sell the toothbrush line to the wholesalers and retail trade. Gillette had already set up a nationwide sales and distribution network for its blades and razors. That coverage included all of urban India (towns with a population of 20,000 or more) and spanned some 200,000 retail outlets in the country. This established and readily available infrastructure was ready for Oral-B's introduction.

THE INDIAN MARKET

India is the second-most populous nation in the world. Its landmass spreads over an entire subcontinent. Politically India is divided into twenty-six states and six union territories, each with its own state government, plus a central government and an elected parliament in New Delhi.

The country is home to some 4,000 cities and towns. India is geographically diverse, with the Himalayas in the north and the huge uninterrupted peninsular coastline in the south. Its huge population of 900 million speaks some fifteen official languages and more than 1,000 dialects. The country also has a number of religions, with all religious groups coexisting under a secular system.

The country has a well-developed media market and an established system of distribution and marketing infrastructure that was adopted by all leading packaged goods companies such as Unilever, Colgate, and even Gillette.

THE TOOTHBRUSH CATEGORY

The Indian market for toothbrushes was already well served before Oral-B's entry. Some 800 million toothbrushes were purchased every year, growing at a rate of approximately 8 percent per year. Toothbrushes were readily available in any grocery store or chemist (pharmacy) or sometimes even in small cigarette vendors just off the main streets.

By far the leading brand in the category was Colgate-Palmolive, which had operated in the market for the last fifty years. The second-largest was Hindustan Lever, a subsidiary of the Unilever group. It was also well established, having operated in the market for decades. In addition, there were literally scores of local entrepreneurial manufacturers and marketers, many of whom were serving local or regional markets.

As with most product categories in India, the toothbrush market was also very price sensitive. More than 75 percent of the market was made up of toothbrushes that sold for less than twelve rupees each (the equivalent of about thirty-three cents U.S.) Largely the local manufacturers served this segment. Oral-B knew they could not make or sell a product at this price and hope to make a profit.

The next segment was the middle price range, between thirteen and eighteen rupees (thirty-six to fifty cents U.S.). This segment represented some 20 percent of sales in volume. Above this was the premium segment, which accounted for only about 5 percent of the market.

THE CONSUMER

As the CM said in one of the first team meetings, "The Indian consumer is interested in the toothbrush she buys for the home about as much as she is in the doormat she places in front of the house." In marketing terms, the toothbrush in India is an extremely low-involvement category to which the consumer hardly gives any thought.

Due to the dominance of toothpaste brands, Indian consumers are more loyal to their brand of toothpaste than to their toothbrush brand. Therefore, prominent toothpaste brands which also market a toothbrush receive a more ready acceptance. Oral-B, however, would be entering the toothbrush category directly, with no supporting toothpaste on which to rely.

The other effect of the dominance of toothpaste advertising was that the Indian consumer believed it was the toothpaste that actually cleaned the teeth and that the toothbrush had a very small role in the cleaning process.

Additionally, Oral-B management was concerned about the relative low priority given to dentists by the Indian consumer. The per-capita population of dentists was very low, and consumers visited the dentist more for remedy than for prevention. This meant that Oral-B could not rely only on its time-tested strategy of working with the dentist population to build its business.

THE ADVERTISING SCENARIO

As expected, leading Indian toothbrush brands benefited enormously from the large advertising outlays used to support the toothpaste brands. Television was the biggest medium for the category, with over 85 percent of the advertising funds being spent in this medium.

Colgate was by far the largest advertiser. Its combined spending behind both the paste and the brush was on the order of 200 million rupees ($5.6 million). Unilever had just introduced its Pepsodent brand a year earlier. Its advertising spent to support paste and brush combined was 140 million rupees ($3.9 million). Lever's other brand—Close-Up—spent over 101 million rupees ($2.8 million) in support of its paste and brush. In addition to all this were the spending levels in advertising by all the other marketers, sometimes in national and often on regional or local media. (Note: Expenditures listed for 1995 were in television advertising only. Other marketing communication activities were in addition to these totals.)

Oral-B was being introduced in India with a launch advertising media budget of $600,000. This further underscored the importance of the quality of communication as the CM and his team prepared to enter the market.

PRODUCT STRATEGY FOR THE LAUNCH

Oral-B had an impressive portfolio of toothbrushes for the Indian market. Given the price sensitivity of the consumer, management decided to launch the basic Oral-B Plus toothbrush at a price of 15 rupees and offer it in a range of colors. The company had earmarked the more sophisticated Indicator and Advantage line of toothbrushes for introduction at a later stage, after the Oral-B brand had been established in the market among both trade and consumers.

LAUNCH OBJECTIVES

Given the market scenario, the Oral-B marketing team had set simple communication objectives.

1. Establish Oral-B as a toothbrush brand in the Indian market.
2. Establish Oral-B as the worldwide leader in quality toothbrushes.
3. Make Oral-B synonymous with dentists worldwide.

It was believed that if these simple objectives could be achieved with all the budgetary constraints outlined earlier, Oral-B would be well on its way to creating a viable business in India.

SELECTED RESEARCH BACKGROUND

On the following pages, selected research and background material is offered that was available to Oral-B's Indian marketing team.

The Study

- Oral-B Laboratories is planning to enter the Indian market with its range of dental care products, primarily toothbrush and dental floss.
- XYZ Research conducted research to understand consumer attitudes and usage of the above-mentioned products.
- A total of 1,523 listing interviews and 1,225 main interviews were conducted across eight centers.
- The target respondents for the listing interview were any adult members (over age fifteen) in a household with monthly income of 500+ rupees.

- For the main interview, the respondent was defined as adult men or women who currently use a toothbrush.

Research Objectives

For the toothbrush:

- estimate penetration of toothbrushes and dentifrices
- brand awareness
- ad awareness
- usage details
- issues relating to purchase
- details relating to incidence of visiting dentist

Key Findings

Toothbrush Penetration
- Nine out of ten persons use only one product to clean their teeth.
- Almost all of the respondents use a toothbrush for cleaning their teeth.
- Apart from the toothbrush, the other products used are finger or datun (wood stick).

SUMMARY TABLE 1
Penetration of Oral Care Products

	Total
Base: All household members	7,539
	%
Solo usage	
Toothbrush only	81
Finger only	10
Datun only	3
Multiple usage	
Toothbrush + finger	2
Toothbrush + datun	1
Not specified	3

Usage of toothbrush increases significantly with an increase in income.

SUMMARY TABLE 2
Toothbrush Usage by Income

	Total
Base: All household members	7,539
	%
Rs 501–1,000	70
Rs 1,000–2,000	82
Rs 2,001–4,000	87
Rs 4,001+	90

Brand Awareness Colgate is the most salient brand, followed by Cibaca. Awareness for all other brands is low.

SUMMARY TABLE 3
Brand Awareness

Base: All repondents (1,225)	Top of Mind	Unaided	Total
	%	%	%
Colgate	55	82	95
Cibaca	19	56	87
Forhans	6	34	74
Binaca	5	23	68
Promise	2	22	70
Ajay	2	9	25
Ajanta	1	10	39
Prudent	1	15	50
Others	3	16	36
DK/CS	8	7	1

Colgate had a higher awareness in big towns and in the west and the south zones.

Not much variation in the awareness for other brands was observed.

Ad Awareness The unaided ad awareness was the highest for Colgate, with half the respondents claiming to have seen the ad on TV. Cibaca was the other brand whose advertising was recalled by more than a third of the respondents. Ad awareness for the other brands was low.

Ad awareness scores do not improve very much, even on prompting.

SUMMARY TABLE 4
Ad Awareness

	Unaided	*Total*
Base: All respondents (1,225)	%	%
Colgate	50	59
Cibaca	32	50
Forhans	20	39
Binaca	11	28
Promise	13	39
Ajay	3	7
Ajanta	4	13
Prudent	12	29
Others	3	9
DK/CS	35	23

Usage Details

Frequency More than three-fifths of the respondents brush their teeth once a day, while more than a third brush twice a day. Incidence of brushing more than twice daily is low.

SUMMARY TABLE 5
Frequency of Brushing

	Total
Base: All respondents (1,225)	%
More than 3 times daily	2
3 times daily	2
2 times daily	33
Once daily	63

Occasion All respondents brush their teeth in the morning. Nearly a quarter also brush their teeth at night before going to bed.

Brand Used Currently Colgate and Cibaca are the two major players being used currently by two-fifths and one-third of the respondents, respectively.

Colgate has a significantly higher penetration in the south (54 percent) and west zones (44 percent). This trend was also observed in the case of brand and ad awareness for Colgate.

Purchase

Factors Influencing Purchase of Toothbrush "Softness of the bristles" emerged as the most important factor followed by "shape of the handle." The other factor was "price," which was considered more important in low-median-income households.

SUMMARY TABLE 6
Factors Influencing Toothbrush Purchase

	Total (Mean Score)
Base: All respondents (1,225)	%
Quality of bristles	
softness	3.6
hardness	2.4
Handle	
shape	2.8
color	2.3
Price	2.5
Recommendation of	
dentist	2.3
shopkeeper	1.6
Same brand as toothpaste used	2.0

Source of Purchase Mostly, toothbrushes are purchased from grocers/general merchants (74 percent). A little over a tenth buy their toothbrushes from chemists.

SUMMARY TABLE 7
Source of Purchase

	Total
Base: All respondents (1,225)	%
Grocer/general merchant	74
Chemist	13
Department store	7
Supermarket	3
Others	3
Not specified	1

Incidence of purchasing a toothbrush from chemists is significantly higher in Bombay, as compared to the other centers. Purchasing from grocers/general merchants is significantly higher in low-median-income households.

Frequency of Purchase Forty-four percent purchase their toothbrush once every two or three months, while 42 percent of the respondents purchase their toothbrush once in more than three months.

SUMMARY TABLE 8
Frequency of Purchase

	Total
Base: All respondents (1,225)	%
More often than once monthly	2
Once monthly	12
Once in 2–3 months	44
Once in 4–5 months	14
Once in 6 months	14
Less often	14

Incidence of Visiting the Dentist Only two-fifths of the respondents had ever visited a dentist. The reason for visiting a dentist is usually "problem-related."

Bibliography

In this book we have used a wide variety of sources. These sources include: references to other works, which are cited in the traditional way; seminar and conference papers; presentations that either or both of us attended; personal experience; and our personal correspondence with a wide variety of companies, professional people, academics, and other knowledgeable individuals. We list the primary references used in each chapter; therefore, some sources may appear in more than one chapter's bibliographic listing. Since we have tried to make this a "working text," we believe this informal use of resources and materials related to each of the individual chapters will be the most useful way of presenting this information to the reader.

CHAPTER 1

Bloomington Convention and Visitors Bureau website: www.bloomingtonmn.org, 1999.

Hill, Sam, and Glen Rifkin. *Radical Marketing: From Harvard to Harley, Lessons from Ten that Broke the Rules and Made It Big*. New York: HarperCollins, 1999.

Kotler, Philip. *Marketing Management: Analysis, Planning, Implementation, and Control*. Upper Saddle River, NJ: Prentice-Hall, 1999.

_____. *Marketing Management: Millennial Edition*. Upper Saddle River, NJ: Prentice-Hall, 1999.

Levinson, Jay Conrad, Seth Godin, and Charles Rubin. *The Guerilla Marketing Handbook*. Boston: Houghton Mifflin Co., 1995.

Perreault, William D., and E. Jerome McCarthy. *Basic Marketing: A Managerial Approach.* 12th ed. Homewood, IL: Richard D. Irwin, 1999.

U.S. Department of Commerce/International Trade Administration. "U.S. Industry and Trade Outlook 1999," pp. 32–39.

Zyman, Sergio. *The End of Marketing as We Know It.* New York: HarperCollins, 1999.

CHAPTER 2

Bartlett, Christopher A., and Sumantra Ghoshal. *Managing Across Borders: The Transnational Solution.* 2nd ed. Boston: Harvard Business School Press, 1998.

Sheth, Jagdish N. *Reflections on International Marketing: In Search of New Paradigms.* Presentation at the American Marketing Association Conference "1998 Marketing Exchange Colloquium." Vienna, Austria: June 22–25, 1998.

CHAPTER 3

Czinkota, Michael R. *Global Marketing.* Forth Worth, TX: Harcourt Brace College Publishers, 1996.

Hamill, Jim, and Philip J. Kitchen. "The Internet (International Context)." In Philip J. Kitchen, ed. *Marketing Communication: Principles and Practice.* Chapter 22. London: International Thomson Business Press, 1999, pp. 381–402.

Keegan, Warren J., and Mark C. Green. *Global Marketing.* Upper Saddle River, NJ: Prentice-Hall, 1999.

Kitchen, Philip J. "For Now We See Through a Glass Darkly: Light on Global Marketing Communications." *Fit for the Global Future.* The Netherlands: ESOMAR, pp. 155–82.

Laswell, Harold D. *Power and Personality.* New York: Norton, 1948, pp. 37–51.

Levitt, Theodore. "The Globalization of Markets." *Harvard Business Review* (May–June 1993).

Lorenz, Chris. "The Overselling of World Brands." *Financial Times* (19 July 1984).

_____. "Why New Products Are Going Global." *Financial Times* (16 July 1984).

Ohmae, Kenichi. *Triad Power: The Coming Shape of Global Competition.* New York: The Free Press, 1985.

Paliwoda, Stanley J. *International Marketing.* London: Butterworth-Heinemann, 1992.

Petty, Richard E., and John T. Cacioppo. *Attitudes and Persuasion: Classic and Contemporary Approaches.* Boulder, CO: Westview Press, 1996.

Schramm, Wilbur D. "How Communication Works." In Wilbur D. Schramm and Donald F. Roberts, eds. *The Process and Effects of Mass Communications.* Urbana, IL: University of Illinois Press, 1976.

Schultz, Don E., Stanley I. Tannenbaum, and Robert F. Lauterborn. *Integrated Marketing Communications*. Chicago: NTC/Contemporary Publishing Group, 1998.

Schwartz, Evan I. *Webonomics: Nine Essential Principles for Growing Your Business on the World Wide Web*. New York: Bantam Doubleday Dell Publishers, 1998.

Shaw, Robert, and Merlin Stone. *Database Marketing*. Aldershot, UK: Gower Press, 1988.

Shimp, Terence A. *Advertising, Promotion, and Supplemental Aspects of Integrated Marketing Communications*. Fort Worth, TX: Harcourt Brace College Publishers, 1997.

CHAPTER 4

American Productivity & Quality Center. *Integrated Marketing Communication*. Houston: American Productivity & Quality Center International Benchmarking Clearinghouse, 1998.

Bartlett, Christopher A., and Sumantra Ghoshal. *Managing Across Borders: The Transnational Solution*. 2nd ed. Boston: Harvard Business School Press, 1998.

Cutlip, Scott M., Allen H. Center, and Glen M. Broom. *Effective Public Relations*. Englewood Cliffs, NJ: Prentice-Hall, 1999.

Davidson, D. Kirk. "Consumers Really Don't Care About Brand Products Owners." *Marketing News* 32, no. 24 (23 November 1998), p. 5.

Dunning, John H. *Multinational Enterprises and the Global Economy*. Wokingham, UK: Addison Wesley Publishing Company, 1993.

Economist, The. "Corporate Eyes, Ears, and Mouth." *The Economist* (18 March 1989), pp. 105–106.

Financial Times. The Global Financial Times (6 November 1998), special insert p. 1.

Keegan, Warren J., and Mark C. Green. *Global Marketing*. Upper Saddle River, NJ: Prentice-Hall, 1999.

Kitchen, Philip J. *Public Relations: Principles and Practice*. London: International Thomson Business Press, 1997.

Kotler, Philip. *Marketing Management: Analysis, Planning, Implementation, and Control*. Upper Saddle River, NJ: Prentice-Hall, 1999.

Levitt, Theodore. "The Globalization of Markets." *Harvard Business Review* (May–June 1993).

———. *The Marketing Imagination*. New York: The Free Press, 1986.

Martin, David. "Chain Reaction." *Financial Times* (17 November 1998), p. 32.

Narisetti, R. "P&G, Seeing Shoppers Confused, Overhauls Marketing." *Wall Street Journal, Europe* (20 January 1997).

Schultz, Don E. "Integrated Marketing Communication: Maybe Definition Is in the Point of View?" *Marketing News* (18 January 1993).

_____."Branding the Basis for Marketing Integration." *Marketing News* 32, no. 24 (23 November 1998), p. 8.

Schultz, Don E., and Heidi F. Schultz. "Transitioning Marketing Communication into the Twenty-First Century." *Journal of Marketing Communication* 4, no. 1 (1998), pp. 9–26.

Sheth, Jagdish N., David Morgan Gardner, and Dennis E. Garrett. *Marketing Theory: Evolution and Evaluation.* London: John Wiley & Sons, 1988, pp. 1-33.

Shimp, Terence A., *Advertising, Promotion, and Supplemental Aspects of Integrated Marketing Communications.* Fort Worth, TX: Harcourt Brace College Publishers, 1997.

Van Riel, Cees B. M., and Chris Blackburn. *Principles of Corporate Communication.* London: Prentice-Hall, 1995, pp. 26–27.

Yip, George S. "Toward a New Global Strategy." *Chief Executive*, Jan/Feb 1996.

CHAPTER 5

American Productivity & Quality Center. *Brand Building & Communication: Power Strategies for the 21st Century.* Houston: American Productivity & Quality Center International Benchmarking Clearinghouse, 1998.

American Productivity & Quality Center. *Integrated Marketing Communications.* Houston: American Productivity & Quality Center International Benchmarking Clearinghouse, 1998.

Bartlett, Christopher A., and Sumantra Ghoshal. *Managing Across Borders: The Transnational Solution.* 2nd ed. Boston: Harvard Business School Press, 1998.

Perreault, William D., and E. Jerome McCarthy. *Basic Marketing: A Managerial Approach.* 12th ed. Homewood, IL: Richard D. Irwin, 1999.

Schultz, Don E., and Jeffrey S. Walters. *Measuring Brand Communication ROI.* New York: Association of National Advertisers, 1997.

Strong, Edward K. *The Psychology of Selling.* New York: McGraw-Hill, 1925.

Taylor, James. Speech at the Meredith Corporation "3rd Annual BrandCom Seminar." New York: June 18, 1998.

CHAPTER 6

American Productivity & Quality Center. *Brand Building & Communication: Power Strategies for the 21st Century.* Houston: American Productivity & Quality Center International Benchmarking Clearinghouse, 1998.

American Productivity & Quality Center. *Integrated Marketing Communications.* Houston: American Productivity & Quality Center International Benchmarking Clearinghouse, 1998.

Schultz, Don E., and Jeffrey S. Walters. *Measuring Brand Communication ROI*. New York: Association of National Advertisers, 1997.

Targetbase Marketing. Presentation Deck. Irving, TX: Targetbase Marketing, 1998.

Williams, Juliet. Class lecture, IMC Program. Northwestern University: October 1997.

CHAPTER 7

Batra, Rajeev, David A. Aaker, and John G. Myers. *Advertising Management*. Englewood Cliffs, NJ: Prentice-Hall International, 1995.

Cohen, William A. *Principles of Marketing Management*. New York: Macmillan, 1991, pp. 268–69.

Goldenberg, Jacob, David Mazursky, and Solomon Sorin. "Identifying the Inventive Schemes of New Products: Towards a Theory of Channelled Ideation." *Journal of Marketing Research*, 1999, to be published.

_____. "Toward Identifying the Fundamental Templates of Quality Ads." Conditionally accepted for *Marketing Science* (2000).

Hamill, Jim, and Philip J. Kitchen. "The Internet (International Context)." In Philip J. Kitchen, ed. *Marketing Communication: Principles and Practice*. Chapter 22. London: International Thomson Business Press, 1999, pp. 381–402.

Hammer, Michael, and James Champy. *Reengineering the Corporation: A Manifesto for Business Revolution*. New York: HarperCollins, 1994.

Institute of Advertising Practitioners, UK. *It Pays to Advertise*. London: IPA, 1996, see De Beers Campaign, Case Study 2.

Keegan, Warren J., and Mark C. Green. *Global Marketing*. Upper Saddle River, NJ: Prentice-Hall 1999.

Kitchen, Philip J., and Colin Wheeler. "Issues Influencing Marketing Communications in a Global Context." *Journal of Marketing Communications* 3, no. 4 (1997).

Kitchen, Philip J., ed. *Marketing Communication: Principles and Practice*. London: International Thomson Business Press, 1999.

O'Guinn, Thomas C., Chris T. Allen, and Richard J. Semenik. *Advertising*. Cincinnati: South-Western Publishing, 1998.

Schultz, Don E., Stanley I. Tannenbaum, and Robert F. Lauterborn. *Integrated Marketing Communications*. Chicago: NTC/Contemporary Publishing Group, 1998.

Shimp, Terence A. *Advertising, Promotion, and Supplemental Aspects of Integrated Marketing Communications*. Fort Worth, TX: Harcourt Brace College Publishers, 1997.

Vakratsas, Demetrios, and Tim Ambler. "How Advertising Works: What Do We Really Know?" *Journal of Marketing* 26 (January 1999), pp. 26–43.

Van Riel, Cees B. M., and Chris Blackburn. *Principles of Corporate Communication*. London: Prentice-Hall, 1995, pp. 26–27.

CHAPTER 8

Advertising Age. "World's Top 50 Advertising Organizations." *Advertising Age* (10 April 1995a, S–18, 1995b, S–20).

Brierly, Sean. *The Advertising Handbook.* London: Routledge, 1995, pp. 45–58.

Byfield, Sheila, and Linda Caller. "Fitting International Brands for Consumers." *Fit for the Global Future.* ESOMAR Seminar. Lisbon, Portugal: July 13–16, 1997.

Crosier, Keith. "Advertising" and "The Argument for Advertising Agency Renumeration." Chapters 26 and 27 in Philip J. Kitchen, ed. *Marketing Communication: Principles and Practice.* London: International Thomson Business Press, 1999, pp. 276–82, 442–58.

Douglas, Susan, and Bernard Dubois. "Looking at the Cultural Environment for International Marketing Opportunities." *Columbia Journal of World Business* 12 (Winter 1977), pp. 102–109.

European Business Readership Survey (EBRS). A *Financial Times* working document based on the 1996 *European Business Readership Survey*, September 1996.

European Media and Marketing Survey 1995/1996. By Inter/view International.

Falke, Heiko, and Axel Schmidt. "The Impact of New Media on the Communication Process." *Fit for the Global Future.* ESOMAR Seminar. Lisbon, Portugal: July 13–16, 1997.

Finney, Mark. "Global Marketing and Advertising." *IPA Media Awards 1992-1995*, London: Institute of Advertising Practitioners, 1995, pp. 171–83.

Fiske, John. *Understanding Popular Culture.* London: Unwin Hayman, 1984.

Keegan, Warren J., and Mark C. Green. *Global Marketing.* Upper Saddle River, NJ: Prentice-Hall, 1999.

Kitchen, Philip J. "The Implications of IMC for International Media Research." Keynote paper for the 3rd International/Objective Research Conference. London: March 4–5, 1998.

Kitchen, Philip J., and Don E. Schultz. " A Multi-Country Comparison of the Drive for Integrated Marketing Communication." *Journal of Advertising Research* 39, no. 1 (1999).

Laspadakis, Andreas. "The Dynamic Role of Sales Promotion." In Philip J. Kitchen, ed. *Marketing Communication: Principles and Practice.* London: International Thomson Business Press, 1999, pp. 303–304.

Levitt, Theodore. *The Marketing Imagination.* New York: The Free Press, 1986.

_____. "The Globalization of Markets." *Harvard Business Review* (May–June 1983).

Meli, Sylvia. Keynote presentation on IMC at the ESOMAR Seminar, Paris: April, 1997.

Perry, Sir Michael. "The Brand–Vehicle for Value in a Changing Marketplace." The Advertising Association, President's Lecture. London:July 7, 1994. Cited in Yiannis Gabriel and Tim Lang. *The Unmanageable Consumer: Contemporary Consumption and Its Fragmentation.* London: Sage Publications, 1995.

Poltrack, David F. "Needed: A New Paradigm for Media Evaluation by Advertisers." *Fit for the Global Future.* ESOMAR Seminar. Lisbon, Portugal: 1997, pp. 129–43.

Rosenshine, Alan "Advertising's Demise Greatly Exaggerated." *Advertising Age* (20 March 1995).

Shimp, Terence A. *Advertising, Promotion, and Supplemental Aspects of Integrated Marketing Communications.* Fort Worth, TX: Harcourt Brace College Publishers, 1997.

Usunier, Jean-Claude. *Marketing Across Cultures.* London: Prentice-Hall, 1996.

CHAPTER 11

Kitchen, Philip J. "The Implications of IMC for International Media Research." Keynote paper presented at the 3rd International/Objective Research Conference, London, March 1998.

Kitchen, Philip J., and Don E. Schultz. "A Multi-Country Analysis of the Drive for Integrated Marketing Communication." *Journal of Advertising Research* 39, no. 1 (1999).

Patel, K. "The World According to Gates." *The Times Higher* (2 April 1999), p. 17.

Schultz, Don E. "Structural Straitjackets Stifle Integrated Success." *Marketing News* (1 March 1999), p. 8.

CASE STUDY 4

Shimp, Terence A. *Advertising, Promotion, and Supplemental Aspects of Integrated Marketing Communications.* Fort Worth, TX: Harcourt Brace College Publishers, 1997.

WCRS. "Orange Proposition—Orange Offers the Future Today." In Philip J. Kitchen, ed. *Marketing Communication: Principles and Practice.* London: International Thomson Business Press, 1999, pp. 89–90.

Index